FLORENTINE CODEX

Florentine Codex

General History of the Things of New Spain

FRAY BERNARDINO DE SAHAGÚN

Book 9 – The Merchants

Translated from the Aztec into English, with notes and illustrations

By

CHARLES E. DIBBLE
UNIVERSITY OF UTAH

ARTHUR J. O. ANDERSON
SCHOOL OF AMERICAN RESEARCH

IN THIRTEEN PARTS

PART X

Chapter heading designs are from the Codex

Published by
The School of American Research and The University of Utah

Monographs of The School of American Research and The Museum of New Mexico
Santa Fe, New Mexico

Number 14, Part X   1959

ISBN-10: 0-87480-006-4 (Book 9)
ISBN-13: 978-0-87480-006-7

ISBN-10: 0-87480-082-X (Set)
ISBN-13: 978-0-87480-082-1

Published and distributed by
The University of Utah Press
Salt Lake City, Utah 84112

To Dudley and Elizabeth Easby, who have shown us how the Aztecs cast and hammered gold, and how they shaped precious stones, we affectionately dedicate this volume.

CONTENTS

LIST OF ILLUSTRATIONS

following page 50

BOOK NINE--THE MERCHANTS

LIBRO NONO DE
los mercaderes, officia
les de oro, y piedras
preciosas, y plu
ma rica

De los Mercaderes

NINTH BOOK, WHICH TELLETH OF THE MERCHANTS AND THE ARTISANS: THOSE WHO WORKED GOLD, AND PRECIOUS STONES, AND PRECIOUS FEATHERS.

INIC CHICUNAUI AMOSTLI, ITECHPA TLA-TOA, IN PUCHTECA, YOAN IN TLACHI-CHIUHQUE, IN QUICHICHIOA COZTIC TEU-CUJTLATL, IOAN TLAÇOTETL, IOAN TLA-ÇOIHUITL.

First Chapter, which telleth of those who founded commerce in Mexico and Tlatilulco.

Inic ce capitulo: intechpa tlatoa, in quitzintique in puchtecaiotl, in mexico ioan tlatilulco.

Behold what was customary in times of old. At the time that commerce began, Quaquauhpitzauac [was ruler]. Those who started the commerce were the principal merchants[1] Itzcoatzin and Tziuhtecatzin. Thus did they engage in trade: they sold only red arara and blue and scarlet parrot feathers.[2] Only these three things did they regard as merchandise.

Izcatqui in iuh tlamanca in ie uecauh: in ipan poch-tecaiotl, ipan otzintic, in quaquauhpitzaoac, in qui-tzintique pochtecaiotl, iehoantin in, in pochtecatlato-que: itzcoatzin, tziuhtecatzin. Inic puchtecatia, in quinamacaia: çan iehoatl in cueçal, ioan cuitlatexo-tli, ioan chamoli: çan i ietlamanisti inic pochtecatti-tiaque.

And the second ruler who came to be installed was Tlacateotl. And also in his time were installed these principal merchants: Cozmatzin [and] Tzompan-tzin. In their time appeared quetzal feathers, [but] not yet the long ones, and troupial[3] and turquoise, and green stones; and capes [and] breech clouts of fine cotton.[4] What was being worn was still all maguey fiber capes, netted capes of maguey fiber, breech clouts, shifts, skirts of maguey fiber.[5]

Auh inic ome motlalico tlatoani: tlacateutl: auh no ipan motlalique, in puchtecatlatoque: iehoantin jn, Cozmatzin, Tzompantzin: ie inpan nez in que-tzalli, aiamo viiac, ioan çaquan, ioan xiuitl, ioan chal-chiuitl, ioan iamanqui tilmatli, iamanqui mastlatl, in nequentiloia, çan oc mochi, ichtilmatli, ichaiatzintli ichmastlatzintli, ichuipiltzintli, ichcuetzintli.

---

1. Corresponding Spanish text: *principales tratantes;* Bernardino de Sahagún: *Historia general de las cosas de Nueva España* (Angel María Garibay K., ed.; México: Editorial Porrúa, S. A., 1956; hereafter referred to as Garibay ed.), Vol. IV, p. 349: *jefes de los traficantes;* Eduard Seler: *Gesammelte Abhandlungen zur Amerikanischen Sprach- und Altertumskunde* (Berlin: Ascher und Co., 1902-1923), Vol. II, p. 1011: *Vorsteher der Kaufmannschaft.*

2. *Cueçalin:* arara, in Eduard Seler: *Collected Works* (J. Eric S. Thompson and Francis B. Richardson, eds.; Cambridge: Carnegie Institution of Washington, 1939), Vol. II, Pts. 3-4, p. 108; parrot with fiery feathers, *ibid.,* p. 63; alo, red guacamaya (sun bird), *ibid.,* p. 47. "*Llama, color rojo vivo, pluma de ese color,*" in Sahagún (Garibay ed.), Vol. IV, p. 331. See also Herbert Friedmann, Ludlow Griscom, and Robert T. Moore (Alden H. Miller, Editor-in-Chief): *Distributional Check-List of the Birds of Mexico,* Pts. I and II (Pacific Coast Avifauna, Nos. 29 and 33; Berkeley: Cooper Ornithological Club, 1950, 1957; hereafter referred to as Friedmann *et al.*) Pt. I, p. 125.

Cuitlatexotli: corresponding Spanish text — "*plumas de papagayos . . . açules.*" "*Azul manchado. Pluma y color de un ave*" (Sahagún, *op. cit.,* p. 332).

Chamoli: "*Ave roja de la región tropical. Pluma fina. Ident. y et. desconocidas*" (*ibid.,* p. 333); probably a parrot (cf. corresponding Spanish text). Seler, *op. cit.,* p. 110, refers to it as a violet or dark red color; in *ibid.,* Pt. 4, p. 52, he writes of *chamotzin* that "female dead were called by another endearing name *chamotzin* 'dark red or ornamental feather' " (quoting Sahagún, X, 29, 12, *MS Acad. Hist.*). Cf. also Eduard Seler, "L'orfèvrerie des anciens mexicains et leur art de travailler la pierre et de faire des ornements en plumes," *Compte-Rendu* de la 8ᵐᵉ Session (Paris: Ernest Leroux, 1892), p. 432 and n. 52.

3. *Çaquantototl:* troupial (*Icterus gularis* Wachl.), according to Seler, *Collected Works,* Pts. 3-4, p. 114; "*Ave de pluma fina, dorada y negra*" (*Gymnostinops Montezumae*), in Sahagún (Garibay ed.), Vol. IV, p. 372; cf. Friedmann *et al.,* Pt. 2, p. 276.

4. Corresponding Spanish text: "*las mātas de algodon, y mastles de algodon.*"

5. *Nequen* in *ibid.*

And the third who came to be installed as ruler was Quauhtlatoatzin. And also in his time were installed these principal merchants: Tollamimichtzin [and] Micxochtziyautzin. And in their time appeared gold lip and ear plugs and rings for the fingers — those called *matzatzaztli* [or] *anillo*; and necklaces with radiating pendants, and fine turquoise, and enormous green stones, and long quetzal feathers; and the skins of wild animals; and long troupial feathers, and blue cotinga and red spoonbill feathers.[6]

And the fourth who came to be installed as ruler was Moquiuixtzin. And also in his time were installed these principal merchants: Popoyotzin [and] Tlacochintzin. And also in their time appeared costly capes — the wonderful red ones, with the wind jewel design; and white duck feather capes; and capes with cup-shaped designs in feathers; and wonderful breech clouts with embroidered ends — with long ends at the extremities of the breech clouts; and embroidered skirts [and] shifts; and capes eight fathoms long,[7] of twisted weave;[8] and chocolate. And all [and] everything [already] mentioned — quetzal feathers, gold, green stones, all the precious feathers — at this time increased, augmented even more. And the reign in Tlatilulco came to an end with Moquiuixtzin. When he died no other ruler was installed in Tlatilulco. Then began only a military government. And here started only military rule in Tlatilulco. Here were the military governors who at that time were installed and given the authority of the displaced ruler Moquiuixtzin. Those who guarded were the commanding general Tziuacpopocatzin, the general Itzquauhtzin, both of whom were royal noblemen; and then the general Tezcatzin, the commanding general Totoçacatzin, both of whom were warrior noblemen, Mexican noblemen.

Auh inic ey, motlalico tlatoani, iehoatl in quauhtlatoatzin: auh no ipan motlalique, in puchtecatlatoque iehoantin in Tollamimichtzin, micxochtziiautzin: auh ie inpan nez, in teucuitlatentetl, ioan teucuitlanacochtli, ioan maxitlaztli: iehoatl in motocaiotia matzatzaztli, anillo, ioan chaiaoac cozcatl, ioan teuxiuitl: ioan ueuei chalchiuitl, ioan viac quetzalli: ioan tequanehoatl, ioan viac çaquan, ioan xiuhtototl, ioan teuquechol.

Auh inic naui, motlalico tlatoani, iehoatl in moquiuiztzin: auh no ipan motlalique, in puchtecatlatoque: iehoantin i, popoiotzin. tlacochintzin: auh no inpan nez, in tlaçotilmatli, in cenca mauiztic, tlapalecacozcaio, ioan xomoihuitilmatli, ioan hihuitica tetecomaio tilmatli, ioan mauiztic mastlatl, tlamachio in iiac, uel iacauiac in imastlaiacaio: ioã tlamachcueitl, tlamachuipilli, ioan chicuematl tilmatli, ilacatziuhqui, ioan cacaoatl. Auh in ie isquich in ic mochi in omoteneuh in quetzalli, in teucuitlatl, in chalchiuitl, in isquich tlaçoihuitl: oc cenca oncan omiequis, otlapiuis: auh in tlatocaiotl tlatilulco ça ica ontlamico, in moquiuiztzin, in icoac omomiquili, aoc ac tlatoani motlali in tlatilulco: vncan otzintic in ça quauhtlatolo. Auh nican vmpeoa, in ça quauhtlatolo in tlatilulco: nican cate in quauhtlatoque, in ipã onmotlalique, in ipetl in icpal, in concauhtia tlatoani moquiuiztzin: in contlapielique, iehoantin i, tlacateccatzintli, tzioacpopocatzin: tlacochcalcatzintli, Itzquauhtzin: omestin tlaçopipilti: auh niman ie tlacochcalcatzintli tezcatzin, tlacateccatzintli, Totoçacatzin: omestin quauhpipilti mexica pipilti.

---

6. *Xiuhtototl*: blue cotinga — *Cotinga cincta* S. *coerulea* (Seler, *op. cit.*, p. 39); *Cyanospiza cyanea, Guiraca coerulea* Sahagún (Garibay ed.), Vol. IV, p. 369. Also cf. Friedmann *et al., op. cit.*, Pt. 2, p. 59.

Teoquechol (*tlauhquechol*): red, rose-colored, or red and white spoonbill or heron (Seler, *op. cit.*, Vol. IV, p. 62; Vol. II, *passim*). In Sahagún (Garibay ed.), Vol. IV, p. 356, *teoquechol* is *Ajaja ajaja*; *tlauhquechol* (p. 364) is the same or *Ajaja rosea*. Also cf. Friedmann *et al., op. cit.*, Pt. 1, p. 53.

7. Corresponding Spanish text: "*mantas de ocho braças en largo.*"

8. "Twisted weave" and "spiral design" are permissible variants.

Second Chapter. Here is told how the merchants began their office, in which they were considered [and] honored as principal [merchants].

And behold, the principal merchants who became the companions of [the governors], those vested with authority, were Quauhpoyaualtzin, Nentlamatitzin, Vetzcatocatzin, Çanatzin, [and] Vei oçomatzin.

And Auitzotzin ruled in Tenochtitlan. Now in his time the merchants had entered [the provinces of] Ayotlan [and] Anauac,[1] [and] there they had been besieged. Four years they remained encircled in Quauhtenanco. In that place war was waged. Those who made war upon them were the people of Tequantepec, Izuatlan, Xochitlan, Amaxtlan, Quauhtzontlan, Atlan, Omitlan, [and] Mapachtepec.[2] These aforementioned cities were all large.

And not these alone contended [and] fought against them, but indeed they massed together all the people of Anauac to fight those besieged in Quauhtenanco. And those who became captives of each of the merchants, they took out of number. Those who had no devices they did not count; they counted only those who had devices; those who came carrying quetzal feather crest devices; shirts of blue cotinga [or] of trogonorus[3] feathers; turquoise mosaic shields; golden, butterfly-shaped nose plates, which they had come wearing; and golden ear pendants which hung from their ears, each extending very wide, reaching their shoulders; and quetzal [and] troupial feather banners, [and] bracelets for the upper arm with sprays of precious feathers. These indeed they counted; these became their captives. Some took twenty, some took fifteen. And as [the enemy] cities fell, as the

Jnic ome capitulo, vncan motenehoa: in quenin iehoantin i puchteca, compeoaltique in intequiuh, inic ipā omachoque, ca tlatoque mauistiq̃

Auh izcate, in inuicalhoan mochiuhque, in puchtecatlatoque: in ontlaliloque petlapan, icpalpan, quauhpoiaoaltzin, nentlamatitzin, vetzcatocatzin, çanatzin, vei oçomatzin.

Auh in tenochtitlan tlatocati, in Auitzotzin: ie ipan in calacque puchteca, Aiotlan, in anaoac, ompa oynpā oalmotzacu: nauhxiuitl in caltzacutimanca in quauhtenanco, in oncan iauchioaloque, in quimoniauchioaia tequantepecatl, izoatecatl, xochtecatl amastecatl, quatzontecatl, atlā omitlan tlacatl, mapachtepeoa: Jnin omoteneuh altepetl, mochi ueuei.

Auh amo çan iioque, in quimonpeoaia, in quimonicalia: çan uel quimonololhuiaia, in ie isquich anaoacatl, inic quimonicalia in oncan tzacutimanca, quauhtenanco. Auh in inmalhoan moch iuhq̃n cecenme puchteca: amo çan tlapoalti in quimacique, in amo tlauiceque, amo quimpouhque, çan iioque in quinpouhque tlauiceque: in onactiuitze quetzalpatzactli, xiuhtotoehoatl, tzinitzcanehoatl, xiuhchimalli, teucuitlaiacapapalotl, in contlalitiuitze: ioan teucuitlanacaztepoztli, in innacaztlan pipilcatiuitz: uel papatlaoac, imacolpan oallaci, ioan quetzalpanitl, çaquanpanitl, machoncotl: o iehoantin in in uel quimonpouhque: in inmalhoan mochiuhque: in aca cacic centecpantli, in aca cacic castolli. Auh in oia altepetl, in ompoliuh anaoacatl: nimā itlan oalcalac in mexicatl.

---

1. Anauac: Gulf of Mexico and Pacific Coast lands, according to Seler, *op. cit.*, Vol. II, Pts. 1-2, pp. 33-34. The corresponding Spanish text refers to *"las proujncias de Aiotlan, y Anaoac."* See also Miguel Acosta Saignes: *Los pochteca: ubicación de los mercaderes en la estructura social tenochca* (Acta Anthropologica, I: 1, México, 1945).

2. See corresponding Spanish text.

3. *Tzinitzcan*: *Trogonorus mexicanus* or *T. ambiguus* Sahagún (Garibay ed.), Vol. IV, p. 366); a bird of black and green feathers (Seler, *op. cit.*, Vol. II, Pts. 3-4, p. 137), or quetzal tail and shoulder feathers (*ibid.*, Vol. V, p. 2). See also Arthur J. O. Anderson & Charles E. Dibble: *Florentine Codex*, Book I (Santa Fe: School of American Research and University of Utah, 1950), p. 18, n. 100. Also cf. Friedmann *et al.*, *op. cit.*, Pt. 2, p. 12. In Book XI of the *Florentine Codex* (fol. 58), it is commented that *"Las plumas de la cabeça casi de todas las preciosas aues se llama tzinitzcan."*

people of Anauac perished, the Mexicans then penetrated among them.

And this was when [the merchants] were ordered to assemble. They said: "O Mexicans, O merchants, O vanguard merchants, the master, the portent, Uitzilopochtli, hath performed his office. We can approach near [and] to our city. No one, therefore, will be arrogant; no one will boast of his valor because of all who have been made our captives. For we came only to seek land for the master, the portent, Uitzilopochtli. And behold the property which we shall have merited, which shall have become the recompense of our breasts and heads, when we come to appear in, when we reach, Mexico: these amber lip plugs, and curved, green, ear pendants with bells, and black staves, and crested guan feather fans.[4] And behold our netted capes and our netted breech clouts,[5] all our possessions, our goods, which will be witnesses of our valor. None of all the merchants, the vanguard merchants, who live in Mexico, who did not come, who did not suffer with us, may take them. It will be our exclusive privilege."

And since they had spent four years there in Ayotlan, their hair fell clear to their loins when they started away.

And when Auitzotzin heard of their renown, when the merchants, the vanguard merchants, who had gone to Ayotlan were already coming, he then commanded that they be met. Indeed, everyone left to go to meet them. Those who took the lead were the fire [and other] priests; then the lords [and] constables.[6] The priests went carrying[7] copal [and] aromatic herbs, [and] blowing shell trumpets. And they went carrying their small bags upon their backs; these were incense bags. And the noblemen [and] constables each went wearing their sleeveless jackets.[8] As they went, they advanced arranged in rows; they formed two files.[9] And they went to meet them there at Acachinanco. When they arrived, they thereupon offered incense to them; they received each of them, as was done in days of old. And when this had

Auh ic uncan in monaoatique, inic mocentlalique: quitoque. Mexicae, pochtecae, oztomecae: ca oconchiuh in itequiuh, in tlacatl, in tetzauitl, in uitzilobuchtli: itloc uel itech tacizque, in tauh, in totepeuh: aiac ic mopoaz, aiac ic moquichitoz, in isquichtin tomalhoan omochiuhque: ca çã otictlaltemolico, in tlacatl in tetzauitl vitzilobuchtli: Auh ca izca in tocococauh, in oticmaceuhque: in telchiquiuh, in totzontecon ipatiuh omochiuh, inic tineztiazque, inic tacizque mexico: iehoatl in apoçonaltentetl, ioan quetzalcoiolnacochtli: ioan xaoactopilli, ioan coxoliecaceoaztli. Auh izca in totilma, colotlalpilli tilmatli: auh in tomastli colotlalpilmastlatl: o isquich in in tasca, in totlatqui, in toneoquichitol iez: aiac uel quicuiz in isquichtin mexico nemi in puchteca, in oztomeca: in amo oallaque, in amo tohoan otlaihiiouique çan toneiscauil iez.

Auh inic nauhxiuhtique, ompa aiotlan: in intzon uel in cuitlacaxiuhian oaluetztia, inic oaleoaque.

Auh in oquicac, in intenio in auitzotzin: in ie uitze in puchteca, in oztomeca in ouiia Aiotlan: niman otlanaoati inic namicozque, uel isquich tlacatl oia, in tenamiquito: iehoantin oteiacantiaque in tlêtlenamacaque, in tlamacazque: niman iehehoantin in tetecuti, achcacauhti: Jn quitquitiaque tlamacazque, copalli, iiauhtli, tecuciztli in quipitztiaque: ioan intotoxi quimamamatiaque, iehoatl in copalxiquipilli: auh in tetecuti, achcacauhti, isxixicol in commahaquitiaque, inic iaque, motecpantiaque, ompantique: auh ompa in quinnamiquito acachinanco: In oacique: niman ie ic quintlenamaquilia, quinnanamicque, in iuh mochioaia ie uecauh. Auh in ie iuhqui: niman ie ic quinuicatze, quiniacantiuitze, in isquichtin otenamiquito, motecpantiuitze, noçac in aquimittaznequi.

4. *Coxoliecaceoaztli*. *Coxolitl*: *Penelope purpurascens* Wagler. Friedmann *et al.*, *op. cit.*, Pt. 1, p. 68.

5. Rank insignia of tradesmen (Seler, *op. cit.*, Vol. II, Pts. 3-4, p. 50); *geknüpfte Tuch mit den Skorpionen*, according to Eduard Seler: *Einige Kapitel aus dem Geschichtswerk des Fray Bernardino de Sahagun aus dem Aztekischen übersetzt* (Caecilie Seler-Sachs, Walter Lehmann, Walter Krickeberg, eds.; Stuttgart: Strecker and Schröder, 1927), p. 31. *Colotlalpilli tilmatli* might also be translated as capes with twisted knots.

6. Cf. Anderson and Dibble, *op. cit.*, Book VIII, p. 55 and n. 9; Sahagún (Garibay ed.), Vol. IV, p. 320.

7. The *Florentine Codex* omits *tlemaitl*, found in the *Real Academia de la Historia MS*, in Bernardino de Sahagún: *Historia general de las cosas de Nueva España* (Francisco del Paso y Troncoso, ed.; Madrid: Hauser y Menet, 1907; hereafter referred to as *Acad. Hist. MS*), fols. 26r-50v.

8. After *conmahaquitiaque*, the *Acad. Hist. MS* has *yuan ymihi yetecõ in q'mahmamatiaq[ue]*.

9. Corresponding Spanish text: *"dos rencles: una de los sacerdotes, y otra de los señores."*

taken place, thereupon all who had gone to meet them proceeded accompanying them, guiding them; came formed in rows. Nor were there any who wished not to see them.[10]

And as they came to reach [Mexico], no one went to his house. They took them at once direct to the palace of Auitzotzin. When they arrived in the middle of the courtyard, thereupon *copal* was cast in the hearth. The ruler Auitzotl came to greet them. He said to them: "O my beloved uncles, O merchants, O vanguard merchants, you have suffered fatigue. Seat yourselves; rest." He went to place them among the lords [and] nobles, those who were arranged there according to rank, the honored ones, his war leaders, the unsurpassed.

And when Auitzotzin had seated himself, thereupon they gave him all which had been taken: the quetzal feather crest devices [and] banners; the troupial feather banners; the blue cotinga, the trogonorus feather shirts; the bracelets for the upper arm with a spray of precious feathers; turquoise mosaic shields; golden butterfly-shaped nose plates; golden ear pendants. These they placed before him. Thereupon they addressed him; they said to him: "O our lord, may it be well with thee. Behold what became the reward of the heads [and] breasts of thy beloved uncles, the outpost merchants, the disguised merchants,[11] the spying merchants in warlike places: this which was not theirs [but] became [the reward] of their starvation, their fatigue. Accept these things which were not theirs."[12]

And then he said to them: "O my beloved uncles, you have suffered fatigue; you are spent.[13] The master, the portent, Uitzilopochtli, willed that you should achieve your goal. And here I see you.[14] Behold your possessions, which became the recompense of your breasts [and] your heads. None will refuse it to you, for it is truly your property, your array. For you went away to merit it." And then he gave them the capes of plaited paper bordered with butterflies, and capes with cup-shaped decorations, and with the stone disc and the carmine colored

Auh in oacico, aiac ichan iah: çan niman quintlamelaoaltique, in itecpanchan Auitzotzin, in oacique itoalnepantla: niman ie ic copaltemalo in tlêquazco, quimonnamiquico in Auitzotl tecutli: quimilhui. Notlatzitzioane, puchtecae, oztomecae: oanquimihiiouiltique, ma ximouetzitican ma ximoceuitzinocan quimontlalito in intlan in tlatoque, in pipilti: in vncan tecpantoque, in mauiztique, in iautachcacahoan: in aiac in huihui.

Auh in onmotlali Auitzotzin: niman ie ic quitlamamaca in isquich malli omochiuh, in quetzalpatzactli quetzalpanitl, çaquanpanitl, xiuhtotoehoatl, tzinitzcanehoatl, machoncotl, xiuhchimalli, teucuitlaiacapapalotl, teucuitlanacaztepoztli, in ispan contequilique: niman ie ic quitlatlauhtia, quilhuique. Totecuiioe, ma ximehuititie: ca izcatqui in intzontecon in imelchiquiuh ipatiuh omochiuh, in motlatzitzihoan, puchteca, hiiaque in naoaloztomeca, in teiaoaloani in iaupan, in aintlaascauil, in intoneuiliz, in inchichinaquiliz omuchiuh, in aintlaacuiuh, ma xocommocuili:

auh niman quimilhui. Notlatzitzioane: oanquihiiouique, oanquiciauhque: oquimonequilti in tlacatl, in tetzauitl in vitzilobuchtli, in ouel anquichiuhque amotequiuh: auh nican amisco amocpac nitlachie. Ca izcatqui in amocococauh, in amelchiquiuh, in amotzontecon ipatiuh omuchiuh: aiac amechcaoaltiz ca nel amasca, amotlatqui ca ooanquimacehoato. Auh niman quinmacac in tilmatli, amanepaniuhqui, tempapaloio, ioan tilmatli tetecomaio, ioan temalacaio, ioan nochpallaxochio, chichicueeçotl: ioan nochpalmastlatl iacauiac. O iehoantin i, inic quinnez-

---

10. *Noçac (noço ac?)*. Cf. Bernardinus Biondelli: *Glossarium Azteco-Latinum et Latino-Aztecum* (Mediolani: Valintiner and Mues, 1869), *noço, neque* (and not). Or *no aço ac?*

11. Corresponding Spanish text: *"somos capitanes, y soldados que disimuladamente andamos a conquistar."*

12. *Ibid.: "emos trabajado y padescido mucho por alcançar estas cosas que no eran nuestras sino que por guerra y con muchos trabajos las alcāçamos."*

13. *Ibid.: "muchas cosas aueis padescido, muchos trabajos aueis passado, como valientes hombres."*

14. *Ibid.: "aueis venjdo sanos, y viuos como agora os veo."* Cf. also Angel María Garibay K.: "Huehuetlatolli," *Tlalocan,* I, 1, p. 34: *"en vuestro rostro, en vuestra frente, yo pongo los ojos."*

flower designs, of eight blotches of blood,[15] and carmine colored breech clouts with long ends. These signified that they had entered Ayotlan. And besides he bestowed capes on them — to each one a bundle of rabbit-fur[16] capes and a boat load of grains of dried maize,[17] and a boat load of beans, and some *chia*,[18] which went to be delivered at the home of each one.

And when war came to pass there at Ayotlan, the merchants, the vanguard merchants, were besieged for four years. At that time, the city yielded; at that time they broke the rampart of eagle [and] ocelot warriors. And all the devices, the quetzal feather crest devices mentioned, all these the merchants assumed; in them they conquered, they completely vanquished, [the foe].

And when the ruler Auitzotzin heard that the disguised merchants were besieged there, then aid was sent. The one who was sent was Moctezuma, who went serving as general. He had not at the time been installed as ruler. And after he had set forth, as he was already on his way, he came upon the news that those who had gone there to Ayotlan, the merchants, had conquered the land. And then the outpost merchants came staying him. They said to Moctezuma: "O our lord, thou hast tired thyself; thou hast suffered fatigue. No longer needest thou reach the place whither thou goest; for it is already the land of the master, the portent, Uitzilopochtli. For thy uncles, the Mexicans, the merchants, the vanguard merchants, have fulfilled their charge." He could only go returning; no longer did he go to wage war. He could only join with them.

And at that time all the land of Anauac was opened up. No longer were the people of Tzapotlan, of Anauac, our foes.

And the quetzal feather crest devices made captive there in Ayotlan were not yet [known] here in Mexico. Later was the time that they appeared, when they had already been carried to Tlatilulco. Auitzotzin adopted them.

And to the principal merchants, disguised merchants [of Tlatilulco], the spying merchants who entered regions of battle,[19] he paid special honors; he

caioti Aiotlan calacque: auh no ioan in quinmacac tilmatli, in cecenme, cecenquimilli in tochpanecaioti: ioan cecem acalli tlaolli, ioan cecem acalli etl, ioan chiē inic caoaloto inchachan.

Auh inic mochiuh iauiotl, in ompa Aiotlan, in impan oalmotzacu in puchteca, in oztomeca: inic nauhxiuitl, ie icoac ia in altepetl: icoac quipetlaque in quauhtenamitl, in ocelotenamitl. Auh in isquich omoteneuh in tlauiztli in quetzalpatzactli: muchi conmaaquique in puchteca, in ipan oquinpeuhque, uel quinpopoloque.

Auh in icoac oquicac in tlatoani Auitzotzin: in ompan oalmotzacu, in naoaloztomeca, niman otlaioa: iehoatl oioaloc in motecuçomatzin, tlacochcalcattitia aiamo tlatocatlalilo in icoac. Auh in oompeuh, in ie iauh: oquinamiquito in tlatolli, ca in ompa iauh Aiotlan, ca ontlalpoloque in puchteca: auh niman quitzacuilico in puchteca iiaque, quilhuique in motecoçoma. Totecuiioe, oticmociauilti, oticmihiiouilti, ca aocmo timaxitiz in ompa timouica, ca ie itlalpan in tlacatl, in tetzauitl, Vitzilobuchtli: ca oquichiuhque in intequiuh in motlatzitzioan, in mexica, in puchteca, in oztomeca: ça oalmocuepato, aoc tle quichioato iauiotl, ça tequitl quimonanato.

Auh ie icoac centlapouh, in isquich anaoacatlalli, in aocac toiaouh omuchiuh, in tzapotecatl, in anaoacatl:

auh in quetzalpatzactli, ompa malli muchiuh in Aiotlan: aiatle catca in nican mexico, quin icoac nez, in ie mamalo tlatilulco, commotlatquiti in Auitzotzin.

Auh in iehoantin in puchtecatlatoque, in naoaloztomeca in teiaoaloani, iaoc calaquini: oc cenca oquinmauizioti teucuitlatentetl in quimonaquili intenco,

---

15. *Chichicue-eçotl.* If *chichicuee-çotl,* "each of eight pieces of cloth."

16. Corresponding Spanish text: *"mantas de tochpanecaiotl."*

17. *Ibid.: "una hanega."*

18. *Ibid.: "cierta medida de chian."*

19. *Ibid.: "Los dichos mercaderes del tlatilulco se llamã tambien capitanes y soldados disimulados en abitu de mercaderes que discurrē por diuersas partes que cercan y dã guerra a las prouincias y pueblos."*

inserted in their lips golden lip plugs to signify to them that they had become his reconnoiterers. And he gave them the precious capes which have been mentioned, and precious breech clouts, which became their reward. Thereafter they tied them on when the great feast day of the month of Tlacaxipeualiztli took place.

This was when all the people about us streamed together [and] collected together here in Mexico when they observed the feast day. Once a year they came to witness it. And when all the rulers who governed cities had gathered together, thereupon began the gladiatorial sacrifice on the round sacrificial stone. Right before them it was performed; they could behold as many four hundreds as there were of captives slain. And also they could see those who were not stout of heart. Also they could see some who caused them somewhat to admire; who tried to be brave. Some still danced. And these rulers assumed as favors the rulers' capes with the cup-shaped designs, and with the eagle's face painted upon them; and red spoonbill feather fans. All rulers who governed cities assumed these as favors. And at the time that there was a gladiatorial sacrifice, they sat there in a protected place for it.

But when it was only in between, when it was not a feast day, the principal merchants, those who bathed slaves, and the disguised vanguard merchants, the slave dealers, put on only the finely woven yucca fiber capes.[20] They always went about wearing these. And the noblemen, at this same time, went about with marvelous, precious capes tied on[21] at the time when such great feast days took place as we came to during a year. But in between, when it was not a feast day, they tied on only the finely woven yucca fiber capes, but they went on using the same method of tying, because the noblemen were very circumspect and punctilious.[22]

And when Auitzotzin commanded the principal merchants, the disguised merchants, the spying merchants, to penetrate some [land], Auitzotzin summoned them. These heeded his command that on his account Anauac was to be reconnoitered. And when they went to the house of the ruler, the lord Auitzotzin, he thereupon gave them his goods — sixteen

inic quinnezcaioti, iehoantin itecunenēhoan omuchiuhque. Auh in tlaçotilmatli oquinmacac, in omoteneuh, ioan tlaçomastlatl. in innetlauhtil muchiuh: quin icoac quimolpiliaia in icoac ueuei ilhuitl quitztiuia in ipan tlacaxipeoaliztli:

ieh icoac in oalcemolinia in cematonaoac, oalmocemacia in nica mexico, in jlhuitl quioalquixtiaia, cexiuhtica in quioalmattiuia: auh in ie isquich in omocemacico tlatoque, in quipachoa altepetl. Niman ie ic ompeoa, inic tlaoâoanoz temalacac: uel imispan mochioaia, uel quimittaia, in quezquitzontli mamalti miquia, auh no uel quimittaia, in aquin amo iollochicaoac, no uel quimittaia: in cequinti oc achiton ic oaltetlamauiçoltia, oalmoquichnenequi, cequintin oc oalmitotia. Auh in iehoantin tlatoque, in quimotlauhtiaia: iehoatl in tlatocatilmatli tetecomaio, ioan xaoalquauhio, ioan tlauhquecholiecaceoaztli, in quimotlauhtiaia: in isquichtin quipachoaia altepetl in tlatoque: auh in icoac tlaoâoano oncan ic moceoaluitoque.

Auh in çan nenmaia, in amo ilhujtl: in quimolpiliaia tilmatli, in puchtecatlatoque in tealtiani: Auh in naoaloztomeca, in tecoanime, çan iehoatl in icçotilmaxixipetztli, mochipa iehoatl quiquentinemia. Auh in pipilti, çan no icoac in quimolpilitiuia in tlaçotilmatli, in mauiztic: in icoac izquitetl ueuei ilhuitl quitztiuia: inic taci ce xiuitl. Auh in icoac nenmanian, in amo ilhuitl, çan no iehoatl in icçotilmaxixipetztli in quimolpiliaia, çan quinamictiuia in innetlalpilil: ipampa in cenca mimatia pipilti, cenca tlanemiliani catca.

Auh in icoac tlanaoatiaia Auitzotzin in campa calaquizque in puchtecatlatoque in naoaloztomeca, in teiaoaloani iaoc, quinoalnotzaia in Auitzotzin: iehoantin concaquia in itlatol, in ipampa tecunenemoaz in anaoac. Auh in oiaque ichan tlatoani Auitzotl tecutli: niman ie ic quinmaca in itlatqui: nauhtzontli in quachtli in qujntiamictia: auh in oconcuito nican

20. Ibid.: "mātas de maguei bien texidas."

21. Quimulpiliaya in Acad. Hist. MS.

22. Corresponding Spanish text: "atauanlas de manera que se pareciessen las mantas que debaxo lleuā en demonstracion de su nobleza por fantasia."

hundred large cotton capes[23] which he entrusted to them as merchandise. And when they went off with it, they bore it here to Tlatilulco. And when they came, then the merchants of Tenochtitlan and those of Tlatilulco assembled. They each exchanged gifts, presented their orations,[24] and [displayed] their rearing and upbringing. Having done this, when the exchange of gifts had been accomplished, when they had animated one another, thereupon they divided up [the capes]. Those of Tenochtitlan took eight hundred large cotton capes, and also those of Tlatilulco took eight hundred. And with the large cotton capes were then bought the rulers' capes, feathered in cupshaped designs, and those of eagle face designs, and striped on the borders with feathers; and rulers' breech clouts with long ends; and embroidered skirts [and] shifts. This clothing was verily the exclusive property of Auitzotzin, [which the merchants carried to Anauac].[25]

And behold what were the goods exclusively of the merchants, those in which they dealt as vanguard merchants, [as] reconnoiterers: golden mountainshaped mitres, like royal crowns;[26] and golden forehead rosettes;[27] and golden necklaces of radiating pendants; and golden ear plugs; and golden covers used by women of Anauac—with these the princesses covered their bodies;[28] and rings for the fingers, called *matzatzaztli*; and golden ear plugs; and rock crystal ear plugs. And the things used by the common folk were obsidian ear plugs,[29] [or] tin, and obsidian razors with leather handles, and pointed obsidian blades, and rabbit fur, and needles for sewing, and shells.[30] All these were prepared as goods exclusively of the merchants, the vanguard merchants, the reconnoiterers, the outpost merchants.

quioalitqui tlatilulco. Auh in ooallaque: niman ic mocentlalia in tenochca puchteca, ioan tlatilulca puchteca, mocepantlatlauhtia, quiquistia in imihiio, in intlatol, in intlacazcaltiliz, in intlacaoapaoaliz. Auh in ie iuhqui, in ommotlatlauhtique, in ommocepanchicauhque: niman ie ic quioalmoxelhuia, ontzontli concui in quachtli tenochca: auh no ontzontli concui in tlatilulca: auh in quachtli niman ic mocoa in tlatocatilmatli ihuitica tetecomaio, ioan xaoalquauhiotilmatli, ioan ihuitica tenoaoanqui, ioan tlatocamastlatl iacauiac, ioan tlamachcueitl, tlamachhuipilli. Jni tlatquitl uel iscoian, iasca, in Auitzotzin.

Auh izcatqui in çan imiscoian intlatqui puchteca, inic onoztomecati, ontecunenemi, tepeio, teucuitlatl: iuhquin tlatocaiotl, ioan teucuitlaisquaamatl, ioan chaiaoac cozcatl, teucuitlatl, ioan teucuitlanacochtli, ioan teucuitlatl tlatzaqualoni, intech monequi in anaoacacihua: iehoantin in cihoapipilti, ic quitzacoa in innacaio, ioan in maxitlaztli, in itoca matzatzaztli, ioan teucuitlanacochtli, ioan teuilonacochtli. Auh in çan maceoalti intech monequi: iehoatl in itznacochtli, amochitl, ioan itztlaeoalli neximaloni, ioan uitzauhqui itztli, ioan tochomitl, ioan vitzmallotl, ioan coiolli. O ca isquich in, inic mochichioaia, in imiscoian intlatqui in puchteca in oztomeca in tecunenenque in iiaque.

23. *Ibid.*: *toldillos.*

24. Cf. *Florentine Codex*, Book VI, fol. 208r.

25. In the *Acad. Hist. MS*, *in quitquiliaya anauac puchteca* follows the word Auitzotzin.

26. Cf. *Florentine Codex*, Book IX, fol. 16v; see also *ibid.*, Book XI, fol. 215r, and Alonso de Molina: *Vocabulario de la lengua mexicana* (Julio Platzmann, ed.; Leipzig: Teubner, 1880), *tlatocayotl.*

27. Alvaro Tezozomoc: *Histoire du Mexique* (H. Ternaux-Compans, tr.; Paris: P. Jannet, 1853), Vol. II, p. 48 — "*bandeau royale*" or "*mitre en papier semé des pierres précieuses.*" Also see *Florentine Codex*, Book IX, fol. 16v.

28. The Aztec term permits such meanings as to lock, stop up, or imprison the body or parts of it.

29. After *itznacochtli*, the *Acad. Hist. MS* has *tepoznacochtli. yuan* (copper ear plugs, and).

30. See Pl. 14, where a *coiolli* is pictured at the bottom. The *coiolli* is a bell of gold or copper in the form of a shell. *Itztlaeoalli*: leather-covered blade if *euatl* is an element; possibly a blade produced by percussion flaking if *eua* is the element: cf. *Florentine Codex*, Book XI, viii, 4.

Third Chapter, which telleth of the offerings which the merchants made when they were going to set out somewhere.

And when they were about to set out, then they sought a good day sign — One Serpent, the straight way, or One Crocodile, or One Monkey, or Seven Serpent. The vanguard merchants who had read the day signs knew on which one they would set out.

And when it was the day before they would set out on a good day sign, thereupon they once and for all washed their heads with soap and cut their hair here in Mexico. And all the time that they went traveling in Anauac, nevermore did they wash their heads with soap [or] cut their hair. They only bathed up to their necks, not submerging in water; all the time they traveled abstaining.

And when night had fallen, when the time of blowing shell trumpets arrived, thereupon they began cutting lengths of paper. First they cut what pertained to the fire [god], whom they called Xiuhtecutli [or] Tlalxictentica. And the paper they cut so that the ends were forked[1] — cut like a woven banner. They tied it to a staff bathed with red. When they had arranged it, then they painted it with liquid rubber. They impaled the [lump of] rubber on a [copper] spit; thereupon they set it on fire. As it continued to burn, so they painted. And thus did they paint the paper: they gave it lips, nose, eyes. It resembled a man. Thus did they make a representation of the fire [god].

Then they cut the [paper] which pertained to the earth [god], whom they called Tlaltecutli. He was bound about the chest with paper; also with liquid rubber they gave him lips, nose, eyes. He also resembled a man.

Then they cut the [paper] which pertained to Yiacatecutli, Cocochimetl, Yacapitzauac. They wrapped completely the stout traveling cane. This same [staff] the merchants worshipped. The vanguard merchants, wherever they went, wherever they penetrated to engage in trade,[2] went carrying their staves. And the

Auh in icoac in ie ompeoazque: niman ie quitemoa in qualli tonalli: iehoatl in ce coatl, vtli melaoac, anoço ce cipactli, anoço ce oçomatli, anoço chicome coatl: in ommotonalpouique oztomeca: iehoantin quimati, in catlehoatl ipan ompeoazque.

Auh in iquac in ie moztla oneoazque in ipan qualli tonalli. Niman ie ic mâmouia moxima in nican mexico: çan iccen iauh in isquich cauitl nemitiui anaoac, aic ceppa mamouia moxima, çan iio moquechaltia amo polaqui: isquich cauitl moçauhtinemia.

Auh in oioac, in oacic tlatlapitzalizpan: niman ie ic quipeoaltia in amaxotla, achtopa quitequia in itech poui in tletl, quitoaia xiuhtecutli, tlalxictêtica: auh in amatl quitequia tlaiopitectli: iuhquin quachpanitl ic tlatectli, quitlacoilpia, tlauhtica ic caltia, in oconcencauhque: niman ie oltica quicuiloa, in olli ic quiço coiolomitl: niman ie ic contlecuinaltia, tlatlatinemj inic tlacuiloa. Auh inic quicuiloa amatl: quitentia, quiiacatia, quistelolotia: iuhquin tlacatl ic tlachie: inic quixiptlaiotia tletl.

Niman iehoatl quitequi, in itech poui tlalli, quitoaia tlaltecutli, amatica tlaelilpilli: no oltica quitentia, quiiacatia, quistelolotia: no iuhquin tlaca tlachie.

Niman iehoatl quitequi in itech poui iiacatecutli, in cocochimetl in iacapitzaoac: iehoatl in otlatopilli, quicencuitlalpiaia: uel iehoatl in quimoteutiaia in puchteca. Jn oztomeca, in campa uia, in campa calaquia, inic ozoztomecatizque, quitquitiuia in intopil, auh in amatl itech pouia, tlanauhçotectli, oltica tlapeiaoalli.

1. Cf. *yopitzontli* in Diego Durán: *Historia de las Indias de Nueva España y islas de Tierra Firme* (Mexico: Andrade y Escalante, 1867), Vol. I, p. 284; Seler, *Collected Works*, Vol. II, Pts. 3-4, p. 63: cap like pointed cone, of Zapotec origin. Also cf. Anderson and Dibble, *op. cit.*, Book I, p. 17 and Pl. 18.

2. *Ozoztomecatizque* so appears in the Aztec text.

paper which belonged with [the staff] was cut into four strips with liquid rubber spilled on it.

Then they cut the [paper] which pertained to One Serpent, the straight way. Thus did they cut it — in the same way, in four strips. Thus did they paint the paper: with liquid rubber they painted on it a serpent. They placed on it its head, and its eyes; they gave it a mouth, a tongue, a neck.

Then they cut the [paper] which pertained to Tlacotzontli [and] Çacatzontli.[3] Thus did they cut the paper, only like a butterfly-shaped lip ornament. And in painting it they only spattered it with liquid rubber.

And when they had prepared [the papers], thereupon the debt [to the gods] was paid at midnight. First they offered, there before the fire [god], what pertained to him. Thereupon they went forth into the middle of the courtyard. There they placed in order the [paper] offerings which pertained to the earth [god], whom they called Tlaltecutli; and One Serpent the one [who was] the way; and Tlacotzontli [and] Çacatzontli. But as the gift of Yiacatecutli they covered the stout traveling canes. The paper never burned. As often as the debt was paid, they always covered [the canes].

And when this was done, when all their offerings were arranged together in the middle of the courtyard, thereupon they entered their home [and] stood before the fire. There they beheaded a quail [to honor the fire]. When they had beheaded it, thereupon, with pointed obsidian blades, they pierced their ears, or they pierced their tongues. When the blood already flowed, they took it with their hands [and] said, "Teonappa," when they cast it into the fire. Thereupon they spattered the papers with it.

When the blood had been offered on [the papers], thereupon they went out into the middle of the courtyard. First they repeatedly cast it; toward the sky they cast their blood. Then there whence the sun came forth, called east, they cast their blood four times. Then there where the sun entered his house, called west, they also four times cast their blood. Then there toward the left hand of the earth, called the south,[4] they also four times cast their blood. Then there toward the right hand of the earth, called the north,[5] they also four times cast their blood. Just there they stopped offering blood to the four quarters.

Niman iehoatl quitequi, in itech pouhqui ce coatl, vtli melaoac: inic quitequi, çan no ie in tlanauhçotectli, inic quicuiloa amatl, oltica quicohoaicuiloa: quitlalia in itzontecon, ioan istelolo, quicamatia, quinenepiltia, quiquechtia.

Niman iehehoatl quitequi, in itech poui in tlacotzontli, in çacatzontli: inic quitequia amatl, çan tempapaloio, auh inic tlacuilolli çan tlaolchipinilli.

Auh in ocõcencauhque, niman ie ic mostlaoa, in iohoalnepantla: achtopa oncan ispan quimanilia, in tletl itech poui. Niman ie ic quiça in itoalnepantla: oncan contecpana in inestlaoal, in itech poui tlalli, quitoaia tlaltecutli: ioan ce coatl, in iehoatl vtli, ioan tlacotzontli, çacatzontli. Auh in iiacatecutli inemac, conquentia in otlatopilli, aic tlatla in amatl, in izquipa mostlaoa çan mochipa conquentia.

Auh in ie iuhqui, in omuchi centecpanque in innestlaoal itoalnepantla; niman ie ic calaqui in inchan, ispan moquetza in tletl: vncan conquechcotona in çoli. In oconquechcotonque, niman ie ic vitzauhqui ic quiço in innacaz, anoço innenepil in quiço. Jn icoac ie qujça eztli, imatica concui quitoaia teunappa in contlaça tleco: niman ie ic ipan quichichipitza in amatl:

in oipan ommiçoc niman ie ic oalquiça in itoalnepantla: achtopa ontlatlaça in ilhuicac, contlaça in iezço: niman ie ompa in tonatiuh iquiçaia, mitoaia tlapcopa, nappa in contlaça iezço: niman ie ompa in tonatiuh icalaquian, mitoaia cioatlampa: no nappa in contlaça iezço: njmã ie umpa in imaopuchcopa tlalli: mitoaia vitznaoacatlalpan: no nappa in contlaça iezço: niman ie umpa in imaiauhcampa tlalli, mitoaia mimiscoa intlalpan: no nappa in contlaça iezço: çan vmpa ommocaoaia, inic nauhcampa ommjço.

---

3. Corresponding Spanish text: *"dioses del camjno."*

4. *Ibid.*: *"se boluja hazia al norte, que dizen ser la mano yzqujerda del mundo*: *a donde llaman vitznauacatlalpan y por otro nomble* [sic] *mjctlampa."* Sahagún's rendition of the directions is correct in Chap. 8.

5. Corresponding Spanish text: *"bolujase hazia al medio dia que dizen ser la mano derecha del mundo y llamanla mimiscoa intlalpan."*

And when this was done, when blood had been offered, when he had made his blood flow, also he spattered it profusely on the papers which lay in the middle of the courtyard. When he came to make blood offerings, then once more he entered his home, stood before the fire, [then took the paper, raised it up — four times he raised it as an offering toward the fire].[6] He spoke to it; he addressed it thus: "May it be well with thee, O thou ocelot warrior, O Tlalxictentica, O lord of the four quarters! May thou in peace accept[7] thy property, thy possessions; perchance in some small thing I have offended thee." [8]

Thereupon he offered the paper to the fire. As he offered it, then he took white *copal* — this was the torchwood[9] *copal*, the legitimate; pungent, odoriferous, very clean, with no rubbish nor dirt. Then he inserted it among the papers, so that they would blaze up well. And he stood watching it closely as it burned, taking good care of it. If the paper only smoked, when it did not burn well, he was much frightened. There he saw that perhaps a sickness would somewhere go to seize him. But if it burned quickly, so that it crackled [and] popped a great deal, he was greatly pleased thereby. He said within himself, "He hath been good to me, the master, our lord. I shall indeed reach the place where I am to go."

And having done this, he thereupon went forth into the middle of the courtyard where the paper [offerings] were laid out. Then he took up [the paper and] stood facing the place whence the sun came forth. Also four times he raised it as an offering; toward all the four quarters he did this. And thus he took up the papers: first he took that which pertained to Tlacotzontli; then the one[10] which pertained to Çacatzontli. Then the one which pertained to One Serpent, the straight way, he laid just on top of them. He bore them all in his arms to lay them on the fire there in the courtyard.

When each one had burned, he then dug into the soil, in the same place, in the middle of the courtyard. There he buried, all together, the paper ashes [including those] burned in his house, having only skimmed

Auh in ie iuhqui in omiçoc, in oconquisti iiezço: no ipan conchichipitza in amatl, vncan mani itoalnepantla: in oommiçoco: niman ie no ceppa calaqui in ichan, ispan moquetza in tletl, quilhuia injc quinotza. Ma ximeuiltitie moceloquichtle, tlalxictenticae, nauhiotecutle: ma iuian xicqualmanili in mocococauh in mascatzin: aço itla oac nimitznoiolitlacalhui.

Niman ie ic commana in amatl in tleco: in ocomman, çatepan concui in iztac copalli, iehoatl in tzioaccopalli, in uel melaoac, in uel iaque in uel chipaoac: in amo tlaçollo, in amo teuhio: niman itlan conaquia in amatl, inic uel cuetlaniz: auh uel quitztimoquetza inic tlatla, uel quimocuitlauiticac intla çan ie pucheoa in amatl, in amo uel tlatla: cenca momauhtiaia: oncan quittaia, in aço cana cocoliztli quicuitiuh: auh intla hiciuhca tlatla in cenca cocomoca, cuecuetlaca: ic cenca papaqui iitic quitoaia, Onechmocnelili, in tlacatl, totecuio, ca uel naciz in umpa niauh.

Auh in ie iuhqui: niman ie ic quiça in itoalnepantla, in uncan mani amatl: niman ie ic concui vmpa itztimoquetza in tonatiuh iquiçaia: no nappa in coniiaoa, nauhcampaisti iuh quichioa. Auh inic concui amatl, achtopa quicui in itech poui tlacotzontli: niman iehehoatl, in itech poui çacatzontli: niman iehehoatl in itech poui ce coatl, vtli melaoac: ça pani quimana, quicennapaloa inic cõmana tleco: in vncan itoalco.

Jn ontlatlac, niman ie ic tlatataca, in çan no oncan itoalnepantla: vncan quicentoca incalitic otlatlac amanestli, çan quisololooa, amo no ie in tleco nestli: Oiui in in muchioaia in ioaltica.

---

6. In the *Acad. Hist. MS*, *tletl* is followed by *nimā ye ic concui in amatl cahcocui nauhpa in coniaua in iuicpa tletl*.

7. Corresponding Spanish text: *"ruegoos que recibais."*

8. *Ibid.*: *"perdoname, si en algo os he offendido."*

9. See Emily Walcott Emmart: *The Badianus Manuscript (Codex Barberini, Latin 241), Vatican Library; an Aztec Herbal of 1552* (Baltimore: The Johns Hopkins Press, 1940), p. 299; also Paul C. Standley "Trees and Shrubs of Mexico," *Contributions from the United States National Herbarium*, Vol. 23, Pt. 3 (Washington: Government Printing Office, 1923), pp. 542-552.

10. *Iehehoatl*: the term so appears in the Aztec text.

them together from the surface, not also [taking] the ashes of the fire [itself].[11] In this manner was it done during the night.

And when it dawned, he thereupon sent emissaries [and] messengers to summon the principal merchants. He assembled all the merchants, the disguised merchants, those who bathed slaves, the slave dealers.[12] And he assembled the youths who traveled, indeed all the old women, his kinsmen, the beloved women,[13] his aunts.[14] And when they had come together, thereupon their hands [and] mouths were washed. When hands had been washed, thereupon food was served. When food had been eaten, then once again were hands [and] mouths washed; thereupon chocolate was served [and] drunk. Then tubes of tobacco were offered them.

And when this was done, then [the host] sat before them; he besought them; he said to them: "Ye have spent yourselves; ye have suffered fatigue. For here in a few words, in a brief utterance, I beseech your revered motherliness [and] fatherliness. For yet, with this, I abandon your beloved water flowers, your beloved neighborhood, your city.[15] Hence have I yet prepared the washing of hands [and] mouths, and grass beds. The trifling purchases are exhibited — the little obsidian knives with leather handles, the little shells, the little needles, the trifling cochineal, the alum. Perhaps the protector of all will strengthen me. This you have received [and] heard."

And when he had thus spoken to them, thereupon the principal merchants of all the *calpulli*,[16] the leaders of each *calpulli*:[17] Pochtlan, Auachtlan, Atlauhco, Acxotla, Tepetitlan, Itztolco, [and] Tzonmolco, the six[18] *calpulli* leaders, who each ruled [and] governed, responded to his words.

When somewhere there were riches [and] the invitation of guests, thus they remained seated by rank, in order:[19] at one side, by the wall on one side, were the

Auh in ooallatuic: niman ie ic tlatitlani tlaioa, in quimonnotza in puchtecatlatoque, quincentlalia in isquichtin puchteca, naoaloztomeca, in tealtiani, in tecoani. Auh in telpuchtinemi uel isquich quicentlalia in ilamatque in inoaiolque in cihoatzhoatzitzinti in iiauihoan. Auh in ocenquizque, niman ie ic tematequilo, tecamapaco, in ontematequiloc, niman ie ic tetlamaco: Jn ontlaqualoc, niman ie no ceppa tematequilo, tecamapaco, niman ie ic teamaco atlioa: niman ie iietl temaco.

Auh in ie iuhqui: niman ic imispã onmotlalia, quintlatlauhtia, quimilhuia. Oanquimociauiltique, oanquimihiiouiltique: ca nican cententica cencamatica nictlatlauhtia, in amotenaniotzin, in amatetaiotzin: ca oc ie nocontlalcauia in amaxochtzin, in amotlaxilacaltzin: auh in amatzin, in amotepetzin: ma oc nicqualchioa in tematequiliztli, in tecamapacaliztli, auh in çacapepechtli: ca omonexiti in tlacocohoaltzintli, in itztlaeoaltzintli in coioltzintli, in uitzmallotzintli, in nocheztzintli, in tlalxocotzintli: aço uel nechonmotlatoctiliz, in tloque, nahoaque: ca iehoatl in anquimocuilia, in anquimocaquitia.

Auh in icoac oiuh quimilhui: niman ie ic quicuepilia in itlatol, in puchteca, tlatoque in izquipetlame, inic cecencalpupan teiacana puchtlan, aoachtlan, atlauhco, acxotla tepetitlan, itztulco, tzommolco: in chicuacenpetlame, cecenme teiacanque tlapachoa.

Jn icoac campa tlacamacho, cohoanotzalo: inic onoque tecpantoque, tlaiaoalotoque, centlapal in calmaieticate in puchtecatlatoque: auh no centlapal, in cal-

11. Corresponding Spanish text: *"cogia la ceniça del papel de tal manera que no tomaua nada de la otra ceniça del fuego, ni tampoco alguna tierra del soelo."*

12. *Ibid.*: *"Los principales mercaderes, capitanes disimulados, y . . . los otros ricos mercaderes que tratauan, en comprar, y vender esclauos."*

13. *Cihoatzhoatzitzinti*: the term is so written in the Aztec text.

14. In the *Acad. Hist. MS*: *"auh in telpuchnemi, uel isquichtin quincentlalia, in ilamatque, in iuanyolque y ciuatzitzinti, inauiuan."*

15. *Amaxochtzin*: it is suggested that this term means *linderos* (limits, boundaries). — Personal communication, Angel María Garibay.

16. A marginal note in Sahagún's hand in the *Acad. Hist. MS* translates *izquipetlame* as *de los barrios*.

17. *Cecencalpulpan*, in the *Acad. Hist. MS.*

18. Seven *calpulli* are listed, although the Aztec text reads "six."

19. Corresponding Spanish text: *"Quando alguno haze combite que se llama tecuanotzaliztli ordenanse los combidados en sus asientos desta manera."*

principal merchants; and likewise at one side, by the wall on [the other] side, were the disguised merchants, the spying merchants in warlike places, seated in order. Closing in [the ends] were the youths.[20]

And the one who was in the very leading position, the principal merchant, came out ahead; he besought, he said to [the host]: "It is well that thou art here. For we have accepted, taken, and heard thy discourse. Be careful in taking to travel, for already thou wilt meet One Serpent, the straight way. Thou mayest somewhere, set foot on the rocky way [or] the mountain trail,[21] [or] with the gods of the road. Travel with care in the plain, in the desert, lest our lord, the protector of all, the master of the heavens [and] of the earth, will somewhere destroy thee. Thou mayest perish in the midst of the forest [or] the crags; thy poor maguey fiber cape [or] breech clout dragged forth; thy poor bones scattered in various places, and thy poor hair streaming out at the place of glory, of renown. As thou goest, go dedicated, indebted, to misery — suffering.[22]

"But if the master, our lord, indeed should nowhere destroy [and] slay thee, endure the unseasoned, the saltless, the briny [food]; the dried tortillas, the coarse *pinole,* the wretched, soggy maize. And likewise nowhere cast slander [or] aspersions at one;[23] make thyself reverent, respectful, to others. If thereby the protector of all should entrust thee something of his riches, his wealth, do not let thyself be arrogant.

"If perhaps somewhere thou goest among others in thy banqueting[24] — perhaps at Tenochtitlan, or Quauhtitlan, or Azcapotzalco, [or] Uitzilopochco, watch thy words; greet others well. And if thou canst reach the city which thou seekest out, be quick to take to the axe, the cutting of wood, the sweeping, the laying of fires, the lighting with torches, the shaking out of [mats], the washing of hands, of mouths, and all the performance of penances, the gathering of fir branches. Go in diligence; be not lazy. Now thou hast heard all."

maieticate, in naoaloztomeca, in iaupan teiaoaloani, tecpantoque: ça tlatzacutoque in telpupuchti.

Auh in iehoatl in uel teiacantica in puchtecatlato, iacattiuh in quitlatlauhtia, quilhuia. Ca ie qualli, ca nican tica, ca otoconanque ca otoconcuique: auh ca otoncacque, in mihiio, in motlatol, ma iiolic xocona in mocxi, ca ie toconnamiquiz in ce coatl vtli melaoac: ma cana toconicxinamic in tecoatl, in quauhcoatl, in tlacotzontli, in çacatzontli: ma iiolic xocontoca in teutlalli, in istlaoatl: aço cana mitzpopoloz in totecuio, in tloque, naoaque, in ilhuicahoa, in tlalticpaque: ma cana xipopoliui quauitl iitic, tescalli iitic: ma oncan uilanto in maiaçoltzin, in momastlaçoltzin: ma cana cecenmanto immomiotzin: auh in motzontzin ma cana momoiaoato: in teiocan in tocaioca, ma umpa popouhto, ma umpa istlauhto in icnopillotl in icnotlacaiotl.

Auh intlaca can uel mitzpopoloz, mitztlatlatiz, in tlacatl, totecuio: ma oaltimaliui, in âcococ in apoiec, in iztaaiotzintli, in totopochtzintli, in xalpinoltzintli, in tlaolpaoaztzintli: auh no ioan ma cana tonteçoquimotla, tonteatlatzicuinalhui, ximoteimacaxili, ximotemauhcaittili: Jntla ie itla ticpielia, in itotonca, in iiamanca, in tloque, naoaque, ma mitznacaztlachielti:

aço cana tontenepanoa tocohoapan, aço tenochtitlan, aço quauhtitlan, aço azcaputzalco, Vitzilobuchco: uel ximotlatolti, qualli ic ximotenochili. Auh intla uel itech taciz in altepetl, in ompa titlamattiuh, ma xoconcuitiuetzi in tepuztli, in quauhtequiliztli, in tlachpanaliztli, in tletlaliliztli, in tlauiliztli in tlatzetzeloliztli, in tematequiliztli, in tecamapacaliztli: auh in isquich in tlamaceoaliztli, in acxoiacuioaliztli, xommopilquitito, ma tontlatlatziuh: ie isquich in ticcaqui.

20. *Ibid.: "sientanse todos juntos a las paredes en sus petates, y icpales a la mano derecha se sientan la gente mas principal por sus grados, y orden de su principalidad como son entre los mercaderes pochtecatlatoque, y a la otra parte que es la mano yzquierda, se asientan los que no son tan principales por los grados, y orden de su principalidad, como es entre los mercaderes de aquellos que llaman naoaloztomeca: las estremidades destas dos partes ocupan los mancebos ordenados por su principalidad."*

21. Cf. *Acad. Hist. MS*, in which a gloss in Sahagún's hand describes *tecuatl* as *camyno pedregoso* and *quauhcoatl* as *camyno môtañoso.*

22. Corresponding Spanish text: *"Rogamos empero n͞ro señor que antes morays en la prosecucion de v͞ro viaje, que no que boluays atras, porque mas querriamos oyr, que v͞ras mͣtas, y v͞ros mastles, estuujessen hechos pedaços por essos camjnos, y derramados v͞ros cabellos: para que desto os quedasse honrra, y fama, que no que bolujendo atras diessedes deshͦrra a vos y a nos."*

23. *Ibid.: "Guardate . . . de off͝eder a nadie con tus palabras o con tus obras."*

24. *Ibid.: "Quando te juntares, con los que no conoces."*

He who thus assembled the principal merchants of all the *calpulli* was one who had already attained his desires, one of many possessions, many goods. But he who was still poor, of not yet very many possessions, goods, summoned only the merchants, the vanguard merchants, of his *calpulli*. And he who was to become leader summoned not only those who heard the discourse; he would take all—as many as wished [to go].

Some were to go for the first time; perchance they were yet young boys whose mothers [and] fathers had [the merchants] take with them. They said: "Let the young boy go with them into the forests [and] grasslands, into places of glory, of renown. For there is the good example;[25] there is castigation. There, perhaps, with their help, he will become prudent, mature, understanding. May he not perish there. What, in truth, will be done? What shall I make of him? Is he perchance a woman? Shall I place, perchance, a spindle, a batten, in his hand?"

And this mother [and] father quite on their own account besought their son. They said to him: "Here thou art, O my son, my beloved youth, my only child. Thou art unfortunate. What in truth shall we do? What shall we make of thee? For this reason did the master, the lord, the protector of all, the master of the earth, create thee, that thou shouldst be a man. Accompany them carefully. Imitate them as they go, as they travel, and when the sauce dish [and] carrying basket are placed before one, [and] drink is offered one. Pay good heed which one is given first place as places are taken before the people; look well how things are arranged."

And when they were about to go, when they were about to start, first, in the house of the one who would lead, who would go as leader of the youths, everything was there assembled; all the loads of merchandise, all the consignments, the possessions of the principal merchants, and the goods of the merchant women, were arranged separately. Right before them all, there they were gathered, there they were assembled, waiting until they were to start. And they assembled all the travel rations, the *pinole*. And they arranged things in the house not by day but at night.

And when they had assembled indeed all the loads, they thereupon arranged them on the carrying frames; they set one each on the hired burden-carriers[26] to

Jn aquin iuh quincentlaliaia y, in puchteca tlatoque, in izquipetlame: iehoatl in ie otlacnopilhui, in ie miec iasca, itlatqui. Auh in çan oc motolinia: in aiamo cenca miec iiasca, itlatqui, çan oc icalpultia in quinnotza puchteca, oztomeca. Auh in aquin tachcauhchiuhtiaz, amo çan icel in quinonotzaia, in quicaquia tlatolli: mochtin in quinuicaz, in quezquintin moioleoa:

in cequintin quin iiopa iazque, aço quin telpuchtepitoton in quinteuicaltiaia in intahoan, in innahoan. Quitoaia, ma teuica in telpuchtontli, in quauhtla, in çacatla, in teniocan in tocaiecan: ca ompa mani in tezcatl, ca ompa hicac in tlauilli in ocotl: ca ompa ca in atl cecec, in tzitzicaztli: aço õpa tepallachiez, mozcaliz, tlacaquiz ma ompa popoliui, tle nellaiz, tle nicchioaz, cuis cihoatl aço malacatl tzotzopaztli imac nictequiliz.

Auh in iehoatl tetatzin tenantzin: çan iscoian in quitlatlauhtia in ipiltzin: quilhuia. Ca nican tica nopiltze, notelpuchtze, nocenteconetzine: timotolinia, tlê nel taiz, tle ticchioaz, ca oic mitzmochiuili, in tlacatl totecuio, in tloque, naoaque, in tlalticpaque, inic toquichtli: ma iuian xonmoteuiquilitiuh, ma tetech xoconitztiuh in iuh huiloa, in iuh ôtlatoco: auh in iuh teispan manalo in mulcaxitl, in chiquiuitl, in iuh teamaco: uel ximotlachielti, in catlehoatl achtopa mocui, inic teispan nequetzalo: uel xicmottili in iuh tlatecpano.

Auh in icoac in ie iazque, in ie ompeoazque: achtopa ichan monechicoa, in aqujn teiacanaz, in tachcauhchiuhtiaz: mochi oncan mocennechicooa, in isquich tlamamalli, in tiamictli, ioan in isquich tetlatquitilli, in imasca in puchtecatlatoque: ioan in intlatqui, in puchtecacihoa, nononqua mochichioa, uel imispan mochintin, oncan mocentlalitoque, vncan cenquiztoque: quichisticate in quenman onpeoazque. Auh mochi quinechicooa: in itacatl, in pinolli: auh quicaltema, amo cemilhuitl, çan ioaltica.

Jn icoac ocenquiz in ie mochi tlamamalli: niman ie ic quichichioa cacastica quiquequetza in tlaqueoaltin quimamazque, achi etic, çan quipantia. Auh in

25. Cf. *Florentine Codex*, Book VI, fol. 204r.

26. Corresponding Spanish text: *"hazian sus cargas en los cacaxtles: y dauan a cada uno destos, que tenjan alqujlados, para que las lleuasen a cuestas, la carga que avia de lleuar: y de tal manera las compasauan, que no eran muy pesadas, y lleuauan igual peso: esto se hazia, por la orden que daua, el que yba por capitan."*

carry on their backs: not very heavy; they put on only a limited amount. And the burden-carrying merchants bore no great weight, only a measured amount. All were thus [laden]. And also this was as those who went as leaders, who guided the train of bearers, had ordered.[27] But [as for] those who were going for the first time, the small boys, they loaded nothing on their backs. They placed upon their backs only the drinking vessels, the gourds.[28]

And when things had been arranged in order in their house, when all were about to go on the road, when darkness had fallen, when it was already night, thereupon all the boats were filled; perhaps two or three boats in which the goods went.

When this had been done, when the boats had been loaded, then those about to embark took their leave. [The leader] seated himself before the people; he said: "Here you are, O noblemen. Your revered feet are benumbed [with age]. Now we leave you; now we proceed to go. For we have received, we have taken, your exhortations, the tears, the compassion which is folded, bound within your bowels, your breasts. For we abandon the entrances [and] the courtyards. And our aunts, our elder sisters, our parents — may they not forget us."

And [the old men and women] thereupon answered their words; they said to them: "It is well. Go your way in peace. Go with no thought of that within your houses [or] at your hearths. For you have heard much of the motherliness [and] fatherliness so that you are bound to the reprimands, the castigation, which have been placed upon you. Do not, somewhere, cast away [or] prejudice the exhortations of your mothers [and] fathers. And you go holding by the hand the unfortunate, small boys. Let them be made to prepare for others the little seats, beds of straw, grass seats. And [instruct them in] all the penances, the fixing of the divisions of the night, the vigils: take care of them; keep them firmly in your grasp. Do not neglect the way of rearing and upbringing."

In this manner — behold — they took final leave of them. When the discourse of each had ended, all thereupon arose. Already a very great fire had been laid, before which lay a green gourd vessel [full] of *copal.* One by one they continued taking the *copal,*

iehoanti quimamazque in puchteca: amo cenca ietic çan tlaiehecolli, çam mochiuhqui. Auh no ic monaoatia in tachcauhchiuhtiazque in quiiacanazque tlamamalli. Auh in quin iopa iazque: in telpochtepitoton aiatle quinmamaltia: çan oc iehoatl in atlioaloni, quinmamaltia, in aiotectli.

Auh in icoac otlatecpanque, in incalitic, in iuh uiloaz vtlica: in onioac in ie tlapoiaoa, niman ie ic tlaacaltemalo, in acalli aço vntetl, aço etetl inic iauh tlatquitl.

Jn ie iuhq̄ in oontlaacaltemaloc: niman ie ic tlanaoatia, in ie onmacalaquizque, teispan onmotlalia, quitoa. Ca nican anmoetzticate pillitzine: amocxitzin cêcêpoatica, ma oc tamechtotlalcauilican, ma oc toniatiuian: ca oticcuique, ca oticanque in amihiiotzin, in amotlatoltzin, in amoxillantzinco in amotozcatlantzinco, cuelpachiuhtica in ilpitica: in choquizço in tlaocollo ma oc tictlalcauican in quiaoatl, in itoalli. Auh in taui, in toueltiuh, in tocotonca, in touiltecca, macuelle techilcahoa.

Auh niman ie ic quincuepilia in intlatol, quimilhuia. Ca ie qualli, ma iiolic xoconanacan in amocxi maca tle xicqualmattiuia in amocalitic in amotlecuilla, ca miec in oanquicacque in naniotl in taiotl, inic oamihilpiloque, in têio in quauhio, in atl itztic, in atl cecec, in tzitzicaztli amotech opachiuh: ma cana anquintlaxiliti anquinchitoniliti, in imihiio in intlatol in amonanhoan in amotahoan. Auh motolinia in amomatitech anquimonantiui in telpopochtzitzinti: ma contetlalilitiuian in teicpaltzintli, in xiuhpepechtzintli in çacaicpaltzintli. Auh in isquich in tlamaceoaliztli, in iohoaltamachiuiliztli in istoçoliztli: xiquincuitlauiltica xiquintlaquauhtzitzquiltica, ma anquizxicauhti in oapaoaloni, in izcatiloni.

Oiui, y, izca iccen quinnahoatiaia. Jn ontzontzonquiz tlatolli: niman ie ic nequetzalo, ie omotlali in cenca vei tletl, xoxouic copalxicalli ispan mani: ceceiaca concuitimani in copalli, contentimani in tleco, nimã ic quiztimani, acalco tlamelahoa: aocac calaqui

---

27. The *Acad. Hist.* MS has *momana* in place of *monaoatia.*

28. Corresponding Spanish text: *"mãdauãlos, que lleuassen lo que se auja de beuer, como pinolli, y las xicaras, y los reboluedores, que eran por la mayor parte, hechos de conchas de tortuga."*

casting it into the fire. Then they went forth [and] proceeded straightway to the boats. None entered the women's quarters, neither did any turn back [or] look to one side. If perchance he had gone forgetting something, he might no more come to take it,[29] nor might they still go to offer it to him. No longer could he do it. Neither did even one of all the old merchants [and] merchant women go following them. When one turned back they thought it an omen of evil — sinful; they regarded it as dangerous. In this manner did the vanguard merchants depart.

cihoapan, ânoac oalmocuepa in ma oalnacaztlachie, in aço itla oquilcauhtia: in ma oc concui, in manoçoc conmacati, aocmo ueliti: anoac quintocatiuh, in isquich tlacatl, in puchtecaueuetque, in puchtecacioa. Jn aquin oalmocuepaia, quitetzammatia, quitlatlaculmatia couicaittaia. Oiui y, inic õpeoaia in oztomeca.

29. *Concui* (*concuique*) in the *Acad. Hist. MS.*

Fourth Chapter, which telleth what the merchants did when they reached where they were going.

And when the merchants had reached Anauac [and] those[1] cities which the rulers of Anauac governed, they thereupon gave them all the items of trade — the precious capes, precious skirts, precious shifts, the property of Auitzotzin, with which they greeted them. And when they had given them these, thereupon the rulers of Anauac gave in return the long quetzal feathers and their tail feathers, and the chili-green ones; and blue cotinga and trogonorus feathers.

And where they entered Anauac was not the place of entry for everyone, because it was the trading area of [the merchants of] Auitzotzin. There went, there entered, only those of Tlatilulco, Tenochtitlan, Uitzilopochco, Azcapotzalco, [and] Quauhtitlan. They always went accompanying one another.

When the merchants had already set out for Anauac, they divided there at Tochtepec. One part entered there into Anauac Ayotlan [and] one part entered there into Anauac Xicalanco.[2] And in this wise was the work divided: those of Tlatilulco were divided into two parts; also those of Tenochtitlan were divided into two parts. Their companions were those of Uitzilopochco, Azcapotzalco, [and] Quauhtitlan.

And as they traveled the road, they went girt for war. They bore their shields, their obsidian-bladed swords, [and] their devices, because they passed through the enemy's land, where they might die [and] where they took captives.

And when they entered there into Xicalanco, they carried the goods of Auitzotzin, all the same ones which have been mentioned, the rulers' capes, the rulers' breech clouts, the precious skirts embroidered perhaps with designs of squared corner stones, or with irregular designs, and embroidered shifts.

And these were the personal property of the merchants: mountain-shaped gold, like a royal crown which the rulers of those places wore, and golden

Jnic naui capitulo, itechpa tlatoa: in tlein quichioaia, in icoac oacique, in cãpa uia puchteca

Auh in oacique in anaoac puchteca: in eehoantin quipachoa altepetl, in tlatoque anaoac: niman ie ic quinmaca in isquich omocôcôuh, in tlaçotilmatli, in tlaçocueitl, in tlaçouipilli: in iasca Auitzotzin inic quimontlapaloa. Auh in oquimommacaque: niman ie ic quioalcuepcaiotia in anaoacatlatoque, iehoatl in uiac quetzalli, ioan totocuitlapiltic quetzalli, ioan chilchotic quetzalli: ioan xiuhtototl ioan tzinitzcan.

Auh in ompa calaquia anaoac, amo mochi tlacatl icalaquian catca: ipampa ca icooapan catca in Auitzotzin, çan iioque in ompa uia, in ompa calaquia, tlatilulca, Tenochca, Vitzilobuchca, azcaputzalca: quauhtitlãcalque: çan mochipa iehoantin inuicalhoan, mochiuhtinenca.

Jn icoac in ie umpeoac anaoac puchteca: vncan moxeloaia in tochtepec, centlamantli vmpa calaquia, in anaoac aiotlan: no centlamantli ompa calaquia, in anaoac xicalanco. Auh inic motequimacaia: occan moxeloaia in tlatilulca, no occan moxeloaia in tenochca: inuiuicalhoan in Vitzilobuchca, in azcaputzalca, quauhtitlancalque.

Auh inic otlatocaia moiaochichiuhtiuia: inchimal, inmacquauh ietiuh, intlauiz, ipampa ca iautitlan in quiçaia: in cana miquia, in cana tlamaia.

Auh in ompa calaquia Xicalanco: in quitquia itlatqui Auitzotzin, çan ie no ie in isquich omito in tlatocatilmatli, in tlatocamastlatl, in tlaçocueitl, in tlamachio aço tetenacazio, anoço chicocueitl, ioan tlamachuipilli.

Auh izcatqui, in imiscoia imasca puchteca: tepeio teucuitlatl, iuhquin tlatocaiotl: commaquia in ompa tlatoque, ioan teucuitlaisquaamatl, ioan teucuitlatlan-

---

1. Eehoantin (iehoantin) so appears in the Aztec text.

2. Anauac Ayotlan and Anauac Xicalanco: the former, Pacific coast lands about Teuantepec; the latter, corresponding Gulf coast lands. Cf. Seler, *op. cit.*, Vol. II, Pt. 1, pp. 34-35. See also *supra*, Chap. 2, n. 1.

forehead rosettes, and golden tooth necklaces, and plaited golden necklaces, and small[3] necklaces of golden flutes, and thin golden necklaces. And these were what the princesses required: golden bowls for spindles, and ear plugs of gold and of rock crystal. But those who were only commoners required obsidian ear plugs, copper ear plugs, and razors of obsidian with leather handles, and pointed obsidian blades, and shells, and needles; [and] cochineal, alum, rabbit fur, birthwort,[4] [and] cosmos sulphureus.[5]

And the merchandise of the leaders, the principal merchants, those who bathed slaves, slave dealers, was slaves, perhaps women, perhaps young boys, whom they sold there.[6] And when they took them, they put their devices on them. If perchance it was a woman they put on devices[7] because they fared forth in warlike lands; they feared our foes of Teuantepec, of Tzapotlan, of Chiapan, when they passed among them.

And when they had come to arrive in the midst of the foe, first they sent messengers [and] emissaries to inform [and] speak to them. And so they journeyed not by day when they traveled, but by night. And when the messengers had arrived, then the rulers of Anauac sent emissaries to meet them. [These] also went girt for war; they went bearing their shields, their obsidian-bladed swords, their devices. Thus they went forth to meet them in the midst of the enemy's land, so that [the merchants] could arrive there [in the province of] Anauac Xicalanco.

And when the merchants reached Anauac Xicalanco [and] the rulers who governed the cities of Anauac, thereupon they gave to each of them all the items of trade—the precious capes, precious skirts, precious shifts, the property of Auitzotzin, with which they greeted them. And then the rulers of Anauac, Xicalanco, Cimatlan, [and] Coatzaqualco reciprocated with the large green stones,[8] round, green, like tomatoes; the cylindrical green stones; then the green

cozcatl, ioan teucuitlacozcapetlatl, ioan xocotic teucuitlatlapitzalcozcatl, ioan pitzaoac teucuitlacozcatl. Auh izcatqui in intech monequia cihoapipilti: teucuitlatzaoalcaxitl, ioan teucuitlanacochtli, ioan teuilonacochtli. Auh in çã macehoalti intech monequia: itznacochtli, tepoznacochtli: ioan itztlaeoalli neximaloni: ioan vitzauhqui ioan coiolli, ioan vitzmallotl: nocheztli, tlalxocotl, tochomitl, tlacopatli, xuchipatli.

Auh in iehoantin, teiacanque puchtecatlatoque: tealtianime, tecohoanime, in intiamic catca, tlatlacoti, aço cihoatl, aço oquichpiltontli, in ompa quimonnamacaia. Auh inic quinuicaia: intlauiz quimonaquiaia, in aço cihoatl conaquiaia in tlauiztli: ipampa ca iautitlan in quiçaia, in quimimacacia toiauhoan tequantepecatl, tzapotecatl, chiappanecatl in intzalan quiçaia.

Auh in ie onacitiui, iaunepantla achtopa ontlatitlani, ontlaihoa, ontlanonotza onteitoa. Auh inic nenemi, amo cemilhuitl: in otlatoca: çan ioaltica. Auh in oacito titlanti, niman oallaihoa in anaoaca tlâtoque: inic quinoalnamiquia no oalmoiauchichiuhtiui inchimal, inmacquauh, intlauiz ietiuitz: inic oncan quinoalnamiquia iaunepantla, inic uel onacia in ompa anaoac Xicalanco.

Auh in oacique puchteca, in anaoac Xicalanco: in iehoantin ompa tlatoq̃, in quipachoa altepetl anaoac: niman ie ic quinmamaca in isquich omococouh in tlaçotilmatli, in tlaçocueitl, in tlaçovipilli, in iasca Auitzotzin inic quimontlapaloa. Auh inic quioalcuepcaiotia in anaoacatlatoque, in xicalanca: in cimateca, in coatzaqualca: iehoatl in uei chalchiuitl, in ololiuhqui quiquiltic tomatic, niman ieehoatl in acatic chalchiuitl, niman ieehoatl in tlacanaoalli chalchiuitl

---

3. Cf. Leonhard Schultze Jena: *Gliederung des Alt-Aztekischen Volks in Familie, Stand und Beruf* (Stuttgart: W. Kohlhammer, 1952), pp. 189, 335, and Molina, *op. cit.,* Spanish-Nahuatl section, *pequeño.*

4. *Tlacopatli.* Medicinal herb, *Aristolochia mexicana,* according to Sahagún (Garibay ed.), IV, p. 361. Francisco J. Santamaría, *Diccionario general de americanismos* (Méjico: Editorial Pedro Robredo, 1942), Vol. III, p. 182, classifies it as *Aristolochya sp.,* or as one of the *plantas compuestas, lostephane heterophylla* Benth., or *Viguiera excelsa* Benth., and Hook; "*o genéricamente de varias especies de esta familia [Aristolochya], como el GUACO.*"

5. *Xochipatli.* "*Hierba florida de medicina. Planta narcótica, medicinal, olorosa. . . . Cosmos sulphureus o Jacquina aurantiaca*" (Sahagún, *op. cit.,* Vol. IV, p. 370). See also Standley, *op. cit.,* Pt. 4, p. 1106.

6. Corresponding Spanish text: "*hombres, y mugeres, y muchachos, y muchachas: y vendianlos en aquella prouincia de xicalanco.*"

7. Ibid.: "*lleuauãlos vestidos, con armas defensiuas, que llamã ichcavipilli, porque no se los matassen los enemigos.*"

8. *Chalchiuitl:* "common jade of green and white color," according to William F. Foshag: "Mineralogical Studies on Guatemalan Jade," *Smithsonian Miscellaneous Collections,* Vol. 135, No. 5 (Washington: Smithsonian Institution, 1957), p. 8.

stones cut on a bias; the well-colored precious green stone[9] which today we call the finest emerald-green jade;[10] and fine bottle-green jadeite,[11] and turquoise mosaic shields; and [stones] with green pyrites in their midst;[12] and large red sea shells, and red coral shells[13] — the very red [ones], and flower-colored shells — the very yellow [ones], and tortoise shell cups[14] — the very yellow [ones], and ocelot-colored tortoise shell cups; and the feathers of the red spoonbill, the troupial, and the blue honeycreeper;[15] and yellow parrot feathers; and the skins of wild animals: this was the black ocelot. All this which the merchants [and] vanguard merchants took there in Xicalanco [and] carried away belonged to Auitzotzin.

And when they came to arrive here in Mexico, then the vanguard merchants placed before Auitzotzin all that which they had gone to get. In this manner traveled the reconnoiterers who exalted the city and the Mexican state; because indeed everywhere they were surrounded by the lands of Anauac. And for that reason Auitzotzin valued them highly. Indeed, he made them like his sons; their very equals he made them. As were noblemen, so also were the merchants, capable and enterprising.

in uel tlapaltic quetzalchalchiuitl, in ascan tiquitoa quetzalitztli, ioan tlilaiotic quetzalitztli, ioan xiuhchimalli ioan quetzalichpetztli tzalaiio, ioan tlapaltecuciztli, ioan tapachtli in uellapaltic, ioan in suchitapachtli in uel coztic, ioan aiotectli in uel coztic, ioan oceloaiotectli, ioan teuquechol, çaquan, ioan chalchiuhtotoli ioan tocihuitl, ioan tequanehoatl: iehoatl in tlatlauhqui ocelotl. O isquich in, in ompa concuia puchteca, in oztomeca: in ompa Xicalanco in quioalitquia, in itech pouia Auitzotzin.

Auh in oacico nican mexico niman ie ispan quitequilia in Auitzotzin: in isquich oquicuito in oztomeca. O iui in, in tecunenemia inic quiuueilique in altepetl, in mexicaiotl ipampa ca nouian tzacuticatca in anaoacatlalli. Auh ipampa in cĕca quintlaçotlaia in Auitzotzin: uel iuhquinma no ipilhoan quinchioaia, çan no quinneneuiliaia, in iuhque pipilti: çan no iuhque in puchteca inic mimatini inic tlanemiliani

---

9. *Quetzalchalchiuitl*: "fine, green, uniformly colored jade that is found among Olmec pieces" (*loc. cit.*). "*Jade fino*," in Sahagun (Garibay ed.), Vol. IV, p. 351.

10. *Quetzalitztli*. The Spaniards called them emeralds; see Molina, *op. cit.* It is translated as green obsidian in Sahagún, *loc. cit.* Foshag, *loc. cit.*, classes it as "probably the finest quality of emerald-green jade, similar to the Chinese *fei-tsui* or imperial jade"; almost transparent, rare.

11. *Tlilayotic quetzalitztli*: in *ibid.*, pp. 8-9, suggesting "the finer qualities of the jade mineral chloromelanite . . . of bottle-green color, or some ot the forms of diopside-jadeite . . . of forest-green color." *Tlilayotic* is the color of black water, according to Sahagún, *op. cit.*, p. 365. Cf. also *Florentine Codex*, Book XI, fol. 207*v*.

12. *Quetzalichtli* is a species of maguey; cf. Rémi Siméon: *Dictionnaire de la langue nahuatl ou mexicaine* (Paris: Imprimerie Nationale, 1885). *Quetzalitzpetztli* might be intended, for green pyrites (*petztli*).

13. *Tapachtli*: red shells or corals, in Sahagún, *op. cit.*, p. 352. Cf. also Molina, *op. cit.* In James Cooper Clark: *Codex Mendoza* (London: Waterlow and Sons, 1938), Vol. II, p. 116: *Spondylus princeps* Gmelin. Also see *Florentine Codex*, Book XI, fol. 211*v*. According to Ignacio Ancona H. and Rafael Martín del Campo, "Malacología precortesiana" (*Memoria* del Congreso Científico Mexicano, México, 1953), Vol. VII, p. 12: "Spondylus americanus o *espóndilo rojo, del Golfo de México, el más abundantamente usado y S. crassisquama o espóndilo de color variable desde el blanco hasta el moreno rójizo, pasando por amarillo, anaranjado y violeta, procedente de las costas de Baja California.*"

14. Corresponding Spanish text: "*paletas de cacao amarillas, hechas de conchas de tortugas, y otras paletas, tambien de tortugas pintadas como cuero de tigre blanco, y negro.*"

15. *Chalchiuhtotol*: *Cyanerpes cyaneus* in Sahagún, *op. cit.*, p. 332 (*ave esmeralda*). For *Cyanerpes cyaneus* (Linnaeus), Friedmann *et al.*, *op. cit.*, Pt. II, p. 235, gives blue honeycreeper.

Fifth Chapter, which telleth how the merchants were given the name of disguised merchants.

And behold, [as to] those known as [and] hence called disguised merchants: when the merchants went into Tzinacantlan before the people of Tzinacantlan had been conquered, to enter so that they did not look like Mexicans, in order to disguise themselves, they took on the appearance of the [natives]. As was the manner of cutting the hair of the people of Tzinacantlan, of Cimatlan, of the Otomi,[1] of the Chontal, just so did the merchants cut their hair to imitate them. And they learned their tongue to enter in disguise. And no one at all could tell whether they were perchance Mexicans when they were anointed with ochre.

And there at Tzinacantlan was where amber occurred and the very long quetzal feathers; because this very place was where all the quetzal birds[2] descended. They came down when spring set in and here ate the acorns of the oak trees. And the blue cotingas [and] the blue honeycreepers came here to eat the fruit of the black fig tree.[3]

And when they caught the blue cotinga, they could not seize it with their hands. They only swiftly plucked, they grasped, a handful of green grass; with it they seized [the bird].[4] For if only with the hands one were to take it, then the blue cotinga's feathers were blemished; the blue became as if soiled.[5]

And the skins of wild animals[6] of all kinds [also] occurred there at Tzinacantlan, in the land of the mountain people.

These disguised merchants were the first who secured all the things mentioned which occurred

Jnic macuilli capitulo itechpa tlatoa in puchteca in quenin tocaiotiloque in naoaloztomeca

Auh izcatqui in omoteneuh, inic mitoa naoaloztomeca: in icoac calacque in tzinacantlan in puchteca, in aiamo peoalo tzinacantecatl, inic calaquia amo necia in aço mexica: inic mispoloaia, quinmopatillotiaia, in iuh moxima tzinacantlan tlaca: mocimatecaxima, ioan mopiochtia ioan mochontalxima çan no iuh moximaia in puchteca, quintlaieecalhuiaia: ioan quimomachtiaia in intlatol inic naoalcalaquia, çan nimã aiac uel quimittaia, in aço mexica tlauhtica in moçaia.

Auh in ompa tzinacantlan, ie umpa in mochioa in apoçonalli, ioan in uel uiac quetzalli: ipampa ca uel oncan intemoian in isquichtin quetzaltotome, icoac in oaltemo xopantla, quioalqua in itlaaquillo aoaquauitl. Auh in xiuhtotome: ioan chalchiuhtotome, vncan quioalqua, in iehoatl itzamatl itlaaquillo.

Auh in icoac câci Xiuhtototl: amo uel inmatica quitzitzquia, çan niman hiciuhca quipitiuetzi, quimomotzotiquiça izçacatl, ic quitzitzquia. Auh intla çan imatica oconan: niman ic poui in ihuiio inic xiuhtototl, ça iuhqui in cuitlatexôtli mochioa:

ioan in tequanehoatl O izquitlamantli, y, in mochioa in ompa tzinacantlan, in tepetlacatlalpan.

Jn iehoantin naoaloztomeca achtopa concuia in isquich omoteneuh, in ompa mochioa. Auh inic con-

---

1. Sahagún (Garibay ed.), X, 29, 52: Otomí youths *se repaban las cabezas, dejando unos pocos de cabellos en los colodrillos . . . que llaman* piochtli. *. . . los hombres ya de edad traían el celebro atusado, como a sobre peine, hasta la media cabeza, y lo demás dejaban con cabellos largos, y llamaban a estos tales* piocheque."

2. After *quetzaltotome*, the *Acad. Hist. MS* has *yuan xiuhtotome, yuan chalchiuhtotome.*

3. *Itzamatl: Ficus cotonifolia (amate prieto)*. Cf. Victor Wolfgang von Hagen: *The Aztec and Maya Papermakers* (New York: J. J. Augustin, 1944), pp. 72 and 40, n. According to Sahagún, *op. cit.*, Vol. IV, p. 338, *Bombax ellipticum* HBK.

4. Corresponding Spanish text: *"quando caçan estas aves . . . no las osan tocar, con las manos: sino roçan de presto heno verde, para tomarlas: de manera que las manos, no lleguẽ a la pluma."*

5. See Sahagún, *op. cit.*, Vol. IV, p. 332: *"Azul manchado. Pluma y color de un ave."* Seler, in "L'orfèvrerie des anciens mexicains," p. 432, refers to *cuitlatexotl* as *les plumes bleues de la queue de l'arara.*

6. After *tequanehoatl*, the *Acad. Hist. MS* has *tlatlauhq'.*

there. And for it they took along obsidian blades with leather handles, obsidian points, needles, shells, cochineal, alum,[7] red ochre, [and] strands of rabbit fur not yet spun into thread.[8] All these were the personal goods of the disguised merchants. For it, they secured all that hath been mentioned: amber, of which were made the labrets and curved lip plugs which the great warriors, the great chieftains required — those who no longer dreaded war; who scorned it; who knew well how war was waged, how captives were taken. And they secured the long quetzal feathers, and the blue cotinga and blue honey-creeper [feathers].[9]

And when, somewhere, the Mexicans, the disguised merchants, were discovered, then they were slain, [for] they were considered ominous; or they barely escaped ambush.[10]

And when now they came, when they returned, likewise they came using their array, their hairdress, their anointing with red ochre. And when they came to arrive at Tochtepec, where they were well thought of, then [and] there they left off their array in which they had traveled, anointed with red ochre; and there also they abandoned their hairdress. And then [and] there they were given[11] their symbols of conquest — the amber lip plugs, and the green, shell-shaped ear pendants; the netted maguey fiber capes; the crested guan feather[12] fans covered with troupial feathers at the bottom; the black staves with tassels of curve-billed thrasher feathers,[13] with which they took the road to arrive here in Mexico.

And when they came to reach their homes, thereupon the disguised merchants sought out the principal merchants; they discussed with them the nature of the places they had gone to see. Accurately did they set forth their account of all that had happened there. And when the principal merchants had heard the exact account, thereupon they led them before the ruler Auitzotzin; before him they set forth all which hath been told which had happened there at Tzina-

cuia iehoatl in itztlaeoalli uitzauhqui: vitzmallotl, coiolli, nocheztli, tlaxocotl tlauitl tochiuitl aiamo tlatzaoalli. O isquich, in, in imiscoian intlatqui in naoaloztomeca: inic concuia in isquich omoteneuh in apoçonalli, tezçacatl, mochioaia ioan tencolli, in intech monequia in ueuei oquichti, in ueuei tiacahoan, in aocmo quimacacia iauiotl; in aoc tle ipã quittaia, in ouel imismacic, in iuh iautihoa, in iuh tetlamaltilo. Yoan in concuia iehoatl in uiac quetzalli: yoan xiuhtototl, ioan chalchiuhtototl.

Auh in icoac campa ittoia in mexica in naoaloztomeca: niman mictiloia, tetzammachoia, auh çan teuquiçaia.

Auh in icoac in ie uitze in ie oalmocuepa: çan iuh tlantiuitze in innechichioal, in innexin, in inneoçaliz tlauhtica. Auh in icoac in oacico tochtepec: cenca mauiztililo, quin oncan quicaoa in innechichioaliz, inic omotlauhoçatinenca, auh no oncan quicaoa in innexin. Auh quin oncan maco: in inneuquichitol in apoçonaltentetl, ioan quetzalcoiolnacochtli, quetzalichaiatl coxoli, hecacehoaztli: çaquantica tlatzinpacholli, xaoactopilli, toztlapilollo, cuitlacochio, in ipan oalotlatocaia, inic oalâcia in nican mexico.

Auh in oacico inchan: niman ie ic quinmottitia in puchtecatlatoque, in naoaloztomeca, quinnonotza in iuhcan otlachieto: uel quimelaoa in intlatol, in isquich ompa mochioa. Auh in oquicacque melaoac tlatolli: in puchteca tlatoque: niman ie ic quiniacana in ispan tlatoani Auitzotzin, ispan quitequilia in isquich omoteneuh, in onpa mochioa tzinacantlan, quilhuia. Totecuioe, tlatoanie: ca izcatõ in ompa mochioa tzinacantla, ca amo oticascauique, inic oticuito, ca

7. *Tlalxocotl* in the *Acad. Hist. MS.*

8. Corresponding Spanish text: *"Unas madejas . . . hechas de pelos de conejos."*

9. Cf. *supra*, Chap. 4, n. 15.

10. Corresponding Spanish text: *"los naturales luego les matauan: y ansi andauã con gran peligro, y con gran miedo."*

11. After *maco*, the *Acad. Hist. MS* has *innechichiualiz.*

12. Cf. *supra*, Chap. 2, n. 4.

13. Sahagún, *op. cit.*, Vol. IV, p. 332: *Toxostoma curvirostra curvirostra* or *Harporhynchus longisrostrus* Scl. Cf. also Santamaría,*op. cit.*, Vol. I, p. 432 *(cuicasoche)*: *"Ave canora de Méjico, de la familia de los túrdidos, con las plumas del pecho y del vientre amarillas y las demás grises o negras en general."* Refer also to *Florentine Codex*, Book II, fol. 36*v*, and Anderson and Dibble, *op. cit.*, Book II, p. 72, n. 18. Cf. also Friedmann *et al.*, *op. cit.*, Pt. 2, pp. 173-79.

cantlan. They said to him: "O our lord, O ruler, behold that which happened there at Tzinacantlan. We have not achieved that which we went to secure. Some were slain because of it; they ambushed thy beloved uncles, the disguised merchants. This is as it was: they sought land for the portent Uitzilopochtli. First these discovered [and] marveled at all the land of Anauac. Secretly they saw [and] entered everywhere in Anauac, to travel inspecting as disguised merchants."

And when Auitzotzin of Tenochtitlan died, Moctezuma, who was also a native of Tenochtitlan, was then installed as ruler. In the same manner he continued the customs, followed the way, honored well the calling of the merchants, the vanguard merchants. He especially honored the principal merchants, the disguised merchants, those who bathed slaves, the slave dealers. He set them right by his side, even like the noblemen, the rulers; like all who had died, who had governed the cities of Mexico [and] Tlatilulco, he rendered them honor.

And the governors [of Tlatilulco][14] and the principal merchants were especially friendly; they greatly esteemed one another. Alike were they in mode of behavior; they loved one another greatly. And thus did the principal merchants, the disguised merchants, conduct themselves: quite apart did they pronounce their judgments; independently were sentences meted out. A merchant, a vanguard merchant, who did wrong, they did not take to someone else; the principal merchants, the disguised merchants, themselves alone pronounced judgment, exacted the punishment, executed the death penalty. There where they congregated was their one house; also one was the house of the governors. Separately they issued their pronouncements, their authority, their rule, their judgments. He who had done wrong they killed, they slew, there at the *quauhcalli,* or anywhere;[15] perhaps indeed in his home they killed—slew—him.

And thus the governors sat [in audience] there at [their] *quauhcalli*; they sat venerated,[16] wearing their golden lip plugs, and blue labrets,[17] and curved green stone lip plugs, and amber labrets,[18] and curved amber lip plugs, and curved blue lip plugs. But the

cequintin ipan omictiloque, oquitzacutiaque in motlatzitzihoan, naoaloztomeca. O ca iui in: inic oquitlaltemolique in tetzauitl vitzilobuchtli achtopa iehoanti quittaia, quimauiçoaia, in isquich anaoacatlalli: in iuhqui topco petlacalco ontlachieia, ỹ çan oc ichtacacalaquia, in nouian anaoac, inic naoaloztomecattitinenca.

Auh in icoac omomiquili Auitzotzin tenochtitla niman icoac ontlatocatlaliloc in Motecuçomatzin, in çan ie no vmpa ichan tenochtitlan, çan no iuh otlamaniti, otlaôtlatocti: uel oquimauizçoti, in puchtecaiotl, in oztomecaiotl: oc cenca tlapanauia inic oquinmauiztili in puchtecatlatoque in naoaloztomeca, in tealtianime, in tecohoanime: uel itloc inaoac oquintlali, in iuh oquinmauiztilitiaque in tetecuti, in tlatoque: in izquintin omomiquilique, in oquipachoco altepetl in mexicaiotl, in tlatilulcaiotl.

Auh in iehoantin in quauhtlatoque ioan puchtecatlatoque, oc cenca omonepannaoatecque, cenca monepantlaçotlaia: çan centetl in inieliz catca, cenca monepantlaçotlaia. Auh inic nenca in puchtecatlatoque: in naoaloztomeca, uel cecni quiuicaia in intlatzontequiliz, nonqua motlatzontequiliaia: in aquin otlatlaco in puchtecatl, in oztomecatl, amo teuic quiuica, çan iehoanti monomatlatzontequiliaia, motlatzacuiltiaia, momictiaia in puchtecatlatoque, in naoaloztomeca: in vncan in necentlaliaia uel centetl incalietica, no centetl incalietica in quauhtlatoque: nonqua quiquistia in imihiio, in intlatol, in intecuio, in intlatocaio, in intlatzontequiliz. Jn aquin otlatlaco quimictia: quitlatlatia, in oncan quauhcali, ioan in çaço campa: aço uel ichan in ompa conmictiaia, contlatlatiaia.

Auh inic onoque in quauhtlatoque: in vncan quauhcali, cenca in omauizçotitoque, conaquitoque, in teucuitlatentetl, ioan xoxouhqui tēzçatl: ioan chalchiuhtencololli, ioan apoçonaltēzçatl, ioan apoçonaltencololli, ioan xoxouhqui tencololli. Auh in puchte-

---

14. In the *Acad. Hist. MS,* *tlatilulco* follows *quauhtlatoque.* See also corresponding Spanish text.
15. See Anderson and Dibble, *op. cit.,* Book VIII, p. 43.
16. Corresponding Spanish text: *"adereçauanse con ataujos de grauedad, y de autoridad."*
17. *Tezçacatl* in the *Acad. Hist. MS*; it is somewhat blurred in the *Florentine Codex.*
18. *Apoçonaltezçacatl* in the *Acad. Hist. MS.*

principal merchants sat wearing golden lip plugs [and] amber lip plugs. With these sat venerated those who in Anauac had entered into the enemy's land, as disguised merchants. Only on feast days did they wear them, as well as their array and symbols of valor.[19]

And thus was it that the work of the principal merchants became precisely that they cared for the market place. They sponsored the common folk, so that none might suffer, might be deceived, tricked, mistreated. These same pronounced judgment upon him who deceived others in the market place, who cheated them in buying and selling. Or they punished the thief. And they regulated well everything: all in the market place which was sold; what the price would be.

And when Moctezuma commanded the merchants, vanguard merchants, the reconnoiterers,[20] to enter, no matter where, if they were besieged [or] slain there, when [the foe] no longer respected the message of Moctezuma,[21] then swiftly he declared war, so that then war should break out. The vanguard merchants went in the lead, appointed by the principal merchants Quappoyaualtzin, Nentlamatitzin, Uetzcatocatzin, Çanatzin, [and] Uei oçomatzin. They issued orders to those who would lead the disguised merchants wherever war was to break out. Indeed in strict command over the disguised merchants who were their leaders was the one called Quappoyaualtzin.[22] He commanded, he summoned those in all the cities about. Here they set out from Tenochtitlan, Texcoco, Uexotla, Coatl ichan, Chalco, Uitzilopochco, Mixcoac, Azcapotzalco, Quauhtitlan, [and] Otompan. From all these parts they came to await, to determine where now they were to go.[23]

And when those of Tlatilulco went to reach a city, they assembled; only one [place] became their home. No one took leave singly; no one could go anywhere alone. And if someone there misused a woman, quickly did they take counsel regarding him; they proceeded to sentence him; they slew him; they killed him.

catlatoque: in conaquitoque teucuitlatentetl, apoço-naltẽtetl, inic momauizçotitoque in ipã anaoac calaquini iaupan, in naoaloztomeca: çan iio icoac in ilhujtl conaquiaia, ioan in innechichioaliz, in inne-uquichitol.

Auh inic catca in puchtecatlatoque in intequiuh mochioaia: uel iehoatl in tianquiztli quimocuitlauiaia, ipan tlatoaia in maceoalli, inic aiac toliniloz xixicoloz, ica necacaiaoaloz, mictiloz: uel iehoantin quitlatzontequiliaia, in aquin tianquizco texixicohoa, teispopoiochioa, in anoço ichtequi, quitlatzacuiltiaia: auh uel quinâmictiticate in ie isquich, in ie mochi tiãquizco monamaca, in quenin patiohoaz.

Auh in icoac tlanaoatiaia motecuçomatzin: izçaçocampa calaquia puchteca, oztomeca, in tecunenẽque: intla impan ooalmotzacu, intla ompa omiquito, in aocmo quiuelcaquilia in itlatol Motecuçomatzin: niman hiciuhca iautlanaoatiaia, inic vmpa iauquixoaz, iehoanti teiacantiuia in oztomeca: tlaisquetzaia in puchtecatlatoque, quappoiaoaltzin, nentlamatitzin, vetzcatocatzin, Çanatzin, vei oçomatzin: quinnaoatiaia in aquique teiacantiazque in naoaloztomeca, in campa iehoatl iauquixoaz, uel quintlaquauhnaoatiaia in inteiacancauh catca in naoaloztomeca: itoca quappoiaoaltzin, quiceniacanaia, quicentlatalhuiaia, in ie nouian altepetl ipan, nican onpeoa tenochtitlan, tetzcoco, uexotla, cohoatl ichan, chalco, vitzilobuchco, miscoac, azcaputzalco, quauhtitlan, otumba. O izquicanin, in nican oalitztoca: quicemitoaia in campa ie uilohoaz.

Auh in icoac oacito in altepetl ipan, in tlatilulca: çan mocentlalia, çan centetl in incal muchioaia, aiac nonqua moquistia, aiac uel icel canpa uia. Auh intla onpa aca cihoatl oquitecac: iciuhca ica mocentlaliaia quitzacutiuia, quitlâtlatia, quimictia.

19. Corresponding Spanish text: "eran tambien insignjas de que erã valientes, de que aujã entrado en la proujncia de anaoac entre los enemjgos."

20. Ibid.: "Los mercaderes y disimulados esploradores."

21. Ibid.: "si alla los prendian o matauan, sin dar buena respuesta, o buen recibimjento, a los que ibã, como mensajeros, del señor de mexico: sino que los prendian o matauan."

22. Ibid.: "en el exercito, que iva: los mercaderes: eran capitanes, y officiales del exercito: elegidos por los señores, que regian a los mercaderes, que se llamauã, quappoiaoaltzin, y Nentlamatitzin, y vetzcatocatzin, y Çanatzin, y vey oçomatzin: ellos dauan el cargo a los que ivã y los instruyan de lo que avian de hazer. Elegian tambien el capitan general, a uno de los principales mercaderes que se llamaua quappoiaualtzin."

23. In campa yeh calacouaz, in the Acad. Hist. MS, follows uilohoaz.

But if only sickness took one, if he died there in Anauac, they did not bury him. They only arranged him on a carrying frame. Thus did they adorn the dead: they inserted a feather labret in his lips, and they painted black the hollows about his eyes; they painted red about the lips with ochre, and they striped his body with white earth. He wore his paper stole; its ends passed under his armpits. And when they had adorned him, then they stretched him on the carrying frame; they bound him there with the carrying frame cords. Thereupon they bore him to a mountain top. There they stood him up; they leaned the carrying frame against [a post].[24] There his body was consumed. And they said that indeed he had not died, for he had gone to heaven; he followed the sun. And just so was it said of those who had died in war; they said that they followed the sun; they went to heaven.

Auh i çan cocoliztli oquicuic: in onpa omic anaoac, amo quintocaia, çan quicacaschichioaia: inic quichichioaia micqui, hiuitēzçacatl conaquiliaia in intenco, ioan quistetlilcomoloa, quintenchichiloa tlauhtica: ioan quiticaoaoana in inacaio, iiamaneapanaliz ieticac, iciacacpa quiquistiliaia. Auh in oconcencauhque: niman ie cacazco conteca, oncan quiilpia cacasmecatica, niman ie ic quiuica in tepeticpac: ompa conquetza quicacastlaxillotia, ompa popoliuia in inacaio. Auh quitoaia ca amo miqui, ca ilhuicac iauh, quitoca in tonatiuh: auh çan no iuhqui impan mitoaia in iaumiquia, quitoaia, quitoca in tonatiuh: ilhuicac iauh.

---

24. Corresponding Spanish text: *"ponjan el cacaxtle leuãtado arrimado a algun palo, hincado en tierra."*

Sixth Chapter, which telleth how the merchants made offerings when they reached their homes, whence they had gone, called the washing of feet.

When he arrived within his house, he entered only by night, not by day. It was always dark when he arrived; also upon a favorable day sign, One House or Seven House. So were the day signs read for them because that which they brought in on the day sign One House, they said, all thus brought in, was the property of the protector of all, the master of the earth, the invisible and untouchable one.[1]

Then swiftly, at night, he entered into [the house] of his leader, in order to present himself to him, to reassure him, because nowhere had our lord destroyed him.

He said to him: "May it be well with thee, O thou brave man! Be relieved in thy heart that I have come to reach [this] land; nowhere did our lord slay me. And at dawn I shall await our mothers, our fathers, the merchants, the vanguard merchants, the exploring merchants. They shall go to drink a little whipped chocolate there in my hut, where I shall await the word of our lord."

And [the other] said to him in return: "Thou hast suffered, thou hast become fatigued, O servant. Thou hast shown mercy to thy mothers [and] thy fathers; [but] not [now] shalt thou acquire [and] hear their words. Rest."

And when he had gone to speak, to converse, with one, then swiftly he cut paper into strips to make the blood sacrifices which pertained to the [god of] fire and to Yacatecutli. Thereupon the debt was paid at midnight. When the debt was paid, thereupon he undertook to secure all which was necessary of food, turkey pasties, meat stewed with maize, turkey stewed with maize, and good chocolate with "divine ear" spice.[2] And the old men, the merchants, the

Jnic chiquacen capitulo, itechpa tlatoa: in quenin puchteca quichioaia tlamanaliztli, in icoac oallacia in campa ohuia, in inchan in mitoa necxipaquiliztli.

Jn icoac in ooalacic in jcalitic: çan iooaltica in oalcalaquia, amo cemilhuitl, çan ic tlapoiahoa in oalaci: no ipan in qualli tonalli, i ce calli, anoço chicome calli, inic motonalpouiliaia, ipampa in contocaia in ce calli: quitoaia ca ie ic cencalaqui in icococauh, in tloque, naoaque, in tlalticpaque, in ioalli, in ehecatl.

Niman iciuhca ioaltica ipan calaqui in iteiacancauh: inic commottitia, coniolpachiuitia, in ipampa acan oquipopolo in totecuio,

quilhuia. Ma ximeuiltitie moceloquichtle: ca ie moiollotzin pachiui, ca otlaltitech nonacico, acan onechtlati in totecuio, auh ma oc tlauizcalpan niquinnochielia in tonahoan in totahoan, in puchteca in oztomeca in iiaque: achitzin texamoiaoaltzintli quimititiui, in oncã noxacaltonco, in onca nictlatolchie totecuio.

Auh quioalilhuia, Otiquihiioui, oticciauh, xolotze: otiquimicneli in monanhoan, in motahoan, aticcuiz aticcaquiz, in imihiio in intlatol, ma ximoceui.

Auh in icoac ontetlalhuito: in ontenotzato, niman ie hiciuhca amaxotla, quichioa in inestlaoal: in itech poui in tletl, ioan iiacatecutli, niman ie ic mostlaoa in ioalnepantla: in ômostlauh, niman ie ic ipan tlatoa in isquich monequiz, in tlaqualli, in totolquimilli, in nacatlaoio, in totollaolli: ioan qualli cacaoatl, teunaçazço. Auh in iehoantin ueuetque: in puchteca, in oztomeca, oc uel iohoan in callaqui: icoac in cooatlan tlauitecoia, in ascã in ipan prima.

1. "Yoalli-Ehecatl, esto es Tezcatlipoca" (Sahagún (Garibay ed.), I, 12, 12); cf. also Anderson and Dibble, op. cit., Book I, p. 9, n. 60. A more literal translation would be "the night, the wind." Cf. also Florentine Codex, Book VI, fol. 210v.

2. Probably teonacazço is meant; see corresponding Spanish text. Teonacaztli, xochinacaztli, or uei nacaztli: "'Oreja divina.' Planta aromática y medicinal. . . . Cymbopetalum penduliflorum," in Sahagún, op. cit., Vol. IV, p. 356; "rosa o especie aromática" in Fr. Bernardino de Sahagún: Historia de las cosas de Nueva España (Miguel Acosta Saignes, ed.; México: Editorial Nueva España, S. A., 1946), Vol. II, p. 303. See teonacascle and sochinacaste in Santamaría, op. cit., Vol. III, pp. 94-95, 156. According to Maximino Martínez, Las plantas medicinales de México (México: Ediciones Botas, 1933), p. 471, "las flores son aromáticas y se usan como tónico estomacal." Emmart, op. cit., p. 315, notes that for its fragrance and flavor, which suggests nutmeg, it was ground and added to chocolate; medicinally, it was used against asthma and flatulence, as relief for the stomach and heart, for "fatigue of those holding public office . . . and in a charm to safeguard the traveler."

vanguard merchants, came into the house when it was still very dark, when they sounded the time at Coatlan, [the hour] which now [is called] prime.[3]

When they had assembled — indeed everyone, the kinsmen and the merchant women, those who ceremonially bathed slaves — thereupon hands were washed, [and] mouths were washed. Thereupon the food came forth. The gift pertaining to Xiuhtecutli came first; they laid in order before [the fire] the severed turkey heads in a sauce dish.[4] Then they laid in order before Yacatecutli the food which pertained to him. And when they had placed these things in order, thereupon food was served; there was eating. When there had been eating, once again hands [and] mouths were washed. Thereupon the sacred cups[5] came forth [with] the chocolate. They said they would drink from the sacred cups.[6] First they also set up a [cup] before Xiuhtecutli, [god of] fire; then also they set one up before Yacatecutli. And when these had been offered, thereupon chocolate was served [the guests] in these sacred cups, and then tobacco tubes were given them for smoking. And when this was done, when all had finished, then the merchants remained seated, that [the host] might give them gifts. In order to produce for the aged,[7] he gave two tortoise shell cups to each of the leaders, but to those who followed them he gave only one each. And he accompanied these with two hundred cacao beans and one hundred [grains of] "sacred ear" spice. And each one [was given] a stirring stick.[8] So did it use to be when the vanguard merchants arrived.

When he had given them these, then he seated himself before them. He said to them: "Here you are. I have gone to perform the carrying of burdens on the back; I have gone using the staff, the carrying frame. Nowhere did the protector of all slay me. Perchance somewhere I have besmirched [and] ruined one. You will take [note of], you will hear of my errors — my faults. Here once again I have beheld your noble presences. And I have come to be near

Jn ocenquizque, in ie isquich tlacatl in hoaniolque: ioan in puchtecacihoa tealtiani, nimã ie ic tematequilò, tecamapaco: niman ie ic oalquiça in tlaqualli, iacattiuh in uentli, in itech poui xiuhtecutli: in ispan conmana, iehoatl in totoltzontecomatl molcaxic ietiuh niman iehehoatl in itech poui in iiacatecutli, ispan conmana in tlaqualli. Auh in ontlaman: niman ie ic tetlamaco, tlaqualo: in ontlaqualoc, oc ceppa tematequilo tecamapaco: niman ie ic oalquiça in teutecomatl, iehoatl in cacahoatl, quitoaia teutecomatl miiz: achtopa no centetl ispan conquetzaia in xiuhtecutli, in tletl: niman ie no centetl ispan conquetza in iiacatecutli: Auh in ontlamanaloc: niman ie ic teamaco iehoatl in teutecomatl, ioan çatepan temaco in iietl, chichinaloni. Auh in ie iuhqui, in otecencaoaloc: ie ic tlaonoc in quinmacaz puchteca, inic quinueuechihoaz in tecomatl, iehoatl in aiotectli ohontetl in quintlauhtiaia teiacanque: auh in quintoquilia ça cecentetl in quimacaia, auh quiuiicaltiaia matlatlacpoalli in cacahoatl, ioan teunacaztli mamacuilpoalli: ioan cecen aquauitl. O iuhqui in: inic oalacia in oztomeca:

In icoac oquimontlamacac: niman ie imispan onmotlalia quimilhuia. Ca nican anmoetzticate: ca onoconchioato in tetlamamaliliztzintli: in tetopil in tecacas oitlã nonaquito: ca acan onechtlati in tloque, nahoaque: aço cana oniteatlatzicuinalhui, oniteçoquimotlac: aanquimocuilizque, aanquimocaquitizque in niiaque in nopalanca, ca nican amitzinco amocpactzinco, ono ceppa nitlachis: auh ono itech nompachiuico, icetzin ometzin, in nonca, in neca, in naui in

3. Corresponding Spanish text: "como agora se tañe al apelde" — first bell-ringing before daybreak in convents of the Franciscan Order — "o a ora de prima" — prime, one of the seven canonical hours.

4. Ibid.: "en caxetes cõ su molli."

5. Ibid.: "Luego saliã por su ordē las xicaras del cacao que llamavan teutecomatl."

6. Acad. Hist. MS: iitiz.

7. Corresponding Spanish text: "estauan cada uno en su lugar sentados, esperando lo que les auja de dar el que los combido, q̃ llamã ellos quinvevechiva: que qujere dezir, don, de viejo venerable."

8. Ibid.: "juntamēte dauã a cada uno doszientas almendras de cacao, y cien granos de aquella especie que llamã teunacaztli: y a cada uno, dauã una paleta de tortuga, con que se rebuelue el cacao: desta manera hazian todos los mercaderes, quando venjan de lexos."

the one or two who are here [and] there: my aunt, my nephew, my kinsmen. Perhaps here the protector of all will destroy, will slay me one of these days. This is what you have heard."

And thereupon they replied, they said to him: "Here art thou. We have eaten, we have drunk the fruits of thy labors in the mountains, the gorges, the deserts; and of thy sighs, thy tears. Perhaps thou hast somewhere sighed, wept, by the will of the protector of all. Here thou hast spread out his property with which he hath favored thee. But even if thou hast here given us food [and] drink, hast thou perchance thus stopped our mouths? Are we therefore afraid of thee? Can our occasion for rearing [and] training perhaps no longer be? Where didst thou get that which thou gavest us to eat [and] drink? Perchance thou didst go somewhere to remove it from one's pot [or] one's dish. Perhaps thou playest *tlachtli* or *patolli,* or thou hast filched some woman's belongings: her goods. Thou hast robbed someone. Perhaps what thou gavest us to eat [and] drink was not [acquired] fittingly, but is dirty, dusty, filthy. This we do not know; but [if so] already thereby thou indeed castest thyself into the river or from a crag; no longer wilt thou have merit nor be deserving. Here we give thee the means of rearing [and] upbringing: fearful punishment, fearful castigation which lieth smoldering, which lieth burning one. What issueth from within one, what settleth upon one, what eateth out our hearts oppresseth thee. [It is] the punishment, the castigation of the protector of all." [9]

And upon this, when they had pressed upon him, had castigated, admonished him, then they besought him; they greeted him, weeping; they charged him not to be presumptuous nor proud, not to attribute his gains falsely to himself when perchance our lord had shown him some little mercy with as many of his goods as he had brought with him: the quetzal feathers, the trogonorus, red spoonbill, troupial, blue cotinga; the duck feathers;[10] or the green stone,

nomach, in nooaiolqui: aço nican nechmopopolhuiz nechmotlatlatiliz, in tloque naoaque, moztlatiz viptlatiz: ca iehoatl in anquimocaquitia.

Auh niman ie ic quicuepilia in itlatol, quilhuia. Ca nican tica: ca otoconquaque ca otoconique, in ipatiuh in tepetl in atlauhtli, in istlaoatl: auh in melciciuiliz, in mochoquiliz, aço cana imatian otelciciuh otichocac, in tloque naoaque: ca nican ticmoiahoa in icococauh inic omitzicnoittac. Auh manel nican titechtlaqualtia titechatlitia: cuis ic titechtentzaquaz, cuis ic timitzimacacizque, cuis aocmo uel quiçaz in totlacaoapaoaia, in totlacazcaltiaia: can oticcuic in titechqualtia, in titechitia: aço cana tecomic tecaxic otimaiauito, aço tohollama, aço tipâpâtohoa: anoço cueie uipille oticnaoalchiuili iasca itlatqui: aca otiquichtequili: acaçomo iuian iectli in titechqualtia in titechitia, aço tzoio, aço teuhio, aço tlaçollo: ca amo ticmati, iece ca ie ic tonmomaiaui in atoiac in tepexic, ca aoc tle momacehoaliez, aoc tle mulhuiliez: nican timitzmaca in tlacaoapaoaloni in tlacazcaltiloni, in tetl in quauitl in uel popocatoc, in uel chîchinauhtoc: motech compachoa in tehiticpa quiquiz, in tecocototztlali, in toiollo conqua: in iatlitzticauh in ialcececauh, in itzitzicaz, in tloque naoaque.

Auh in ie iuhqui in oitech conpachoque: in oconquisti in quauhio i teio, in teahoaliztlatolli: çatepan quitlatlauhtiaquichoquiztlapaloa, quicaoaltia inic amo atlamatiz, inic amo mopoaz inic amo quimotlatquitocaz, in aço itla oquitlaoculi in totecuio, in quesquich itlatqui ooalietia: in quetzalli, in tzinitzcan, in teuquechol, in çaquan, i xiuhtototl, in xomoihuitl: anoço chalchiuitl aço apoçonalli, aço atzaccaiotl, aço aquauitl, anoço tequanehoatl: aço cacahoatl, aço teuna-

9. *Ibid.:* "*aquj has recebido la doctrina que los padres deuen dar a sus hijos, que son reprehensiones, y castigos, duros, y asperos que pungen, y llagan lo interior del coraçon, y de las entrañas: y sõ estas reprehensiones los açotes, y hurtigas con que castiga nr̃o señor dios.*" Tetl, quauitl: cf. Molina, *op. cit. Uel popocatoc, in uel chîchinauhtoc:* cf. *Florentine Codex,* Book VI, cap. xliii, *in popocatiuh, in chichinatiuh* —"*se dice de aquel que habla . . . de reprehension . . . de manera que causa temor a los que lo oyen*" In iatl itzticauh in ialcececauh: cf. loc. cit., *in atl itztic, in atl cecec topan quichiua in totecuio* —"*Agua fria, agua helada enuia nuestro señor. . . . se dice . . . de la pestilencia, o hambre, y otras aflicciones. . . . Afligenos señor como con agua fria y con agua helada.*" Itzitzicaz: cf. Bernardino de Sahagún: "Memoriales con escolios," *Historia general de las cosas de Nueva España* (Francisco del Paso y Troncoso, ed.; Madrid: Hauser y Menet, 1905), Vol. VI, cap. iv, p. 206, *tzitzicazuia* —"*herir con hortigas, o costigar con palabras penosas.*"

10. *Xumutl: cierto pato* (Molina, *op. cit.*). Tezozomoc, *op. cit.,* Vol. I, p. 363, defines *xomome* as "*oiseaux qui resemblent par la forme à des perdrix d'Espagne, mais qui sont noirs comme le jais.*"

or the amber, or the stoppers for gourds, or stirring sticks; or the skins of wild animals; perhaps the cacao beans or the "divine ear" spice which he had gone to secure when he had gone practising trade as a disguised merchant. With these [words] the old merchants brought [those who returned prosperous] to tears; they humbled them; they sternly admonished them not to disregard, not to neglect our lord.

But he who had been thus counseled was not thereby offended. He felt no anger over it. Much did he abase himself; verily, he appreciated it. He answered them weeping; he said to them: "O beloved noblemen, I thank you for the favor you have shown me; you have left me consolation. I have given [and] left you affliction. Who am I? Who do I think I am that I should consider looking into your noble bowels, your noble breasts, which are as secret places? Perhaps I shall ignore your valued words; perhaps somewhere I shall forget you — cast you aside, I who am without merit, perverse. Here I use vainly, I waste, [the gifts of] the protector of all. Rest."

And these old men who thus admonished him did not waste their words. They esteemed them highly. The old men [and] the old women did not offer them purposelessly, even if their utterance was [only] one word, one syllable. That which was worth being carried off, being borne away, was taken to heart.

And so they spoke to one when some little thing appeared,[11] when he made profits, when he desired advice. He said: "Behold, our lord hath given me of his noble creations, his noble possessions. Perhaps yet I shall live well; perhaps already I become perverse. Perchance already I become proud. May I hear the means of good rearing, of good upbringing; may the old men come; may I hear their valued words."

In this way spoke the well reared, the well trained, the well taught. And thus [the old men] gave one their discourse; as hath been told. The words of training came forth only by drink and food, so that no one might live in evil. Not without purpose did they eat [and] drink. For verily so splendid was considered the position of the merchant, the vanguard merchant, that none lived a perverse life. The words of the old merchants were well regarded, well treasured.

caztli in oquicuito, inic onaoaloztomecatito. O iehoatl in, in quinchoctiaia inic nentlamatia in puchteca ueuetque: cenca uel quinanaoatiaia, inic amo quitlaauilquistiliz, in amo quitlaauilmachiliz totecuio.

Auh in iehoatl nonotzalo amo quitecococamati: amo quitlauelchioa: cenca iê mopechteca uel quicnelilmati, quinchoquiznanquilia, quimilhuia. Pillitzine: oannechmocnelilique, otlacauhqui in amoiollotzin, cocoliztli namechnocuitiliz, namechnetlalcaoaltiliz: ac nehoatl ac ninomati, in nontlachie in amoxillantzinco, in amotozcatlătzinco: in iuhqui topco petlacalco: aço noconauilmatiz in amihiiotzin in amotlatoltzin, aço cana namechonnolcauililiz, namechonnotlaxililiz in nitlapaltontli in nitlaueliloc: ca nican nictlanenpolhuia, nictlaauilquistilia, in tloque, nahoaque, ma ximoceuitzinocan.

Auh in iehoantin ueuetque: inic tenonotzaia, amo quinenquistiaia in intlatol, cenca quitlaçotlaia: amo quitenenmacaia in ueuetque, in ilamatque, in manel cententli cencamatl intlatol: uel ipan moolpiticatca, in tlatconi, in tlamamaloni.

Auh inic quiteilhuiaia: hicoac in itlatzin onmonexiti, in oquinênesti in momonotzallani, quitoa, Ca izcatqui onechmomaquili in totecuio: itlachihoaltzin iiascatzin ac açoc uel ninemi, aço ie nitlauelilocati, aço ie teisco teicpac ninemi: ma oc niccaqui in tlacazcaltiloni in tlacaoapaoaloni, ma oalhuian in ueuetque, ma niccaqui in intlatoltzin.

O ihui in, in quitoaia in qualtin tlazcaltiltin: in uellaoapaoalti, in tlanonotzalti. Auh inic quitemacaia in imihiio in intlatol, ie omito, in çan atica i çan tlaqualtica, in onca quiçaia in nezcaliliztlatolli, inic aiac tlauelilocanêca, amo çan quinêquaia, amo çã quinemia, in atl, in tlaqualli: ca nel ic omauizçotoca in puchtecaiotl, in oztomecaiotl, inic aiac otlauelilocanenca, cenca onemalhuiloc: uel omopis in intlatol puchteca ueuetque.

---

11. *Acad. Hist. MS*: *in itlahtzin.*

And how they returned from Anauac, how they followed the roads, how they came back, we have already told. Not purposelessly did they come. Wherever there was a pyramid place, there they went to pay their debt, to perform penances, at places where debts were paid in the desert, until they reached Itziocan, where they stopped. They there sought a favorable day sign; [perhaps still ten or still twenty days they awaited the good day sign].[12] And when it was a good day sign, at once they quickly traveled, so that indeed upon [that day sign] they might enter their homes. Not by day but by night they swiftly entered by boat.

And as to their goods, no one could see how much there was; perhaps they carefully hid — covered up — all the boats. Not at one's [own] home did one arrive, [but] perhaps at the house of his uncle or his aunt, or of his elder sister; or it was only someone else's house into which he went — one who was of good heart, who told no lies, who held his peace, who lived in humility, in sadness. Nor was he a thief; he was prudent. And when he had quickly come to unload what he had acquired, then swiftly he took away his boat. When it dawned, nothing remained.

And this owner of the goods did not acknowledge them; he did not take the goods himself; he did not claim them as his own. He only said, speaking to those whom he charged with guarding them: "Here it is. Thou must guard it. Do not say, 'Perhaps these are his property or his goods which we are given to guard'; only the possessions of the principal vanguard merchants have been brought here by me."

And there in the cities, perhaps in Tochtepec, or Anauac, or Xoconochco,[13] into as many cities as he bore their goods, neither did he acknowledge them. He did not claim the goods, the property, as his own. He only told them: "They are not my goods which I have carried; they are the goods of our mothers, our fathers, the merchants, the vanguard merchants."

In this manner did the vanguard merchants live. They were very moderate; they did not exalt themselves. They only went about abasing themselves, seeking neither praise nor fame. Only humbly, saddened, did they live. They did not seek honor [and]

Auh inic oalmocuepaia anaoac: inic oalotlatocaia, inic oaluia, ie oticteneuhque, amo çan nen oalhuia: in izquican têtzaqualli, çan onca oalmostlauhtiui, oallamaceuhtiia, in istlahoacan: inic oallacia itziocã, oc oncan motlalia, oncan quittaia in qualli tonalli[, açoc mahtlacilhuitia, anoçoc cempoualilhuitia in quichie qualli tonalli]. Auh in ie ipan qualli tonalli: çan niman icoac oaltotocatiuetzi, inic uel ipan oalcalaquia in inchan, amo cemilhuitl, çã iohoaltica in acaltica oalcalactiuetzia.

Auh in intlatqui: aiac uel quittaia in quesquich, in aço cemacalli, cenca quitlatiaia, quitlapachoaia: amo inchan in oallacia, aço iitla, aço iiahui ichan, anoço iueltiuh, anoço çan aca ichan in ipan oalcalaquia: iehoatl in aquin qualli iiollo, in amo ihiztlacati, in amo monônonotza: i çan itolol, imalcoch ic nemi, in amono ihichtequi, in uel mimati. Auh in oconquistiuetzico in tlapanaui: niman hiciuhca quiuicatiquiça in iacal in ooallatuic atle mantoc.

Auh in iehoatl tlatquioa: amo quimomachitoca, amo quimascatia, amo qujmotlatquitoca: çan quitoa quimilhuia in quintlapieltia: nican ca oc xicmopielican, ma anquitoti aço iasca aço itlatqui, in techpieltia, çan nioalitquitiloc: imasca intachcaoan oztomeca.

Auh in ompa altepetl ipan: in aço tochtepec, anoço anaoac, xoconochco, in quesquich quitqui itlatqui, amo no quimomachitoca, amo quimotlatquitoca: amo quimascatoca, çan quiteilhuia. Ca amo notlatqui in onicqualitquic: ca intlatqui in tonahoan in totahoan, in puchteca in oztomeca.

O iui in, inic onenca oztomeca, cenca omomalhuitiaque: amo mopantlazque, çan omotlanitlaztiaque, amo mîtollanque, moteneoallanque: çan intolol inmalcoch ic onenque: amo quinectiaque in mauizçotl, in teniotl: çan imahaiaçoltzin ietinenca: cenca

12. After *tonalli*, the *Acad. Hist.* MS includes material inserted here in the Aztec text in brackets.

13. *Xoconochco*: Cf. R. H. Barlow: *The Extent of the Empire of the Culhua Mexica* (Berkeley and Los Angeles: University of California Press, 1949), p. 97: "In the State of Chiapas, at the approaches of Guatemala, lay the costal province of Xoconochco."

fame. They walked about wearing only their miserable maguey fiber capes. They greatly feared notoriety, the praising of one. It was for this reason that Moctezuma, as hath been told, especially esteemed the old merchants, the disguised merchants, those who ceremonially bathed slaves, the slave dealers. He made them like his sons.

But when now they corrupted their way of life, when they no longer were of good heart, then he was as if saddened. Then the chieftains, in envy, falsely, by means of false testimony, with imagined deeds, condemned the disguised merchants,[14] in order to slay the innocent, so that by means of [their goods] the shorn ones, the Otomí warriors, the war leaders, might be sustained. Thus, through them, their dignity, their patrimony, advanced [and] spread.[15]

quimacacia in teihtolli, in teiecteneoaliztli: ipampa ca in iehoatl Motecuçoma: ie omoteneuh, in oc cenca quintlaçotlaia in puchteca ueuetque, in naoaloztomeca, in tealtianime, in tecohoanime: in iuhquima ipilhoan quinchioaia.

Auh in icoac in ie itlacauhtiuh in innemiliz: in aocmo qualli iniollo, in ça iuhqui nentlamati, in ça iztlacatiliztica, tetentlapiquiliztica, tetlanaoalchichiuiliztica: in quintlatzontequiliaia naoaloztomeca intiachcahoan, inic quinmictiaia, in atle intlatlacul: çan nexicoliztica inic inca mozcaltiaia in quachichicti, in otomi, in iautachcahoan: inic inca ohoalotlatocatia, inic ooalmacantia in intecuio, in intlatocaio

---

14. In the *Acad. Hist. MS*, the term is *tiahcaua.*

15. Corresponding Spanish text: *"quando se altiuecian, y desuanecian, y se maluauan, con el favor, y honrra, de las riqueças: el señor entristeciase, y perdialos, el amor: y buscaualos, algunas ocasiones, falsas, o aparentes, para abatirlos, y matarlos: aunque sin culpa, sino por odio, de su altiuez, y soberuja, y con las haziendas dellos, proueya a los soldados viejos de su corte, que se llamavan quachichicti, y otros otomj, y otros, yautachcavan: y con aquellos sustentauan su fausto, y su pompa."* — For *ooalmacantia,* the *Acad. Hist. MS* has *ovalmaantia.*

Seventh Chapter, which telleth how these merchants at that time held a banquet.

He who held a banquet, when his possessions, his goods, were already many; when already he had attained his fortune, his wealth; when our lord had shown him mercy, thereupon took counsel with himself; he spoke thus: "Behold, our lord, master of the earth, protector of all, hath shown me mercy [with] his property, his possessions, his goods. May our lord for a little while show me his mercy; may I not lose, may I not dissipate my wealth,[1] nor neglect the master, our lord. And now may I behold the presence of the poor old men, the poor old women; and our mothers, our fathers, the old merchants, the principal merchants. And the one [or] two poor, destitute, who are my kinsmen: may I assemble them; may I still acknowledge them."

And when he had thus spoken, thereupon he spread out his possessions, his goods, in order to display all which was to be used when needed. First he set down for this purpose the cacao beans, the "divine ear" spice, the tubes of tobacco, the turkeys, the sauce dishes, the carrying baskets, the earthen cups, the wood or the combustible cane to burn, on which the tamales would cook. All this he placed in the house.[2] And when indeed all [and] everything was at hand which would be needed, when he was dissatisfied with nothing more, thereupon he had the people forget [their preoccupations]; he notified the old men, the old women, and all who were to assist him, the kinsmen and the singers; seven at a time he informed them.[3]

And he served the food precisely on a favorable day sign, perhaps One Crocodile or Seven Monkey. [The readers of the day signs] reckoned which, of all the day signs, would be a good time; they did not choose at random.

Jnic chicome capitulo: itechpa tlatoa, in quenin iehoantin puchteca: in iquac quichioaia cuicuicaliztli.

In aquin cuicuicaia: icoac in ie miec iasca itlatqui, in ie quitta inecuiltonol, inetlamachtil: in ie oquitlaocoli totecuio: niman ie ic moiolnonotza, ie quitoa. Ca izcatqui, in onechmotlaocolili in totecuio, in tlalticpaque, in tloque naoaque: in icococauh in iascatzin in itlatquitzin: ma moztla ma uiptla nechonmotlaocolili in totecuio, manoce nitlapolo, ma nitlaatocti, ma nictlachitonili in tlacatl totecuio: Auh in ascan ma imisco, ma imicpac nitlachie in icnoueue in icnoilama: auh in tonanhoan in totahoan, in puchteca ueuetque, in puchtecatlatoque: auh in cetzin vmetzin in motolinia, in icnotlaca in nooaniolque, ma niquincentlali, ma oc niquimoniximati.

In oiuh quito y, niman ie ic quimoiaoa in iasca in itlatqui, inic quinestia in isquich popoliuiz, in tetech monequiz, achtopa ic tlateca, in cacaoatl, in teunacaztli, in ietl, in totoli, in mulcaxtli, in chiquiuitl, i çoquitecomatl, in quauitl anoço tlâchinolacatl in tlatlaz, in itlan icuciz tamallj, muchi quicaltema. Auh in ie isquich in omochi nez: in isquich monequiz, in aoc tle quitequipachoa. Niman ie ic temulcaoaltia: quinmachitia, in ueuetque, in ilamatque: ioan in isquichtin quipaleuizque in ioaniolque: ioan in cuicanime, chicometica in quitecaquitia.

Auh in uel icoac tetlaqualtia: ipan in qualli tonalli, aço ce cipactli, anoço chicome oçomatli, quipouhtiuh in iquin qualcan iez cemilhuitonalli, amo çan quiliuizuiaia.

---

1. See Molina, op. cit., tlaatoctiani.

2. Corresponding Spanish text: "compraua mucho cacao: y tambien aquella especie muy oloroso, que se llama teunacaztli, o vei nacaztli: la qual molida se beue con el cacao, y otras especies, que molidas se beuen con el cacao: compraua tambien muchas gallinas, y gallos de papada y mucha loça, toda la que era menester, para serujcio de la comida y tambien chiquujtes de muchas maneras, y xicaras de barro, para beuer, y palos para reboluer el cacao, y mucha leña para gujsar la comjda, y cañas de mahiz o otras cañas que se llamã tlachinollacatl para cozer los tamales." — The Acad. Hist. MS has quicacaltema instead of quicaltema.

3. Corresponding Spanish text: "los cantores, y dançadores del areyto."

In this manner was it done in days of old, in order that a banquet be held. First they selected those who were wise, able, prudent; the agile, not the halt; the very honorable, the well-spoken, the strong, the gracious hosts; those of good bearing [and] appearance, not cowardly, nor bewildered, nor shy; those of stalwart gaze. These were the ones chosen; the lesser ones were not required there; only the seasoned warriors, the brave warriors, the men of war, who distributed [and] with their hands disposed of the flowers, the tobacco, the food, the chocolate, and were the welcomers, attendants, receptionists, ushers.

The tobacco server,[4] to perform his task, bore the tobacco [tube] in his right hand; thus he held it: there where it was sealed off; not by the tube [end].[5] And he went bearing the bowl for the tobacco tubes in his left hand. First he offered one the tobacco tube. He said: "My beloved noble, here is thy cane of tobacco." Then [the guest] took it up; he placed it between his fingers to smoke it. This denoted the spear thrower or the spear; war equipment; valor. And the bowl for tobacco tubes stood for the shield, wherefore he bore it in his left hand. He went holding it only by its rim, to carry it. He laid it before perhaps the commanding general, or the general; perhaps the *atempanecatl*;[6] all the lords, and the eagle warrior guides, or the noblemen: indeed all who were invited.

And then they followed with the flowers. To carry them one held in his right hand the "shield flower,"[7] and there in his left he grasped the "stick flower."[8] For this reason did he hold [the "shield flower"] in his right hand: the one to whom the flowers were offered stood facing the flower server, and so he took the "shield flower" in his left hand and he took the "stick flower" from him with his right hand. The "shield flower" represented a shield.

And then they followed with the food. To carry it one held the sauce dish in his right hand, not holding it by its rim, but only going resting it in the palm of his hand. And there in his left hand he went bear-

O ie iui in: in mochioaia in ie uecauh inic cuicuicoia: achtopa quīpepenaia in mimatini, in mozcaliani, in tlanemiliani, in mocxiiehecoani, in amo icximimiquini: in cenca tlamauiztiliani, in qualli intlatol, in chicaoac, in coanezqui: in moch quitquiticac in innacaio, in itlachieliz in amo ismâmaui, in amo ismimiqui: in acan mistzacuilia in uel imicxitlan tlachie: iehoantin in in pepenaloia, amo çan tlapaltontli in oncan monequia: uel iehoantin in tequioaque, in tiacahoan, in oquichtin: in quimoiaoaia in inmac popoliuia, in suchitl, in ietl, in tlaqualli, in cacaoatl: auh in tenamiqui in techie in tecalaquia in tetlalia.

Jnic quichioa itequiuh in teiiemaca: imaiauhcampa in quitqui in iietl inic quitzitzquia, oncan in ipan tlapepechollo, amo ipan in acatl. Auh in iopuchcopa quitquitiuh in iecaxitl iacachto contemaca in ietl, quitoa Nopiltzintzine nican catqui macatzin: niman quioalcuilia imapiltzalā quiteca, inic quichichina, quinezcaiotia in atlatl, in anoço tlatzontectli, in iautlatquitl, in oquichtiliztli. Auh in iecaxitl quinezcaiotia in chimalli: ipampa in iopuchcopa quitqui, çan inacacic quimantiuh inic quitqui: ispā conmanilia, in aço tlacateccatl, in anoço tlacochcalcatl, aço atēpanecatl, in ie mochintin tlatoque: ioan quauhiacame anoço pipilti, in ie isquich tlacatl tlanotzalli.

Auh niman iehehoatl quitoquilia in suchitl inic quitqui imaiauhcampa in quitzitzquia in chimalsuchitl: auh in iopuchcopa onpa quitzitzquia in quauhsuchitl: ipampa in ompa quitzitzquia in imaiauhcan. Ca in iehoatl suchimaco: ca quisnamictimoquetza in tesuchimacac: auh inic quioalcuilia in chimalsuchitl iiopuchcopa: auh in imaiauhcampa ompa quioalcui in quauhsuchitl. Jn iehoatl y, in chimalsuchitl quinezcaiotia in chimalli.

Auh niman iehehoatl quitoquilia in tlaqualli: inic quitqui imaiauhcāpa quitzitzquia in mulcaxitl, amo itenco in quitzitzquia: çan imacpalnepantla quimantiuh. Auh in iopuchcopa, ompa quitquitiuh in chi-

---

4. *Ibid.*: "*dauan las cañas de humo.*"

5. *Ibid.*: "*tomavan la caña, en la mano derecha: no por la caña que estaua descubierta, sino por la parte que estaua con el carbon.*"

6. See Chap. 10, n. 10.

7. *Chimalxochitl*: probably *Helianthus annuus* L., in Sahagún (Garibay ed.), Vol. IV, p. 334.

8. *Quauhxochitl*: "*Planta parasitaria, usada como medicina. . . . Indefinida,*" in *ibid.*, p. 350. Santamaría, *op. cit.*, Vol. I, p. 421, defines it, however, as "*Otro nombre vulgar que en Méjico se da a la planta apocinácea conocida también por* Tabasqueña (Plumeria rubra)."

ing the basket well filled with tamales. Neither did he take it by its rim; only on the palm of his hand did he set the basket.[9]

And then they ended with the chocolate. To carry it one placed the cup in his right hand. He did not go taking it by its rim, but likewise went placing the gourd in the palm of his hand. And the stirring stick and gourd rest he went bearing there in his left hand.

These were to pay honor to the lords. But those who followed, all [were served with] only earthen cups.

quiuitl, uel tentiuh in tamalli, amo no itenco cana: çan no imacpalnepātla in quiquetza chiquitl.

Auh niman iehehoatl in cacahoatl, ça ontlatzacuia, inic quitqui imaiauhcampa quiquetza in tecomatl, amo itenco cantiuh, çan no imacpalnepantla quiquetztiuh in aiotectli. Auh in aquauitl: ioan aiaoalli, ompa quitquitiuh in iopuchcopa.

Iehoatl in: inic quinmauiztiliaia in tlatoque: auh in quitoquiliaia çan mochi çoquitecomatl.

---

9. *Chiquiuitl* in the *Acad. Hist. MS.*

Eighth Chapter, which telleth how he who held the banquet performed the act of offering, to pay the debt [to the gods], when the singers were about to begin to dance; and what they did during the night.

And when they were about to begin, when the singers were about to start dancing, first they laid offerings before Uitzilopochtli; they gave him his gifts of flowers, of tubes of tobacco. They laid them down at the landing [of the pyramid] in an eagle vessel.[1] And later they continued making offerings in each of the temples called Uitznauac, Pochtlan, Yopico, [and] Tlamatzinco, on the altars. The placing of offerings ceased there at the home of [those who provided the banquet]. There in the middle of the courtyard, before the ground drum,[2] where lay a covering of straw, they laid offerings of "shield flowers," of necklaces [and] garlands of flowers. And there they laid an offering of two bowls for tobacco tubes on which they set the tubes of tobacco which lay burning.

And when the offering had been made, thereafter was begun the singing. A little sunlight [remained] when they started singing. First all whistled through their fingers. When the host heard it, then all [and] each of the women residing there, and his neighbors, who heard the whistling through the fingers, sighed, kissed the earth, [and] said: "The master, our lord, hath spoken." With only one of their fingers they kissed the earth.[3] Then quickly, swiftly, they took the incense ladle.[4] With it they scooped up fire on which they spread white *copal;* this was the torchwood *copal,* the legitimate, the odoriferous, with no rubbish nor dirt; very clear. They said it was his fortune.[5]

Thereupon went into the courtyard one who was to offer incense.[6] They took a quail to him. When he had arrived where the ground drum stood, he

Jnic chicuey capitulo, itechpa tlatoa in quenin quichioaia tlamanaliztli, inic mostlaoaia, in iehoatl quichioaia cuicuicaliztli, in icoac ie compeoaltizque cuicanime mîtotizque: ioan in tlein quichioaia in ioaltica.

Auh in ie compehoaltizque, in ie peoazque mitotizque cuicanime: achtopa ontlamanaia in ispan, Vitzilobuchtli conmana in inuen, in suchitl, in ietl, vncan conteca in apetlac quauhxicaltica. Auh çatepan tlâtlamana in izquican teupan mitoaia, vitznaoac, puchtlan, iopico, tlamatzinco, momozco: ça ompa ommocaoa in inchan ontlamana, oncan in itoalnepantla, ispan in ueuetl, in oncan onoc çacapechtli ipan in conmamana in chimalsuchitl, in suchicozcatl, in icpacsuchitl: auh oncan conmana yn iecaxitl ontetl, oncan contêteca in ietl tlatlatlatoc.

Auh in ontlamanaloc: niman ie ic peoalo in cuico, oc achiton tonatiuh in quipeoaltia in cuica: achtopa mapipitzoa. Jn oquicac in tecoanotzani niman ie helcîciui, ontlalqua, mochintin in isquichtin cihoa, oncan onoque ioan in icalnaoactlaca, in quicaquia, mapipitzoliztli, quitoaia. Omonaoatili, in tlacatl totecuio: çaz çe in inmapil ic ontlalquaia. Niman iciuhca quicuitiquiça in tlemaitl, ic cosxopiloa in tletl, oncan conteca in iztac copalli, iehoatl in tzioaccopalli, in uel iaque in amo tlaçollo, in amo teuhio, in uel chipaoac, mitoaia itonal:

niman ie ic iauh in tlenamacaz, in itoalco quitquilitiui in çolli; in icoac oonacic in oncan icac ueuetl, niman quiteca in tlemaitl: achtopa conquechcotona

---

1. Corresponding Spanish text: *"en su oratorio, en un plato grande de madero pintado."*

2. *Ibid.: "delante del atambor, y teponaztli en un estrado de heno, que estaua delante del atambor, y teponaztli."*

3. In the *Acad. Hist. MS, ontlalquaia* is followed by *auh i yehuatl ilhuichiuaya.*

4. Corresponding Spanish text: *"un incenssario, como caço."*

5. *Ibid.: "dezian, que era su suerte."*

6. *Ibid.: "luego salia al patio de la casa un satrapa y un sacristanejo, lleuauale unas codornjzes."*

then set down the incense ladle. First he beheaded the quail. He cast it on the ground; there it moved, fluttering. He observed closely where it would proceed to go. If it went [north] toward what they called the land of the dead, the right hand of the earth,[7] [the host] was much frightened thereby. He took it as an omen of evil. He said: "Already I shall take sick; I am about to die." But if it went there whence the sun came forth [east], or where the sun entered his house [west], or toward the left hand of the earth [south], he was much gladdened thereby. He said: "The protector of all[8] hath no anger; there is yet reward for me."

Thereupon [the priest] took his incense ladle; he stood facing the ground drum. Four times he raised his incense ladle there toward where the sun came forth, called east. And the second place where he offered incense was there where the sun entered his house, called west; he also raised his incense ladle four times. And the third place where he offered incense was there toward the left hand of the earth, called south; he also raised his incense ladle four times. And the fourth place where he offered incense was there toward the right hand of the earth, called north; he also raised his incense ladle four times. To all parts he offered incense. And when he had offered incense, he cast the coals into the hearth; he brought in only the incense ladle.

And when they who provided the banquet had offered incense, thereupon came out those who were to dance: the commanding general[9] [and] indeed all the shorn ones, the Otomí [warriors], the seasoned warriors, the masters of the youths. But the principal merchants did not dance; they only sat; they remained watching, because it was these who gave the banquet. And the aged merchants received the people with flowers, with tubes of tobacco, [and] paper garlands, with turquoise mosaics, and fine maguey fiber plumage glistening with flecks of mica.[10]

At the very first, mushrooms had been served. They ate them at the time when, they said, the shell

tlalpan contlaça, oncan tlapapatlatztinemj: uel quittaia in campa iê itztiaz: intla ompa itztiuh, in quitoaia mictlampa, in imaiauhcan tlalli, cenca ic momauhtiaia: quitetzammatia quitoaia. Ca ie cocoliztli niccuiz ie nimiquiz. Auh intla tonatiuh [yquiçayampa itztiuh, ahnoço] icalaquian anoço iiopuchcopa tlalli itztiuh, cenca ic papaquia, quitoaia: ca aiatlei in iqualan tloque ca oc onca in nomacehoal.

Niman ie ic concui in itlema quisnamictimoquetza in ueuetl, nappa in coniiaoa in itlema in ompa oalquiça tonatiuh, mitoaia tlapcopa. Auh inic occan tlatotoniaia, ompa in icalaquian tonatiuh, mîtoaia cihoatlanpa, no nappa in coniaoa in itlema. Auh inic escan tlatotoniaia, vmpa in iopuchcopa tlalli, mitoaia vitznaoatlalpa, no nappa in coniahoa in itlema. Auh inic nauhcan tlatotonia ompa in imaiauhcampa tlalli, mitoaia mimiscoa intlalpan, no nappa in coniaoaia in itlema. O izquican in in tlenamacaia: auh in ontlenamacac, in tlesuchtli tlêquazco contema, çaiio in quicalaquia tlemaitl.

Jn ontlatotoni in tecoanotza, niman ie ic oalquiça in mitotizque, in tlacateccatl, in ie mochintin quaquachicti, in otomi, in tequioaque in titiachcahoan. Auh in iehoantin puchtecatlatoque amo mitotia, çan onoque mopistoque: ipampa ca iehoantin in tecooachioa. Auh in puchtecaueuetq̃ jehoantin tenamique, in suchitica, in ietica, in amacozcatl xiuhtezcaio: auh in ichquequetzalli pepeiocio metzcuitlatica,

vel iacattiuia in tequaltiloia nanacatl in quiquaia, icoac in quitoaia tlâtlapitzalizpan aiamo tle tlaqualli

---

7. Cf. notes 4 and 5, Chapter 3. — After *tonatiuh, the Acad. Hist.* MS has *yquiçayampa itztiuh, ahnoço.* It is inserted in the Aztec text here in brackets.

8. In the *Acad. Hist.* MS, *nauaque* follows *tloque.*

9. After *tlacateccatl,* the *Acad. Hist.* MS has *tlacochcalcatl.*

10. Possibly mica. See Nardo Antonio Reccho: *Rervm Medicarvm Novae Hispaniae Thesavrvs sev Plantarvm animalivm mineralivm mexicanorvm historia ex Francisci Hernandez* (Rome: Vitalis Mascardi, 1651), p. 336: *"Mezcuitlatl . . . qui in praetenues quoque secari consueuit laminulas, ex aureo colore purpurascentes. Quae quantumuis in igne commorentur, neque exuruntur, neque . . . incalescunt."* Cf. also p. 895; and *Florentine Codex,* Book XI, fol. 214v.

trumpets were blown. They ate no more food; they only drank chocolate during the night. And they ate the mushrooms with honey. When the mushrooms took effect on them, then they danced, then they wept. But some, while still in command of their senses, entered[11] [and] sat there by the house on their seats; they danced no more, but only sat there nodding.

One saw in vision that already he would die, [and] there continued weeping. One saw in vision that he would die in battle; one saw in vision that he would be eaten by wild beasts; one saw in vision that he would take captives in war; one saw in vision that he would be rich, wealthy; one saw in vision that he would buy slaves — he would be a slave owner; one saw in vision that he would commit adultery — he would be struck by stones -- he would be stoned; one saw in vision that he would steal — he would also be stoned; one saw in vision that his head would be crushed by stones — they would condemn him; one saw in vision that he would perish in the water; one saw in vision that he would live in peace, in tranquillity, until he died; one saw in vision that he would fall from a roof-top — he would fall to his death. However many things were to befall one, he then saw all in vision: even that he would be drowned.

And when the effects of the mushrooms had left them, they consulted among themselves and told one another what they had seen in vision. And they saw in vision what would befall those who had eaten no mushrooms, and what they went about doing. Some were perhaps[12] thieves, some perhaps committed adultery. Howsoever many things there were, all were told — that one would take captives, one would become a seasoned warrior, a leader of the youths, one would die in battle, become rich, buy slaves, provide banquets, ceremonially bathe slaves, commit adultery, be strangled, perish in the water, drown. Whatsoever was to befall one, they then saw all [in vision]. Perhaps he would go to his death in Anauac.

And when the division of the night arrived, when it was exactly midnight, the one who provided the banquet thereupon paid his debt [to the gods]. He burned paper spattered with rubber; he did as hath

quiquaia, çan oc iio, in cacahoatl conia ioaltica. Auh in nanacatl necuio in quiquaia: in icoac ie intech quiça nanacatl, in oncan mitotia, oncan choca: Auh in cequintin in oc iniollo quimati, in oncan inieian motlalia caltech aocmo mitotia, ça oncan oaltolotimotlalia.

Jn aca conmottilia ie miquiz, oncan chocatica: in aca conmottilia iaumiquiz: in aca conmottilia tequanqualoz: in aca conmottilia tlamaz iauc: in aca conmottilia iehoatl in mocuiltonoz in motlacamatiz: in aca conmotilia tecohoaz tlacaoa iez, in aca conmottilia tetlaximaz, tetzotzonaloz tetepacholoz: in aca conmottilia ihichtequiz no tetepacholoz: in aca conmottilia tequatepachoz quitzacutiaz: in aca conmottilia atlan miquiz: in aca conmottilia iehoatl in iuian iocosca monemitiz ipan miquiz: in aca conmottilia tlapanco oaluetziz mictiuetziz. J çaço quesquich tepan mochioaz: mochi oncan conittaia, in anoço ilaquiloz.

Auh in oquincauh nanacatl: mononotza quimolhuia in tlein oconmottilique. Auh in iehoantin in atle oquiquaque nanacatl: no quiquimonittilia in tlein inpan mochioaz: ioan in tlein quichiuhtinemi cequinti in aço ihichtequi, in aço tetlâtlaxima. Jz çaço quezquitlamantli in isquich omito in tlamaz, in tequioacatiz, in telpuchiiacatiz, in iaumiquiz, in motlacamatiz, in tecohoaz in cuicuicaz in tealtiz, in tetlaximaz in moquechmecaniz, in atlan miquiz in ilaquiloz: in çaço tlein inpan mochioaz, muchi oncan conittaia in aço anaoac miquitiuh.

Auh in oacic ioalli xeliui, in ie uel ioalnepantla: in iehoatl tecoanotza: niman ie ic mostlaoa, iehoatl in amatl quitlâtia tlaolchipinilli, iuh quichioa in oiuh mito tlacpac. Auh ie no ceppa icoac atlihoa, aço oppa

11. In the *Acad. Hist. MS, calaqui* follows *quimati.*
12. For *in oc*, the *Acad. Hist. MS* has *in ahço.*

been told above.[13] And once again chocolate was drunk; two or three times during the night chocolate was served. And so they danced all night; indeed they sang until the dawn broke — perhaps the plain one, or the version of the Uexotzinca, or of the Chalca.[14] And the gifts which have been mentioned — flowers, tubes of tobacco — [and] the ashes remaining from the incense ladle, they buried all there in the middle of the courtyard. As they buried it, they said: "We put the maguey thorns [and] tubes of tobacco in the earth. Our children [and] grandchildren shall eat; they shall drink; they will not perish forever."

anoço espa in iohoan teamaco: iuh ce iohoal in mitotia, uel iuh tlatui, in queoa aço tlamelauhcaiotl, anoço uexotzincaiotl anoço chalchicacuicatl. Auh in omoteneuh in uentli: in suchitl in ietl, in tlenamacnestli mochi oncan quitocaia in itoalnepantla. Jnic quitocaia quitoaia uitztli, in ietl tictlalaquia quiquazque quizque in topilhoan, in toshuihoan amo cempoliuiz.

---

13. Chapter 3.

14. In the *Acad. Hist. MS* and in the corresponding Spanish text, *chalcacuicatl*. Cf. Angel María Garibay K.: *Historia de la literatura náhuatl* (México: Editorial Porrúa, 1953), Vol. I, pp. 151 *et seq.*, and p. 232; *Abside*, II (1937) and V (1940); Antonio Peñafiel (ed.): *Cantares en idioma mexicano* (México: Oficina Tipográfica de la Secretaría de Fomento, 1904); Leonhard Schulze Jena: *Alt-Aztekische Gesänge* (Gerdt Kutscher, ed.; Stuttgart: W. Kohlhammer, 1957), pp. 169 *et seq.*

Ninth Chapter, which telleth what they did when it was about to dawn, and what they did when the sun arose.

And when the dawn was about to come, when the morning star emerged, when already a little of the brightness of the dawn appeared, when already it lightened, then quickly — swiftly — they buried the ashes of the incense ladle, the flowers, the tobacco. The guests showed much concern; they feared that someone of vicious life might come. They said: "He will make [the ashes] vile." It was well understood that these were those who lived in concubinage, the adulterers, the thieves, those who constantly played *tlachtli*, those who constantly played *patolli*, the drunken, the besotted. They feared these.

And when they had buried [the ashes], thereupon there was singing with the two-toned drum; they intoned a song after the manner of Anauac, or the flower song.[1] And when the sun came forth, thereupon food was served to each and every one. They served food to all the people. They passed no one by. Each one ate [and] drank by himself; flowers [and] tubes of tobacco were given to them and to the poor old men, the poor old women. Then later all the guests entered. And the women bore their dried grains of maize, each one a small basket [of them] which she carried [and] rested on her shoulders. They said: "We shall leave tamales." And thus they went there where they kept themselves apart: they formed themselves in separate groups of perhaps five, or six, or ten: howsoever many would be in procession. And when they arrived there where they kept themselves apart, then they entered the women's quarters, where they watched the others. They took places by the door, holding the grains of maize in the folds of their skirts.[2] Then they placed [the maize] on reed mats, and then they served them food.[3] And when they ate, they served them no

Jnic chicunaui capitulo: itechpa tlatoa in tlein quichioaia in icoac ie tlatuiz: ioan in tlein quichioaia in icoac oalquiça tonatiuh.

Auh in ie tlatuitiuitz, in ooalcholo uei citlalin, in icoac ie achi tlauizcalleoaz, in ie tlachipaoa: icoac hiciuhca contocatiuetzi, in tlenamacnestli, in suchitl, in ietl: cenca quitlaçotlaia, quimimacaxiltiaia in tlacohoanotzalti, in aço aca teuhiotiuitz, tlaçollotiuitz, quitoaia: quiteuhiotiz quitlaçollotiz. Jnic momelaoacacaqui: iehoantin in momêmecatiani in tetlaxinque in ihichtequi in oollama, in pâpâtoa, in tlaoanque in socomicque: iehoantin in, in quimimacaxiltiaia.

Auh in ocontocaque: niman ie ic teponazcuico, iehoatl in queoa anaoacaiotl, anoço supancuicatl. Auh in ooalquiz tonatiuh: niman ie ic tetlamaco, ceceiaca quintlamaca in isquich tlacatl, aiac ipan quiça, cececcan in tlaqualo atlioa tesuchimaco, teiiemaco. Auh in icnoueuetque, in icnoilamatque: quin icoac calaquia in isquichtin tlanotzalti: auh in cihoa intlaul ietiuh, cêcentzinpetlaio in quitqui in quequechpan quiquequetzaia quitoaia titamalcahoazque. Auh inic uia, in ompa mopiazque mocecentlamantilia aço mamacuiltin: anoço chichiquacemme, anoço matlatlactin momana, i çaço quezquintin mantiazque. Auh ino onacique, in ompa mopiazque: niman ie calaqui iz cihoapan, in techiê, tlaquetzaltitlan mani, quimoncuixanoltitimani in tlaolli: nimã petlapan quintlalia. Auh nimã ie quintlamaca. Auh in ontlaquaque: aocmo cacaoatl in quinmacaia, ça atulli chianpitzaoac, puchtecaio caxitl, inic quinmacaia tiçatica tlacujlollo.

---

1. Cf. Garibay, *op. cit.*, Vol. II, p. 403.

2. *Xanaltihtimani* in the *Acad. Hist.* MS.

3. Corresponding Spanish text: *"En entrando en las casas donde suelen juntarse, los combidados que estan cercados de un patio, como celdas: ponjanse, cada uno en su aposento: estas mugeres, yendo a la casa del combite: yban de cinco, en cinco, y de seis, en seis: entravan a la casa de las mugeres donde hazen la comjda, y ponjanse, cabe las puertas, donde hazian pan: y tenjan alli el mahiz, que avian traydo: y despues hechauanlo sobre un petate: y luego les dauan comjda."*

chocolate, but only *atole* with *chía*. They served it to them in a merchant's plate with a design in white.

First the women did thus: each one carried a cape of maguey fiber [that the one who provided the banquet might] secure wood. They showed [this] favor to the giver of the banquet, in order to place it on him. Such was customary for all who gave banquets or died; they wrapped them in capes; so they placed them on.

And for the entire day there was [entering[4] and] lingering. Now there was no more dancing; when the singing had ceased, it was precisely time to eat. And when [a host's] banquet was over, when food had been served, on the morrow once again food [and] drink were served. Tubes of tobacco [and] flowers were provided. Only the chosen ones did he summon to eat and drink.[5]

But if nothing remained of the flowers, tubes of tobacco, food, [or] chocolate at the time of the distribution of the leftovers, so the old men considered of him who fed the people, nothing more would be to his merit; nothing more would be his reward. Always it resulted that the master, our lord, became irritated. But if there remained flowers, tubes of tobacco, food, chocolate, carrying baskets, sauce dishes, earthen cups, they thereby saw that once again banquets would be held; that they were not ended. They said: "Our lord, the protector of all, hath been merciful to us. There is still the reward, the merit, of the youth, the young boy; he will still prosper."

Then once again they set [the host before them]; they admonished him; they gave him the reprimands, the counsel, of the elders — the punishment, the castigations; they impressed upon him the words of torment which penetrated his entrails even as wood smoldered [and] smoked.[6] Thus they continued to belabor him in order to lengthen his life.

And when they had set forth the means by which they reared [and] instructed, then they besought him; they said to him: "Here thou art. Take heed. Our lord hath poured forth his possessions. Not in *tlachtli* nor in *patolli* hast thou entered. One [or] two of thy mothers, of thy fathers, came to eat [and] drink as they required. For thou hast recognized

Inic quichioaia cihoa achtopa onquauhcaoaia, cecentetl in ichtilmatli quitquia, in cõtlaoculiaia cuicuicaz, inic ipan ontlatecaia: mochi tlacatl ipan mochioaia, in aquique cuicuicaia, anoço momiquiliaia, quinquimiloaia, inic inpan tlatecaia.

Auh uel iuh cemilhuitl in nepielo, aocmo netotilo in mocaoaia cuicatl çan tlaqualizpan. Auh in icoac onquiz itecoanotzaliz, in ontlaqualoc, çan imoztlaioc in oc ceppa tlaqualo atlioa, teiiemaco, tesuchimaco: ça tlapepentli in quinotza in atli in tla.

Auh intlacaioc tle mocaoaz in suchitl in ietl in tlaqualli in cacaoatl, in icoac apeoalo: ic quittaia in ueuetque, aoc tle imâcehoal iez, aoc tle ilhuil iez in iehoatl tetlatlaqualtia, çan iccen onquiça mochîchîctiuh in tlacatl totecuio. Auh intla omocauh in suchitl in ietl in tlaqualli in cacaoatl, in chiquiuitl, in mulcaxitl, in çoquitecomatl: ic quittaia in oc ceppa mochioaz tecooanotzaliztli in amo poliui, quitoaia. O techmocnelili in totecuio: in tloque naoaque, oc onca ilhuil imaçeoal, oc tlamauiçoz in telpuchtontli, in tlapaltontli.

Niman ie no ceppa quioallalia quinonotza, quimaca in teiô in quauhiô: in ueuetlatolli, in atl cecec, in tzitzicaztli itech quipachoa in uel tecocotlatolli, in teiticpa quiquiz in iuhqui quauitl pôpocatoc chichinauhtoc, ic quiuiuitequi inic quiuecapanilhuia in inemiliz.

Auh in oconquisti tlacahoapaoaloni tlacazcaltiloni çatepan quitlatlauhtia, quilhuia. Ca nican tica tle ticmati: ca oconmomoiauh in icococauh in totecuio: ca amo tlachco, patulco otictlali, ca oconquaco, ca oconico ca ointech onmonec, in cetzin in ometzin in monahoan in motahoan: ca oimisco, omicpac tontlachis, otiquimonisima: auh cuis ic tatlamatiz cuis ti-

---

4. In the *Acad. Hist. MS, in calacoua* follows *cemilhuitl*. Since its omission alters the sense of the passage, it is here inserted in brackets.

5. *Tlaqua* in the *Acad. Hist. MS.*

6. Cf. *supra*, Chap. 6, n. 9.

[and] acknowledged them in their presence. Shalt thou therefore perchance by presumptuous, proud, ignominious? Shalt thou rather deliver thyself to comforts? Quickly take up, without fail, the staff [and] the carrying frame. Let it be that somewhere in the desert, the plains, at the foot of a tree, at the base of a crag, thou perish; that thy bones go scattered, thy hair outspread, thy poor rags, thy poor maguey fiber cape, thy wretched breech clout dragging. For in truth it is a battle for us, the vanguard merchants. For we have made the master, our lord, great in honor — in glory — we who are thy mothers [and] thy fathers. And if there is yet some reward [and] merit for us, thou shalt return here; we shall see thee; we shall behold thy presence. Remember nothing within thy house. Continue to travel. Do not stumble against the sticks, into the grass.[7] Go carefully. Take heed, O my beloved son! All this we do to our satisfaction, to gird thee, we thy fathers [and] thy mothers."

mopoaz, cuis misco mocpac ticmanaz: cuis noce ie tlatotonian, ie tlaiamaiã tonmotecaz, ma xoconcuitiuetzi, ma itlan xonaqui, in topilli in cacastli: ma cana teutlalli istlaoatl iitic, quauitl itzintlan, tescalli itzintlan xipopoliui: ma cana cecenmanto in momiiotzin ma cana momoiaoato in motzontzin: ma cana viuilanto in motzotzomatzin, in maiaçoltzin, in momastlaçultzin. Ca nel toiautiliz, in toztomeca: ca uei in oticmauiçoque, in oticmauiçalhuique, tlacatl totecuio, in tehoanti in timonahoan in timotahoan. Auh intla oc itla tolhuil tomacehoal: ca tioalmocuepaz, ca timitzittazque, misco mocpac titlachiezque: maca tle ticqualilnamiquiz in mocalitic: ma xoconcenmattiuh in nenemiliztli, maca tle toconicxinamiquiz in tlacotl in çacatl: ma iuian xoniatiuh, tle ticmati nopiltze: ie isquich tonequistil ticchioa, ic timitzquimiloa in timonahoan, in timotahoan.

---

7. Corresponding Spanish text: *"no tengais miedo a los tropeçones del camjno, ni a las llagas, que hazen en los pies, las ramas espinosas, que nacen en el camjno."*

Tenth Chapter. Here is told of still another feast celebration (which was called "the bathing"). It was especially the merchants who performed it. And when this took place, they observed a feast day; they slew slaves.

When the merchants ceremonially bathed slaves, it was in [the month of] Panquetzaliztli.[1] And when they washed the bathed one, when they slew the slave, they bought [him] there at Azcapotzalco, in the market place; there was the selling place of the slaves. Those who sold them were slave dealers.

Thus did they array the men. First they placed on, they tied about them precious capes [and] precious breech clouts, and shod them in sandals; these were the very fine sandals. And they inserted lip shafts[2] or amber lip plugs in their lower lips; they put leather ear plugs, with pendants hanging from them, in their ears. And they cut their hair in the manner of seasoned warriors, and placed garlands of flowers about their heads, and gave them "shield flowers."[3] And they placed in their hands tubes of good tobacco. They went about sucking [the tubes and] smelling [the flowers] in the market place. There they went about dancing.

And those who sold women [slaves] likewise adorned [them]. They put on them good shifts, those with overspread flowers, or decorated with downy yellow parrot feathers; and their skirts were the ones with the irregular design, or the design of squared corner stones; and they cut their hair, just cutting [it a little below the ears];[4] and they put their necklaces, their garlands of flowers, on them. And they gave them "shield flowers" and tobacco tubes. With these they went dancing, sucking [the tobacco tubes, and] smelling the flowers.

And the slave dealer hired men who sang and beat the two-toned drums. These beat the drums, the two-toned drums, [and] intoned the songs for

Jnic matlactli capitulo: onca mitoa in oc centlamantli ilhuichioaliztli, (in mitoaia tealtiliztli): oc cenca iehoantin quichioaia in puchteca. Auh in icoac y, ilhuiquistiaia, quinmictiaia tlatlacoti.

Jn iquac tealtiaia in puchteca: pan in panquetzaliztli: auh in caltiaia, iehoatl in tlaltilli, in quimictiaia tlacotli, ompa quimoncohoaia in azcaputzalco in tianquizco ompa innamacoian catca in tlatlacoti: iehoanti quinnamacaia in tlacanecuiloque catca.

Jnic quinchichioaia in oquichti, achtopa quincencaoaia, quimonilpiliaia in tlaçotilmatli, in tlaçomastlatl, ioan quincactia iehoatl i cenca qualli cactli, ioan tlamitentetl, anoço apoçonaltentetl in quimonaquiliaia intenco ioan cuetlasnacochtli ihtipepeiocio in quimonaquiliaia innacazco, ioan quintequioacaximaia, ioan quimjcpacsuchicozcatiaia, ioan quinmaca chimalsuchitl: ioan qualli in ietl inmac quintequilia, tlâtlâchichintinemi, tlanecutinemi in tianquizco, oncan miihtotitinemi

Auh in iehoanti cihoa quinamacaia: çan no iuh quichichioaia quimonaquiaia, in qualli vipilli, in suchimoiaoac, anoço xoxoloio: auh in incue iehoatl in chicucueitl, anoço tetenacazço, ioan quixima, çan quintlâtlâtzontequilia, ioan insuchicozqui imicpacsuchiuh, quimonaquiaia, ioan chimalsuchitl, ioan iietl impā mitotitinemi, tlachichintinemi tlanecutinemi.

Auh in iehoatl tlacanecuilo, quimontlaqueoaia in teponazcuicanime: iehoantin quītlatzotzonilia, quinteponacilhuia, quincuicatlaxilia in tlatlacoti: cenca

---

1. The *Acad. Hist. MS* reads: *Nican ompeua in tealtiliztlahtulli.*
2. *Tlamītentetl* in *ibid.*
3. See Chap. 7, n. 7; corresponding Spanish text: *"sus rodelas, en las manos, de flores."*
4. *Ibid.: "cortauanlas, los cabellos por debaxo de las orejas, vna mano o poco mas, todo alrededor."*

the slaves. They took pains that they should dance well there in the market place. Each of the slave dealers grouped his people separately.

And one who would buy a slave very carefully considered which one he would take. He sought one who was of good understanding; who sang well; who made his dance accompany [the beat of] the two-toned drum; and who was pleasing of countenance, of sound body, very clean, without blemish; nowhere scarred [nor] swollen with bruises, [nor] of shuffling feet, afflicted by wens [or] depressions on the forehead, etc.;⁵ one who was well disposed in body, who was very healthy, slender, in all parts like a round, stone column.⁶ Thereupon [the buyer] reached an agreement with the slave dealer on how much the price of his slave would be.⁷

If he were not highly skilled as a dancer, his price was thirty large capes. But if he danced well, if he were clean of body, his price was forty large capes.

And when [the buyer] bought the slave, the slave dealer took off all which was on him — the precious cape, the precious breech clout, the fine sandals. And if it were a woman, he took all from her — the precious skirt [and] the precious shift. And the slave dealer took all the flowers [and] tubes of tobacco. Only a few he sold in good capes, breech clouts, sandals, the good skirts, the good shifts. [Others] he left quite bare. But the slave buyer, already acquainted with the customs, took with him capes, breech clouts, skirts, shifts — these were not very choice; there he provided them with breech clouts, capes, sandals,⁸ shifts, in which to bring them back with him.

And when he had made him arrive, then he placed [the slave] in a wooden jail during the night. And when it had dawned, he brought him out. To a woman he gave unspun cotton; perhaps she might yet spin as she was waiting her death, to which they were to condemn her. But for a man he did nothing.

And when the one who would be a bather of slaves began, he first built houses; he erected perhaps three or four houses, on whose flat roofs his bathed ones would always go about dancing.

quincuitlauiltiaia, inic uel mitotiaia, in oncan tianquizco, nononqua quinmanaia in intlacaoan, in tlacanecuiloque.

Auh in aquin tecohoaz cenca uel motlâtlattiliaia, in ac iehoatl canaz. In oquittac i cenca mimati: in cenca uel cuica: in quiuicaltia, inetotiliz teponaztli: ioan in qualli ixaiac, in qualli inacaio, in cenca chipaoac, in acan quenami, in acan titiquiltic, xixipuchtic, cocomotztic, quaxiquipiltic, quatatacaltic, Etᵃ. Jn ipanoca uel mîmati inacaio, in uellacamelaoac, in iuhqui cuillotic, in anoce ipanoca temimiltic, nimã ie ic quitennonotza in tlacanecuilo in quezqui ipatiuh itlacauh.

Jn amo cenca mîmati ic mitotia in ipatiuh cenquimilli onmatlactli. Auh in qualli ic mîtotia in chipaoac inacaio in ipatiuh onquimilli in quachtli.

Auh in icoac oconcouhque in tlacotli: in iehoatl tlacanecuilo, mochi quicuicuilia in itech ocatca in tlaçotilmatli, in tlaçomastlatl, in tlaçocactli. Auh intla cihoatl: mochi quicuicuilia in tlaçocueitl, in tlaçouipilli: auh in suchitl in ietl mochi concui in tlacanecuilo: çan ipan quinnamacaia in qualli tilmatli, in qualli mastlatl, in qualli cactli: in qualli cueitl, in qualli vipilli, uel quinpepetlaoa. Auh in tecoanime, ie iuh ietiuh in iollo: quitqui in tilmatli, mastlatl, cueitl, vipilli: iehoatl in amo cenca qualli, ompa quinmastlatia, quintlalpilia: quincactia quinuipiltia, inic quinoalhuica.

Auh in oconaxito: niman quauhcalco quitlalia in ie iohoa: auh in otlatuic, quioalquistiaia in cihoatl, ichcatl quimacaia, açoc tzaoaia inic quichistica in imiquiz, inic quitlatzontequiliz: auh in oquichtli amo tle quichioaia.

Auh in icoac compeoaltiaia in aquin tealtiz: achtopa mocacaltiaia, in quiquetzaia ical aço etetl anoço nauhtetl: inic mochipa itlapanco mîtotitinemizque itlaaltilhoan.

<hr>

5. After *quatatacaltic*, the *Acad. Hist. MS* has *quametlapiltic, quachitahtic, quaxomachtic, quapatztic*.

6. Corresponding Spanish text: *"al que via que mejor cantaua, y mas sentidamẽte dançauan, conforme al sõ, y que tenia buen gesto, y buena disposicion: que no tenja tacha corporal, ni era corcobado, ni gordo demasiado . . . y que era bien proporcionado, y bien hecho, en su estatura (en la letra se ponẽ otras particularidades, que contienen muy buenos vocablos [)]."*

7. *Yntlacauh* in the *Acad. Hist. MS*.

8. *Ibid.: quincuetia.*

And when his possessions were very many, when he had been able to attain the things of the world, when in no wise did anything impede him,[9] when indeed there was everything which was to be consumed, when nothing displeased him, when all was at hand, when everything appeared for others to eat, then he would present capes as gifts: these were capes with plaited paper ornaments and with carmine-colored flowers, made with eight blotches of blood, and with orange flowers; and netted capes; and capes with whorl designs; capes with spiral designs; and long, narrow ones, two fathoms long. The capes were at hand, perhaps eight or twelve hundred of them, which were to be used. And of breech clouts perhaps four hundred were at hand: the precious breech clout with long ends, and the one of coyote fur, or perhaps the netted one, or the tawny-colored one; [or] perhaps white breech clouts.

All these precious capes and breech clouts mentioned were given as gifts to the great chieftains: the commanding general, the general; the *quauhnochtli,* the fearless warriors, the Otomí warriors, the *mixcoatlailotlac,* the *ezuauacatl,* the *maçatecatl,* the *tlillancalqui,* the *ticociauacatl,* the *tezcacoacatl,* the *tocuiltecatl,* the *atempanecatl,* the lord general — indeed all princes of the reigning family.[10] To these the bather of slaves gave gifts according to their liking. And then he gave gifts to the principal merchants,[11] to those who bathed slaves, and all the disguised merchants, the spying merchants who entered regions of battle, the slave dealers. Thus were they given gifts: the chosen few received precious capes [and] breech clouts as gifts. Then gifts were given merchants from the cities around, of which there were twelve, whom they invited. They were those who bathed slaves, the chosen few.

And then he gave gifts to all the women who bathed slaves. They received as gifts skirts: the one with the heart design, and with whorl [or] spiral designs; and shifts: the one with the downy feather pendants, [or] the one painted like stone vases, and the shift with the design of an eagle head in a setting,

Auh in icoac in cenca ie miec in itlatqui: in ouel quicnopilhui in tlalticpacaiutl: in çan niman aoc tle quimamimictia, in ie mochi onca in isquich popoliuiz: in aoc tle quitequipachoa, in omochi nez in oic tlatecac, in quitetlauhtiz in tilmatli: iehoatl in amanepaniuhqui, ioan nochpallaxochio chicueçotl, ioan vitztecollaxochio, ioan tlalpiltilmatli, ioan tlatzcallotl, ilacatziuhqui, ioan canaoaca onmatl, in tilmatli necia, aço ontzontli, anoço etzõtli in popoliuia. Auh in mastlatl, aço centzontli in necia: iehoatl in tlaçomastlatl iacauiiac, ioan coioichcamastlatl, aço tlalpilmastlatl, anoço quappachmastlatl, aço iztac mastlatl.

Jn izquitlamantli omoteneuh tlaçotilmatli, tlaçomastlatl: iehoantin quimotlauhtiaia in ueuei tiacahoa, tlacateccatl, tlacochcalcatl, quauhnochtli, in quaquachicti in otomi in imiscoatlailotlac, in ezoaoacatl, in maçatecatl, in tlillancalqui, in ticociaoacatl, in tezcacoacatl in tocuiltecatl, in atenpanecatl, in tlacochcalcatl tecutli, in ie mochintin tlaçopipiltin. O iehoantin i in intech monequi in quintlauhtiaia tealti. Auh niman iehoantin in quintlauhtiaia in puchtecatlatoque, in tealtianime, ioan in isquichti in naoaloztomeca, in teiaoaloani, iautitlan calaquini, in tecoanime: inic motlauhtiaia çan ipan mopepenaia, in quimotlauhtiaia: iehoatl in tlaçotilmatli, in tlaçomastlatl: niman iehehoatl in quimotlauhtiaia, in ie nouian altepetl ipan puchteca, matlactepetl omome, in quinnotzaia: iehoantin tealtianime çan ipan mopepenaia.

Auh niman iehoãtin in quimontlauhtiaia: in ie mochintin cihoa, in tealtianime, in quimotlauhtiaia cueitl: iehoatl in iollo, ioan tlatzcallotl, ilacatziuhqui: ioan vipilli iehoatl in putõcapipilcac, texicalicuiliuhqui, ioan isquauhcallo vipilli, tenmalinqui. O isquich in, in quitetlauhtiaia tealtiz.

---

9. After *quimamimictia, quicximimictia* follows in *ibid.*

10. English equivalents are difficult to assign. Some idea of distinctions in rank are suggested as follows in Clark, *op. cit.,* Vol. III, pp. 63-65, although there is some overlapping: *tlacateccatl, tlacochcalcatl, ticociaoacatl, tezcacoacatl,* and *tocuiltecatl* are grouped as *hombres valientes; quauhnochtli, tlillancalqui, atenpanecatl,* and *ezoaoacatl* as *executores; mixcoatlailotlac* as *justicia como alto* and *ezoaoacatl* as *alcalde;* and *quaquachicti, otomi,* and *tlacatecatl* as holding their rank *de haber cautivado en las guerras.* See also Anderson and Dibble, *op. cit.,* Book II, pp. 102, 114; Book VIII, p. 62; Book XII, pp. 9, 112; Seler, *op. cit.,* Vol. II, Pt. 3, p. 86; and Juan de Torquemada: *Segunda parte de los veinte i un libros rituales i monarchia indiana* (Madrid: Nicolas Rodrigues Franco, 1723), p. 352.

11. The corresponding Spanish text refers to *puchteca tlailotlac — jefe de los traficantes de tierra extraña,* in Sahagún, *op. cit.,* Vol. IV, p. 349.

with a border of twisted cords. All these, he who would bathe slaves gave them as gifts.

And then he prepared all the grains of dried maize which would be needed. In wooden bins he put them. And the beans he also piled into wooden bins,[12] and the wrinkled *chía*[13] [and] small *chía* seeds. Using bins he placed about all things required to assist them, that they might not go hungry, that they might drink — that there would be what all might drink; [and] merchants' vessels in which *atole* topped with squash seeds might be served. And chilis he placed in [containers of] matting; and he laid out salt, perhaps forty or sixty [jars of it]. And he arranged to buy tomatoes; daily he bought tomatoes with perhaps twenty small capes. And then he provided turkeys, perhaps eighty or a hundred of them. Then he bought dogs to provide the people as food, perhaps twenty or forty. When they died, they put them with the turkeys which they served; at the bottom of the sauce dish they placed the dog meat, on top they placed the turkey as required. And then he provided the cacao beans, perhaps twenty sacks of them, as required. And then he provided the chocolate beaters, perhaps two or four thousand of them; then the sauce dishes,[14] the large baskets, the earthen cups, the merchants' plates, the wood, the charcoal. All this he packed into the house. Then he paid for the water which was consumed daily, perhaps three or four boats of it. The value of a boat [of water] was one small cape given [for it].

The value of one small cape was one hundred cacao beans; this was the one [known as] *tototlaqualtequachtli*. And the value of the following small cape was eighty cacao beans. And finally the value of the last small cape was sixty-five cacao beans.[15]

And when this was done, when the things were prepared, when all was at hand that was mentioned and told of, then he set out for Tochtepec, where resided together the merchants, the vanguard merchants, of every city: inhabitants of every city. There, together, were the houses of each one[16] from Tenochtitlan, Tlatilulco, Texcoco, Uexotla, Coatl ichan,

Auh niman iehoatl quicencaoa in isquich tetech monequiz in tlaolli, quauhcuezcomatl ic quimâmâna, ioan in etl, no quicuecuezcomatema: ioan chientzotzol, chianpitzaoac, cuezcontica quiquêquetzaia: intech monequia in isquichtin quipaleuiaia, inic amo apizmiquizque: inic tlaiia, inic tlaioaloia, puchteca caxitl inic temacoia atulli aiohoachpani: ioan chilli, mochi petlatica quiquequetzaia, ioan iztatl quimanaia, aço ontecpantli, anoço etecpantli: ioan tomatl quicouhtiuia, in cecemilhuitl ic tomacohoa, aço cêquimilli in tequachtli. Auh niman iehoatl quinestia in totolin: aço nauhtecpantli, ano macuiltecpantli. Niman iehoatl in quicohoaia chichi in ipan tetlaqualtiaia aço centecpantli, anoço ontecpantli in miquia quiuicaltiaia in totolin in ipan tetlamacaia, tlani quitlaliaia mulcaxic in chichinacatl, ça pani quitlaliaia in totolnacatl, in tetech monequia. Auh niman iehoatl in cacahoatl quinestiaia: aço centecpanxiquipilli in tetech monequi. Auh niman iehoatl quinestia in acaquauitl, aço macuiltzontli, anoço matlactzontli. Niman iehoatl in mulcaxitl: in chiquiuitl, in çoquitecomatl, in puchtecaiocaxitl, in quauitl, in tecolli: mochi quicaltema. Niman iehoatl quipatiotia in atl: in cecemilhuitl popoliuia, aço eacalli anoço naoacalli: in cemacalli ipatiuh catca, centetl in tequachtli momacaia:

in centetl tequachtli, ipatiuh catca, macuilpoalli in cacaoatl, iehoatl in tototlaqualtequachtli: auh in quitoquilia uel iehoatl in tequachtli nappoalli ipatiuh catca in cacaoatl: auh in ça iequene tlatzacuia tequachtli, Epoalli onmacuilli in cacaoatl, ipatiuh catca.

Auh in ie iuhqui, in otlacencauh, in omochi nez, in isquich omoteneuh in omito: niman ie ompeoa in tochtepec in ompa cemonoque in puchteca in oztomeca in ie nouian altepetl ipan, in ie nouian altepetl ipan tlaca: onca cemonoca in ical, cecentetl ic catca, in tenochtitlan, in tlatilulco, in tetzcuco, in uexotla, in coatl ichan, in chalco, in suchmilco, in

12. *Quiquauhcuezcomatema* in the *Acad. Hist. MS.*

13. Anderson and Dibble, *op. cit.*, Book VIII, p. 67; Sahagún, *op. cit.*, p. 333, translates as "*Semilla de salvia molida y diluída en agua, usada como medicina.*"

14. Corresponding Spanish text: "*caxetillos que tienen tres pies, para serujcio de la comjda.*"

15. The Spanish text implies a distinction, which does not appear in the Nahuatl column, among *tototlaqualtequachtli* (first grade, fine, small capes, at 100 cacao beans), *tequachtli* (second grade, fine, small capes at 80), and *quachtli* (third grade, large capes, at 60 — not the 65 mentioned in the Nahuatl text).

16. The *Acad. Hist. MS* reads: *cecentetl y catca.*

Chalco, Xochimilco, Uitzilopochco, Mixcoac, Azcapotzalco, Quauhtitlan, Otompan.

In order to gain their livelihoods, they went penetrating everywhere, from city to city; precisely there at Tochtepec they turned back. For the inhabitants of these cities could not enter the province of Anauac. Only the Mexicans of Tenochtitlan [and] of Tlatilulco entered, with their companions, the inhabitants of Quauhtitlan [and] Uitzilopochco.[17]

Vitzilobuchco, in miscoac, in azcaputzalco, in quauhtitlan, in otumba:

inic motlaiecultitinenca in nouian altepetl ipan calactinenca, çan oncan oallacuepaia in tochtepec. Auh in altepehoaque: amo uel calacque in anaoac, çanioque in calaquia in mexica in tenochca, in mexica tlatilulca inuicalhoan quauhtitlacalque, Vitzilobuchca.

---

17. Corresponding Spanish text: "*yba luego a tochtepec, donde ay gran cantidad de mercaderes, y tratantes, y a todos los otros pueblos, donde aujan mercaderes: los quales todos tenjan sus casas, o posadas en Mexico, y en el tlatilulco, y los de vexotla, y de tetzcoco, y de coatl ichan, y de chalco, y de xochimjlco, y de vitzilobuchco, y de Mixcoac, y de azcaputzalco, y de quauhtitlan, y de otumba: los quales todos son tratantes en las proujncias remotas, que estan hasta tochtepec. Los mercaderes de otros pueblos no entrauan en la proujncia de anaoac: solos los Mexicanos, y del tlatilulco y sus compañeros que eran los de vitzilobuchco, y de quauhtitlan: entrauan en esta proujncia de Anaoac: yba a todos los pueblos a combidar, para el banquete.*"

ILLUSTRATIONS

BOOK IX

quechol ihcoatl ipepech mochioa,
oçan ienoie itlapacho tlauhque
chol, aueço tla tlapalpilli ihuitl
auh imtoztli ipepech mochioa inaz
tlapalli ihuitl, cannoie quimope
pechoa in tozcuicuil, in ihuitl in
motzinhoa coztlapilli, çan mopa,
mocoztiaps, mocozpa tleco icuicie
ipan quaqualaca in tlapalli, çantla
calli, tlaxxocotl monamictia auh
eakpan motequiz quiuia, inicac in
omotzquis quiui, inic omocencauh,
iniz quicac icac tlapepechtott, imi
hui tlaoatzalli, inienouian omote
tecac, omotzacoaz, impan ichcatl
mepan tlacuilolli, çatzpan moçoloa
Auh inicoac centzel momamaçoa
paltontli ipan moçoloa in amatl,
oceppa ipan micuiloa in omoctzi
cuic machiotl, intlacuicuitl o
mochiuh ichcatl ipan tecaui iui
huitlachioalli, ipan mocencaloa
inahuitl oapalli, aço xuchitlacui
lolli, aço quillacuilolli, anoço itla
tlaxiptlaiotl inmochioaz, inaço
quenami tlamachtli, intlauelitta
lli. Inicac omicuilo, inomotla

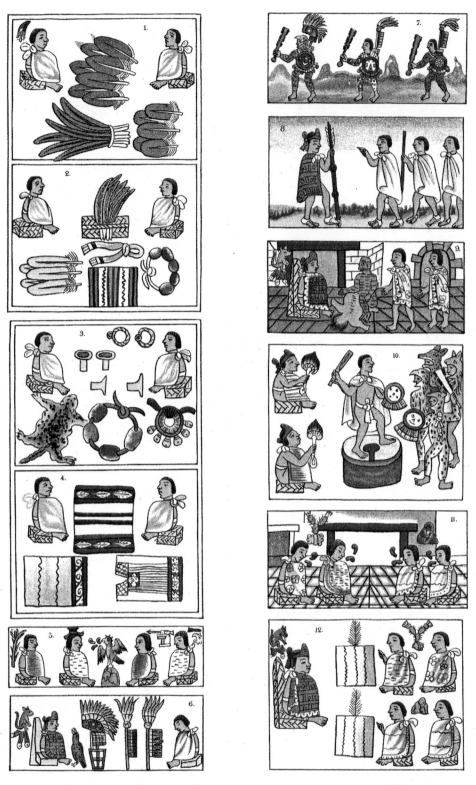

— *After Paso y Troncoso*

1–4. Merchants and their goods (preceding Chapter 1). 5. The four military governors of Tlatilulco (Chapter 1). 6. A merchant before Auitzotzin with the quetzal feather crest device, the quetzal feather banner, and the troupial feather banner (Chapter 2). 7. Merchants in battle array (Chapter 2). 8. The successful warring merchants meet Moctezuma (Chapter 2). 9, 10. Tlacaxipeualiztli scenes (Chapter 2). 11. Merchants of Tenochtitlan and Tlatilulco in conference (Chapter 2). 12. Merchants before Auitzotzin (Chapter 2).

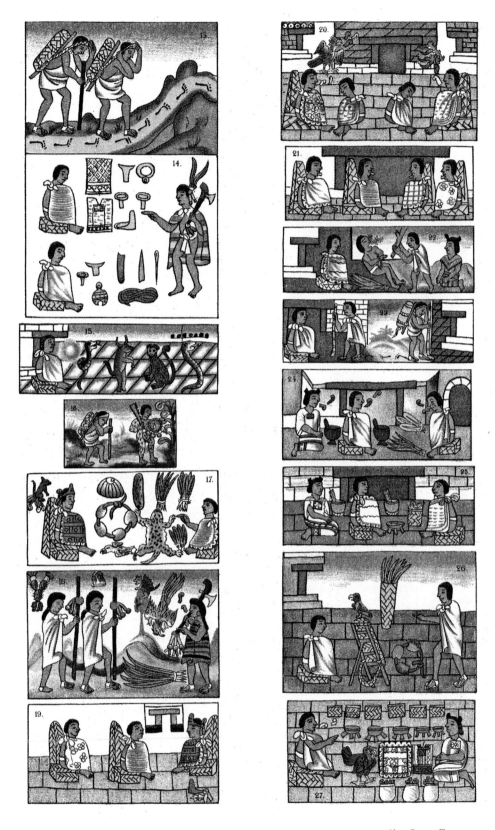

— *After Paso y Troncoso*

13. Merchants on the road (Chapter 2). 14. Merchants and their wares (Chapter 2). 15. Favorable day signs (Chapter 3). 16. Merchant carrying wares into Anauac (Chapter 4). 17. Merchant presenting goods to Auitzotzin (Chapter 4). 18. Disguised merchants in Tzinacantlan (Chapter 5). 19. Merchants before Moctezuma as ruler (Chapter 5). 20–22. Merchants' courts and punishments (Chapter 5). 23. Returning merchant (Chapter 6). 24, 25. Listening to the admonitions of the elders (Chapter 6). 26. Merchants' equipment (Chapter 6). 27. Preparations for a banquet (Chapter 7).

28, 29. Banquet scenes (Chapter 7). 30. Offerings of flowers and tobacco to Uitzilopochtli (Chapter 8). 31. Musicians (Chapter 8). 32. Food offerings (Chapter 8). 33. Gifts given to banquet guests (Chapter 9). 34. Listening to the admonitions of the elders (Chapter 9). 35. Buying slaves in Azcapotzalco (Chapter 10). 36. Arraying of slaves (Chapter 10). 37. Turkey and dogs for banquet food (Chapter 10). 38. Merchants from Tenochtitlan and Tlatilulco (Chapter 10). 39. The array of the sacrificed slave (Chapter 14). 40. Offerings of food to Totec (Chapter 15). 41. Mixing clay and charcoal for core (Chapter 16).

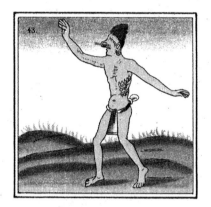

— *After Paso y Troncoso*

42. Shaping the charcoal and clay core (Chapter 16). 43. A Huaxtec (Chapter 16). 44. Turtle, bird, and fish (Chapter 16). 45. Golden ornament with bells (Chapter 16). 46, 47. Melting, rolling, and application of wax (Chapter 16). 48. Application of charcoal and water paste (Chapter 16). 49. Application of outer covering of coarse charcoal and clay (Chapter 16).

— *After Paso y Troncoso*

50. Melting the gold (Chapter 16). 51. Washing the finished object in alum solution (Chapter 16). 52. Application of "gold medicine" (Chapter 16). 53. Polishing (Chapter 16). 54–56. Chasing and other gold-work (Chapter 16). 57. Charcoal and clay core work (Chapter 16).

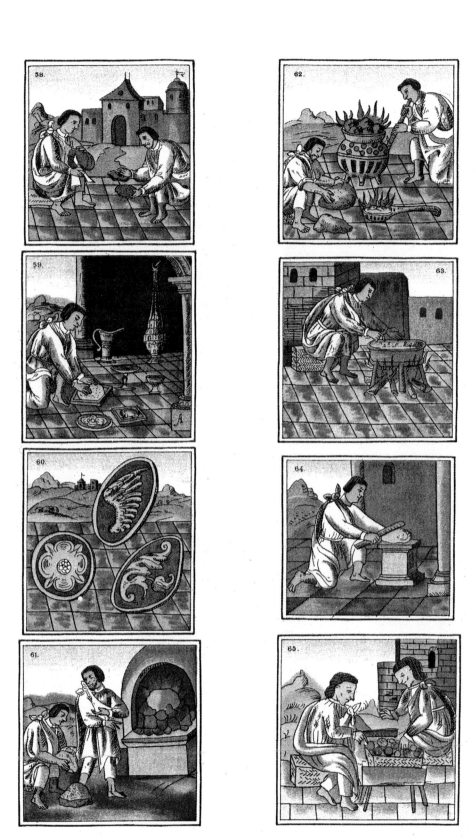

58. Charcoal and clay core work (Chapter 16). 59, 60. Gold objects (Chapter 16). 61, 62. Melting and casting gold (Chapter 16). 63. Washing in alum solution (Chapter 16). 64. Rubbing (Chapter 16). 65. The work of the lapidary (Chapter 17).

— *After Paso y Troncoso*

66–69. The work of the lapidary (Chapter 17). 70. Feather artisans (Chapter 18). 71. Macuil ocelotl (Chapter 18). 72. Xiuhtlati and Xilo (Chapter 18). 73. The bearing of maize stalk staves (Chapter 18). 74. Coyotl inaual (Chapter 19).

— *After Paso y Troncoso*

75. Dedication of girls to the goddesses (Chapter 19). 76. Yacatecutli and Coyotl inaual (Chapter 19). 77. Feather artisans at work (Chapter 19). 78. Feather-bearing merchants before Auitzotzin (Chapter 19). 79–83. Feather devices and their making (Chapter 20).

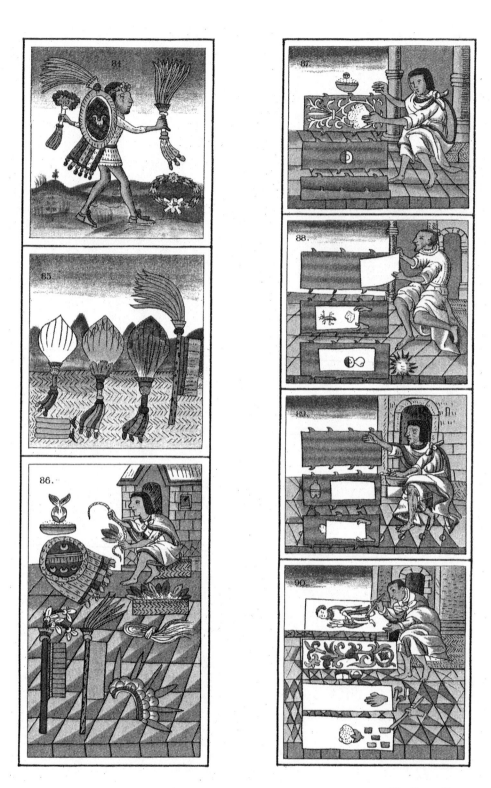

— *After Paso y Troncoso*

84–86. Feather devices and their making (Chapter 20). 87–90. Cutting patterns and designing (Chapter 21).

— After Paso y Troncoso

91, 92. Cutting patterns and designing (Chapter 21). 93–95. Glue-hardening process (Chapter 21). 96. Dyeing feathers (Chapter 21).

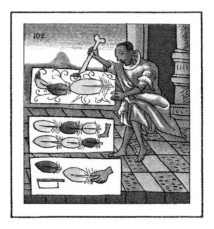

97–102. Final affixing of feathers (Chapter 21).

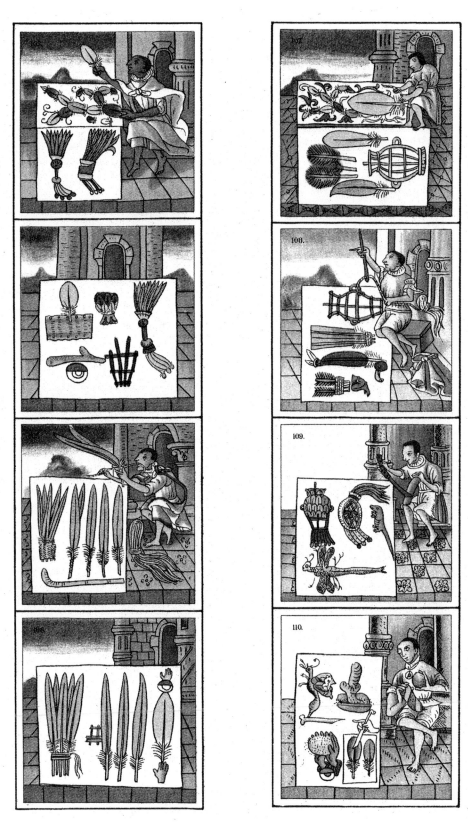

— *After Paso y Troncoso*

103. Final affixing of feathers (Chapter 21). 104–110. The frame-and-cord method (Chapter 21).

Eleventh Chapter. Here is told what was done when the holding of a feast was determined: he went to invite the other merchants to banquet there at Tochtepec.

And when he who was to bathe slaves came to reach Tochtepec, he thereupon entered the house of those of Tlatilulco. What he was to give as gifts, and the chocolate beaters, he caused to be carried on the backs [of carriers].[1] Then he went directly to where the god of the vanguard merchants, named Yacatecutli, was. Quickly he swept the place before [the god]; he spread out a reed mat. When he had spread it out, he thereupon swiftly unpacked what were the vestments of Yacatecutli; then he unwrapped the stout traveling canes. If he were to bathe one, [or] two, [or] three, [or] four slaves, he took that many [staves] — very good ones which had good bases. And when he had taken them, he bound them together; he set them up where [the god] stood. He covered them with their corresponding array, [and] laid down paper on the reed mat before the staves. And thus did he who would bathe slaves make it known whether he would bathe two — a man [and] a woman, [or three — two men and a woman],[2] [or] four — two men [and] two women. And on [the staves] he would place capes; these were the coyote fur ones with a cup design worked with feathers, [and] with the red eye border; and the breech clout with long ends; and the skirt with the squared corner stone design, [or] of irregular design; and the shift with the design of radiating flowers, or the one with yellow parrot feathers. He placed all there before [the image of] Yacatecutli, so that it might be seen there what he would place on the bathed ones. There was where he spread his fame to incite others.

And when he had laid down [the offering], he thereupon entered the house where [the merchants] of Tlatilulco were; then he quickly ordered food, turkeys, [and] chocolate to be prepared. And when

Jnic matlactli oce capitulo, vncan mitoa: in tlein mochioaia: in icoac mochioaiaia ilhuitlaliztli, uiia quincoanotzaia oc cequintin puchteca, in ompa tochtepec.

Auh in oacito in tochtepec, in iehoatl tealtiz: niman ie ic calacqui in ichan tlatilulca, quimamalia in quitetlauhtiz, ioan acaquauitl, niman ie ispan tlamelaoa in uncan ca inteuuh in oztomeca: itoca iiacatecutli. Ihciuhca tlachpana ispan conteca petlatl. Jn ocontecac, niman ie ic quixitinia in itlaquen ieticac in iiacatecutli: niman ic quitotoma in otlatopilli, intla ce, intla ome, intla ei, intla naui caltiz, izqui conana: iehoatl in uel qualli in uel xocpale. Auh in ocona, niman ie ic quilpia: conquetza in oncan icaia, conquentia in itlatqui ieticac, in amatl ispan contema petlapan in otlatopilli. Auh inic tealtiz, oncan quitemachitia: intla ome caltiz, ce oquichtli, ce cihoatl: [auh yntla yehy caltiz. ome oquichtli: ce ciuatl] auh intla naui caltiz, ome oquichtli, ome cihoatl. Auh in itech quitlalizque in tilmatli: iehoatl in coioichcatl, tetecomaio, ihuitica tenchilnaoaio: ioan mastlatl iacauiiac, ioan cueitl, tetenacazço, chicocueitl, ioan vipilli suchimoiaoac, anoço xôxôloio: mochi on oncan contlalia in ispan iiacatecutli inic oncan ittoz, in iuhqui intech quitlalizque tlaaltilti, vncan ca, quitemauiçoltiaia inic teioleoaia.

Auh in ocontlali: niman ie ic calaqui in calitic in oncan cate tlatilulca: niman ie ic tlanaoatia, hiciuhca mochioa in tlaqualli, in totolin, in cacaoatl. Auh in omocencauh in isquich tetech monequiz: niman ie ic

---

1. Referring to *quimamalia*, the corresponding Spanish text reads: *"lleuaua consigo tamemes, que lleuauā las cargas a cuestas."*
2. The phrase in brackets appears in the *Acad. Hist. MS.*

all that would be required had been made ready, then invitations were issued. He invited the vanguard merchants, those who bathed slaves, the slave dealers. Those of the twelve cities he summoned; at midnight they came in. And when they had gone to assemble, when already all [were there], thereupon hands were washed. When hands had been washed, thereupon food was served; there was eating. And when they had eaten, once again hands were washed [and] mouths were washed. Thereupon chocolate was served, tobacco tubes were offered; afterwards gifts were given the guests.

And when he who would bathe slaves had provided for the guests, thereupon he went to offer incense. He had quail carried for him.[3] If he were to bathe two [slaves], he slew two quail; and if he were to bathe three, [or] four, that many quail did he slay. He placed himself before the fire, whereupon he beheaded the quail; with his hands[4] he cast them into the fire. After this he offered incense. Four times he raised it in dedication toward where the sun came forth. To all four directions he did likewise.

And when he had thus offered incense, he thereupon seated himself before the guests. He had confided in one of the men; this one he caused to speak, to plead for him. He said: "You have come together, indeed each [and] all of you, the inhabitants of the cities; you, the merchants; you, the vanguard merchants; you, who have come here suffering affliction, with effort, in pain of heart [and] body; you, who are my eagle and ocelot warriors;[5] who are needy, poor; who place no value upon your breasts [and] your heads in assailing the crags, the gorges, the mountains, the deserts. Somewhere you have sought out the riches, the wealth of the protector of all. And behold here the reward of the gorges, the mountains, the deserts; let not the property, the goods of the master our lord be somewhere destroyed; let it not escape. [Your host] wisheth to behold the presence of[6] the master, the portent, Uitzilopochtli; he wisheth to behead for him one of his slaves.[7] Behold all this which you are to take to appease your hearts, you who are inhabitants of the cities; you who are merchants, vanguard merchants."

tenotzalo, quinnotza in oztomeca, in tealtianime, in tecoanime: matlactepetl omome in quinnotzaia, ioalnepantla in calaquia. Auh in ocenquiçato, in ie mochi tlacatl: niman ie ic tematequilo, in ontematequiloc, niman ie ic tetlamaco, tlaqualo: auh in ontlaqualoc, ie no ceppa tematequilo, tecamapaco: niman ie ic teamaco, teiiemaco, çatepan tetlauhtilo.

Auh in otecencauh in tealtiz: niman ie ic iauh in tlenamacaz: quitquilia in çollin: intla ome caltiz, ontetl çolin in quimictia. Auh intla ey, intla naui caltiz izquitetl çolin quimictia: ispã onmoquetza in tletl: nimã ie ic conquechcotona in çolin, icamac contlaça in tletl: niman ie ic tlenamaca, nappa in conjiaoa in tonatiuh iquiçaia: nauhcampaisti iuh quichioa.

Auh in ie iuhqui in ontlenamacac. Niman ie ic teispan onmotlalia, ce tlacatl itech mocahoa: iehhoatl quitlâtalhuia quitlatlatlauhtilia, quitoa. Ca oticenquiçaco, in ie tisquich in ie timochi: in tahoa in titepehoa, in tipuchtecatl, in toztomecatl: in nican tiquihiiouico, in ticciahuico, in toneoaco, in chichinacaco in moiollo in monacaio: in tinoquauh in tinocelouh, in titoxonqui in tioâçonqui: in atictlaçotla in melchiquiuh, in motzontecon, inic ticmotla in tescalli in atlauhtli, in tepetl, in istlaoatl: can ca in tictemoa in itotonca in iiamanca, in tloque, in nahoaque. Auh izcatqui in ipatiuh in atlauhtli, in tepetl, in istlaoatl: ma cana ontlapolo, ma cana temac contlaz, in iascatzin, in itlatquitzin, in tlacatl totecuio. Auh ca isco icpac ontlachieznequi in tlacatl in tetzauitl, in Vitzilobuchtli. Cetzin contomiliznequi in icooauh in itotouh. O ca isquich in, in ticmocuilia: ic pachiui in moiollotzin, in tahoa in titepehoa: in tipuchtecatl in toztomecatl.

3. Corresponding Spanish text: *"algun su criado que yva con el, lleuaua codornizes."*

4. Read *imac.*

5. In the *Acad. Hist. MS, tinocelouh* is followed by *yn tiquauhtlacatl, yn tiçacatlacatl* — you who are people of the forests and of the grasslands.

6. Corresponding Spanish text: *"quiere hazer algun serujcio, y mostrar agradescimjento."*

7. *Concotoniliznequi,* in the *Acad. Hist. MS.* The phrase is metaphorical.

And thereupon the leading merchants, the leaders who governed in each of the cities,[8] responded to the words. They said: "O our lords, O merchants who are here present, we have received, we have accepted the weeping, the tears. For you have revealed that which in secret hath lain bound up, enclosed: the reward of the eagle [and] ocelot warriors. For here we contemplate that which hath been accorded us by the grace of the master, our lord, the protector of all."

And when it was finished, thereupon [the host] took his leave of the house of the merchants. Then he set forth taking that which would be the feathered staff.[9] And then he came to reach his home here in Mexico.[10]

Auh niman ie ic quicuepa in tlatolli: in puchteca-tlatoque in izquintin cecen altepetl ipan tlapachooa: teiacaiana, quitoa. Totecuioohoane puchtecae: ca nican anmonoltitoque, ca otoconanque, ca otoconcui-que, in choquiztli, in ixaiotl: ca otocontlapouhque in toptli, in petlacalli, in oilpitoca, in otzacuitoca, in ipatiuh in quauhtli, in ocelotl, ca nican tontlachia ipaltzinco in tlacatl totecuio, in tloque naoaque: otechmocnelili.

Auh in ie isquich: nimã ie ic tlanaoatia in ichan puchteca, niman ie ic oalpeoa quitquitiuitz in ihuito-pilli iez: auh in oacito in ichã in nican mexico.

---

8. Corresponding Spanish text: *"los mercaderes, y principales Mexicanos, y tlatilulcanos, que son señores de aquellos doze pueblos."* *Teiacaiana*: *teyacana*, in the *Acad. Hist. MS.*

9. Corresponding Spanish text: *"baculo, ataujado, con borlas de pluma rica."*

10. *Ibid.*: *"venjase para su tierra Mexico, y tlatilulco."* After *Mexico*, the *Acad. Hist. MS* has *tlatilolco.*

Twelfth Chapter. Here is told what the one who determined the holding of the feast prepared in his city when he returned from the invited guests.

Then he quickly prepared what would be required for the principal merchants, the disguised merchants. First he notified three [of them]: Quappoyaualtzin, Uetzcatocatzin, [and] Çanatzin. He gave them food, drink, tubes of tobacco, gifts. He gave them the things [already] mentioned which pertained to the disguised merchants: capes with plaited paper ornaments and precious breech clouts with long ends.

And when he had prepared these things for them, he then seated himself before them; he said to them: "O noblemen, you will pardon me that I trouble you. For, behold, you have received, you have grasped [my words], that I wish to behold the presence of the portent, Uitzilopochtli, because somewhere some of the wealth of the master, our lord, hath been shown me. Somewhere I shall make use of it; I shall cast it into the water; I shall reap a profit. With this you are content."

Thereupon they besought him; they said to him: "O youth, thou who art here, who are we? Who do we think we are that thou shouldst reveal the secrets of the master, our lord, the portent, Uitzilopochtli, that here we have heard thy weeping, thy sorrow? During these past few days — during this past year, these past two years — thou hast on this account lived dedicated to this. Perhaps it is only thy childish, thy foolish act that thou committest. Do not live stupidly. Perhaps thou art not equal to it. Do not do things poorly. Do not commit an outrage; do not bring shame to us, the merchants, the vanguard merchants, the outpost merchants, the bathers of slaves, the slave dealers. Perchance thou hast not beforehand prepared a repast, placed in order all which one would require. Let us behold that which is hidden away, for verily we are the old men."

On this, he gave them an account of all that hath been mentioned which would be consumed.

Jnic matlactli omome capitulo, oncan mitoa: in tlein oquicencauh, in iehoatl in aquin quichioaia ilhuitlaliztli, in ipan ialtepeuh ipan in icoac oalmocuepaia in tlacoanotzalti.

Niman hiciuhca qujcencahoa, in intech monequiz, in puchtecatlatoque, in naoaloztomeca: çan oc eintin in quincaquitia, quappoiaoaltzin, Vetzcatocatzin, çanatzin, quintlaqualtia, quimatlitia, quimiiemaca, quintlauhtia iehoatl in quinmaca in omoteneuh, in intech poui in naoaloztomeca, in amanepaniuhqui, ioan tlaçomastlatl iacauiiac.

Auh in oquimoncencauh, niman ie imispan onmotlalia, quimilhuia. Pillitzine: namechnotlalcaoaltiliz, namechnotlapololtiliz, ca izcatqui: anquimanilia, anquimocuilia, ca isco, icpac, nontlachieznequi, in tetzauitl, in Vitzilobuchtli: anca cana cetzin, omonexiti, in icococauh, in tlacatl totecuio. Cana nontlapoloz, nontlaatoctiz, nontlachitoniz: ca ic pachiui in amoiollotzin.

Niman ie ic quitlatlauhtia: quilhuia. Telpuchtle, ca nican tica: ac tehoantin, ac titomati: in nican tictlapoa, in itop, in ipetlacal, in tlacatl, totecuio, in tetzauitl in uitzilobuchtli: ca nican ticcaqui in mochoquiz, in motlaocol, in ie macuil, in ie matlac: in ie cexiuh, in ie oxiuh: ic timotequipachotinemi, aço çan mococoneio, micnopillo timaitia, ma aoncan tinen: acaçomo titenamic, ma auel ticchiuh, ma çan tontlapinauhti, ma titechpinauhti, in puchteca, in oztomeca, in jiaque, in tealtianime in tecoanime: acaçomo achtopa oic titlatecac, otitlacencauh, in isquich tetech monequiz, ma tontlachiecan in topco, in petlacalco: ca nel iehoatl inic tiueuetque.

Niman ie ic quinpouilia in isquich omoteneuh, in popoliuiz:

When their doubts had been satisfied, they thereupon said to him: "O youth, thou hast made preparations for the protector of all. Set out very carefully. Be not lazy; be not sluggish. Be not dismayed; be not disheartened. Choose thy words with care; be deliberate in speech.[1] Be careful in others' hands. Thus do we allay thy fears. Four times shalt thou serve food. The first time is when thou shalt perform [the ceremony called] *teyolmelaua*.[2] The second time is when thou shalt perform [the ceremony called] *tlaixnextia*. The third time is when thou shalt perform [the ceremony called] *teteualtia*.[3] The fourth time is when thou shalt perform [the ceremony called] *tlamictia*. Take care on this occasion not to covet others' property [and] goods. [Of this] we first warn thee."

Once again he said to them: "O noblemen, you have shown me favor. Your hearts have been saddened. Would I somewhere reject your counsel? May you speak as your hearts wish; may your motherliness, your fatherliness come to be heard, received, grasped!"

Then they said to him: "It is well, O child. Let us now read a good day sign." Then they sent a messenger who summoned a reader of the day signs; one who exclusively read the day signs for one — who in it gained his livelihood.

And when they saw a good day sign, the days which governed us, then they said: "Let it be at this time: One House, or Two Flower, or Two Monkey." Whichever good day sign they would take, precisely at this time he who would bathe slaves started his preoccupation.

And when the old merchants were satisfied, finally, they took their leave of him. They said to him:[4] "O my son, O child, we have been satisfied. We have received, we have accepted thy weeping, thy affliction. Do not be presumptuous over it; do not be proud. Do not offend others. Respect the unfortunate old men, the unfortunate women, the miserable, the poor; take pity upon them. Give one somewhere perchance a poor, worn, breech clout, a miserable netted maguey cape; tie, wrap them about him; give him something to drink. For he is the representative of the master, our lord. For this thou shalt

in oiniollo, ompachiuh niman ie ic quilhuia. Telpuchtle: ca otocontlachielique, in tloque naoaque, uel iiolic ximoquetza: ma momamimic, ma mocximimic, ma titlacuetlaxo, ma timoçoçotlauh, ioan ma itla iliuiz motlatol, ma ticiuhcatlato, iiolic temac xonotiuh, ca ic timitziolpachiujltia: ca nappa in titetlaqualtiz. Jnic ceppa icoac in titeiolmelaoaz: inic oppa icoac in tontlaisnestiz: inic espa icoac in titeteualtiz: inic nappa icoac in titlamictiz: ma cana oncã tiqueleui in teasca, in tetlatqui, achto timitznemachtia:

ie no ceppa quimilhuia. Pillitzine: oannechmocnelilique, otlaocos in amoiollotzin: aço cana nocontlaçaz in amihiiotzin, in amotlatoltzin: ma xicmitalhuican, in quen connequiz in amoiollotzin, ma cacoqui, ma cuihoaloqui, ma analoqui, in amotenaiotzin, in amotetaiotzin:

Niman ic quilhuia, ca ie qualli xole: ma oc ticpoacan in qualli tonalli niman ic tlaihoa, connotza in tonalpouhqui çan ic catca in tetonalpohuiliaia, oncan motlaiecultiaia.

Auh in oconittac in qualli tonalli: in cemilhuitl techitquia, niman quitoa, ma icoac y, i ce calli, anoço ome suchitl: anoço ome oçomatli in çaço catlehoatl canaz, qualli tonalli: uel ipan in compehoaltia, in inetequipachol in iehoatl tealtiz.

Auh in iiollo ompachiuh, in puchtecaueuetque: ça iccen connahoatia, quilhuia. Nopiltze, xole: ca otoiollo ompachiuh, ca otoconanque, ca otoconcuique, in mochoquiz, in monetequipachol, ma ic tatlama, ma ic timopouh: ma ic teisco teicpac tinen, xoconimacaci in icnoueue, in icnoilama, in aoalnecini, in icochca in ineuhca: ioan in motolinia xictlaocoli aço cana mastlaçoltzintli aiaçoltzintli, xicmaca, xiquilpilj, xictlaquenti, xicatliti: ca ipatilloã in tlacatl, totecuio: ic timonemitiz in tlalticpac: ma tinen, ma ticemilhuiti ma achi tictoca: inin timitzilhuia intlacamo iuh ticchioaz tioalispopoiotiz, tioallanquatzico-

1. *Acad. Hist. MS*: *iliuiztiquito*.
2. Corresponding Spanish text: *"quando de nuevo an de llegar: tus combidados, y los significares la fiesta que as de hazer."*
3. *Ibid.*: *"quando los esclauos se ataujaren de sus papeles, y se hiziere la cerimonja que se llama teteualtia."*
4. After *quilhuia*, the *Acad. Hist. MS* has *ca nican tica*.

be given life on earth. Live [long];[5] may thy days be long. Mayest thou in some way follow this which we tell thee; if thou dost not do thus, thou shalt become blind; thy knees, thy legs will become crippled. For truly this thou hast sought from the master, our lord. For he looketh into stones [and] wood. Take care not, somewhere, to covet another's wife, another's daughter. Begin a good, a righteous [life]. All is done to our satisfaction."

liuiz, tioalcocototzauiz: ca nel iehoatl in otictemoli, in tlacatl totecuio, ca tetl, ca quauitl iitic motlachieltitica, ma cana tiqueleui tecioauh, teichpoch: xocompeoalti in qualli iectli, ie isquich in tonequistil mochioa.

Thirteenth Chapter. Here is told how they began the feast and what was then done.

Then he who undertook [the banquet] began what now was to be done in his house. The many prepared tamales were specified as to certain sizes. All about in the cities were hired those who made tamales. They went with turkey hens to enter his home.

And when all which would be required had been arranged, thereupon were summoned those who for the first time were to hear the information, so that he might announce to them that he would bathe slaves. He summoned [guests from] twelve cities.

First he arrayed his bathed slaves. He gave them what pertained to them: the capes, the breech clouts, the skirts, the shifts along whose borders they had placed the trimming. He added leather ear plugs with their pendants, or long, curved labrets. He added crushed paper which they had sown with fine, pointed quetzal feathers, bound about with red cord to place them in their ears. And on their ankles he placed rattles; on the edges of [a band of] ocelot skin he laid shells. On each ankle he bound them on. And he tied "shining hair strands" about their temples, which were decorated in this way: alternating [strips of] turquoise [and] gold, reddish coral shells, [and] black mirror stones. From the tips [of the strips] they hung bits of hair.[1] Hence was it called "shining hair strands."

Then he assembled them. He did nothing but make them continue dancing. Now they nevermore abandoned the flower necklaces, the garlands of flowers, the shields of flowers, the tubes of tobacco. Every day he decked them with flowers. They did nothing but continue to smell [the flowers], to smoke [the tobacco tubes].

And in just the same way he adorned the women. He put on them the good shifts, the good skirts, the good sandals, and [gave them] the flowers, the to-

Inic matlactli omei capitulo, oncan mitoa: in quenin conpeoaltiaia ilhuichioaliztli, ioan in tlein vncan muchioaia.

Niman ie conpeoaltia in ipan tlatoa: inic mochioaz in icalitic, amo çan quesquich in mochioa tamalli, motamachioa inic ueuei, nouian tlapatiotiaia in altepetl ipan, in mochioaia tamallj oaltotollotiuh, inic oalcalaquia ichan.

Auh in omocecauh in isquich monequiz: niman ie ic tenotzalo, in iancuican mocaquiz tlatolli, inic teiolmelaoaz in tealtiz: matlactli omome altepetl in quinotza.

Achtopa quinchichioa in itlaaltilhoan quinmaca in intech poui in tilmatli, i mastlatl, in cueitl in uipilli, in cuetentli, conaquia in itenco: quiuicaltiaia cuetlasnacochtli, itipepeiocio, anoço tezçacanecuilli, quiuicaltia amapatlachtli quitotocaticac quetzaliacauitztli, chichilicpatica, in quicuicuitlalpiaia, in conaquiaia innacazco: ioan imicxic quitlalia in tzitzilli, iehoatl in oceloehoatl, itenco quitecaia coiolli, ontlapalisti in imicxic quimihilpiliaia, ioan petzotzocolli in incanaoacan quimihilpiliaia inic tlacuilolli çan tlatlatlapantli in xiuitl teucuitlatl, tapachtli, tezcapoctli, iiacac quipipiloa aquitoton tzontli: ipampa in motocaiotia petzotzocolli,

niman ic quicenmana in ça ic nemi mitotitinemi: aoquic quicahoa in suchicozcatl, in icpacsuchitl, in chimalsuchitl in ietl cecemilhuitl in mosuchitia: çan ic nemi in tlanecutinemi, in tlachichintinemi.

Auh in cihoa, çan no iuh quicencahoa quimonaquia in qualli uipillj, in qualli cueitl, in qualli cactli: auh in suchitl in ietl in suchicozcatl, in icpacsuchitl:

---

1. Corresponding Spanish text: *"les colgauã en las sienes un cuero amarillo, pintado con tiras de oro, y tiras de turquesas entrepuestas las unas a las otras, en las estremidades deste cuero, colgauan vnas auaneridas, coloradas; entrepuestas, unas piedras de espejo: y tambien unos cabellos, entrepuestos a las avaneras, y a las cuẽtas de espejo: y por esso se llamaua petzotzocolli."* — In *Einige Kapitel*, Seler defines *tezcapoctetl* as pyrites, and links them to the indumentary of Tezcatlipoca (p. 108, n. 1).

bacco tubes, the flower necklaces, the garlands of flowers. And their hair braids [were tied with] many-colored, loose cotton threads of red, yellow, blue, black, twisted into a rope with white feathers.

And when he had arrayed them at midnight, first he gave them food [and] drink. Then he placed them on reed mats, on woven reed seats; at the entrance to the house he placed them so that all the guests would see them there.

This was [the ceremony] called *teiolmelaoa*.[2] It was still night when [the guests] left, when they entered, when food [and] drink were served, when flowers, tobacco tubes, [and] gifts were given. There was constant going [and coming].

And the second time that he summoned guests was when it was [the ceremony called] *tlaixnextia*. In just the same way was it done as hath been told.

And the third time that he summoned guests was when it was [the ceremony called] *teteualtia,* when he put on the heads of his bathed ones what were known as the *anecuyotl*;[3] this was a turquoise device, made with feathers[4] — indeed made of all kinds of feathers, like a feather headdress of white feather pendants, which became his hair. And his ear plugs were wooden, painted of many colors. And as his nose pendant there issued a broad piece of obsidian. And his godly jacket, which he put on, ended at his thighs. Its raveled border was feathered,[5] and in blue, black, red, it was designed with skulls, with a field of bones;[6] and he was bound about the waist with a rich sash. And on [each of] his shoulders they placed a prairie falcon's wing.[7] These were paper prairie falcon wings; he bound on each shoulder the paper which was wrapped about the base [of the wings. The paper was] painted with red, with black, with flecks of iron pyrites strewn over it.[8] And an arm band [was] on one arm; on their wrists, there on the left they had placed what was like a maniple. And he gave them obsidian sandals, on which they walked.

auh in itzonipilhoaz tlatlapalicpatl chichiltic coztic, texotic, tliltic, iztac ihuitl inic tlamalintli catca.

Auh in oquimoncencauhque, ioalnepantla achtopa quintlaqualtia quimatlitia: niman oncan quimontlalia in petlapan, in icpalpan, calixac in quinoallalia inic oncã quimittazque, in isquichtin tlacoanotzaltin:

iehoatl inic mitoa teiolmelaoa, oc iohoan in pehoa calacoa in ontlaqualo in onatlioa in onnexochitilo, in onneiietilo, in onnetlauhtilo, çan ic oalquixoaticac.

Auh inic oppa tenotzaia: icoac in ontlaisnestia, çan no iuh mochioaia in omito.

Auh inic espa tenotzaia: icoac in teteualtia, icoac quimonaquiaia in imicpac, in itlaaltilhoan, mitoaia anecuiotl, iehoatl in ihuitl tlachioalli, xinapallotl, uel isquich in nepapan ihuitl ic tlachioalli, iuhquin tzoncalli, iztac ihuitl inic tlapilollo in itzon mochioaia: ioan inacoch, quauhnacochtli, tlatlatlapalicuilolli, ioan iacapilol, itzpatlactli ipã quiçaia: ioan iteuxicol in conaqujaia, imetzpan tlami, ic tenpoçonqui potonqui: auh inic tlacuilolli texotli tlilli, tlapalli, tzotzontecomaio, oomicallo: ioan inic mocuitlalpiaia xiuhtlalpilli: auh in iaculpan contlatlalilia tlômaitl, iehoatl in tlôtli iiamatlapal, nenecuc in iaculpan coniilpilia, amatl inic tlatzinquimilolli tlacuilolli tlapaltica, tliltica, apetztli ipan tlapipixolli, ioan matacastli centlapal in imaquechtlan contlaliliaia, ompa in iopuchcopa, iuhquin manipulo: ioan itzcactli in quinmacaia, in ipan nenemia.

---

2. Corresponding Spanish text: *"Esto es lo que se dixo arriba, que se publicaua el combite, toda la noche comjan y beujan los que yvan, y venjan en aquella casa."* See *teyolmelaua* in Chap. 12.

3. Cf. Anderson and Dibble, *op. cit.,* Book I, p. 69.

4. The *Acad. Hist. MS* has *xiuapallotl.* See Molina, *op. cit., uapaua (guarnecer algo).*

5. Corresponding Spanish text: *"con vnas orillas deshiladas."*

6. *Ibid.: "huessos de muertos, puestos en quadra."*

7. *Falco mexicanus* Schlegal. Friedmann *et al., op. cit.,* Pt. I, p. 65.

8. *Ibid.: "Estauan . . . rebueltas con papel los cabos dellas, y asidas a la xaqueta: estaua pintado, aquel papel de diuersas colores entrepuestas, colorado, y negro, rebuelto con marcaxita."* — After *tliltica,* the *Acad. Hist. MS* has *texotica;* and, for *matacastli, moxotaztli.*

And also at that time he summoned their companions and priests of tangled hair, who would continue looking after the bathed ones when they were to die. All the time they would continue to guard them. And he summoned his two face-washers, who took care of the bathed ones, women in whose presence they indeed died. And all three of these, the escorts, the priests of tangled hair, the face-washers, all were given gifts. He gave them capes with carmine colored flowers, and breech clouts with long ends, and sandals. And the ceremonial bathers gave the women as gifts their skirts, their shifts; and they painted their faces; they pasted them with colored feathers.

Auh no icoac quinnotzaia in iteancahoan: ioan ipaoacauh, in quimocuitlauitinemizque in tlatlaaltilti, in icoac miquizque, isquich cauitl quīpistinemizque: ioan omentin quinnotzaia iteixamicahoa in quinmocuitlauiaia tlatlaaltilti cihoa uel imispan in miquia. Auh in iehoantin, in ietlamanistin in teananime, in paoaque, in teixamique, mochinti motlauhtiaia: iehoatl in quimomacaia in nochpallaxochio, ioan iacauiac mastlatl ioan cactli. Auh in cihoa, incue, inuipil, in quintlauhtiaia tealtianime: ioan quixaoa, quipotonia, tlapalihuitica.

Fourteenth Chapter. Here is told how they slew the slaves at the time that they observed the feast day.[1]

And the fourth time that he invited guests was at the time when, on the morrow, the bathed ones were to die. While the sun was still a little strong they took them before [the temple of] Uitzilopochtli. There they caused them to perform the *xalaquia* [ceremony].[2] There he made them drink the "obsidian medicine." This they called the god's wine. When they had drunk, then they brought them away. No longer did they bring them carefully. It was indeed as if they had drunk a great deal of wine; they were, in fact, quite drunk. No more did they enter the home of the one who bathed slaves; rather, they took them there to the *calpulli* temple. There they placed them in [the *calpulli* of] either Pochtlan or Acxotlan. There they had them hold vigil all night, singing, dancing.

And when it was midnight, when [it was the time to] blow shell trumpets, [to] draw blood, those who fasted, the priests, then quickly placed [the victims] before the hearth, where a straw mat lay spread out. On it they placed them. Then forthwith he who bathed slaves arrayed himself; he put on his godly sleeveless jacket, just like the ones the ceremonially bathed ones had put on, and the round pleated paper flower, with papers, painted papers, and his foam sandals. When he had quickly arrayed himself, then they put out the fire. In the dark they fed [the victims] amaranth seed dough placed in honey. They fed them four mouthfuls cut with maguey fiber thread.

And when they had fed them, then they came taking[3] some hair from the crowns of their heads. A man came blowing, sounding, a whistle; it came saying, "Chich." He came with it only in order that they swiftly proceed to remove hair from the crown

Inic matlactli onnaui capitulo, vncan mitoa in quenin quinmictiaia tlatlacuti: in icoac ilhuitlaia.

Auh inic nappa tenotzaia: icoac in ie iuh moztla miquizque tlatlaaltilti, oc achi uei in tonatiuh, in quinhuica ispan Vitzilobuchtli, in ompa quimoxalaquiaia, ompa quioalitia in itzpatlactli: iehoatl in quitoaia teuctli, jn oconique niman ie ic quinuicatze: aocmo quimamattiuitze, uel iuhquinma cenca miec vctli oquique: uel ic ihuintique, aocmo ompa calaqui in ichan tealti, ça umpa quinuica in calpulco, umpa quimontlalia in aço puchtlan, anoço acxotlan, in uncan quintozçauiaia, ceioal in cuica: mîtotîtinemi.

Auh in icoac ioalnepantla: in ie tlapitza miçoc, in moçauhqui, tlamacazqui: niman hiciuhca quintlalia tlecuilisquac, in oncã onoc petlatl, ipan quintlalia. Niman hiciuhca mochichioa in tealti: conmaquia iteuxicol, çan no iuhqui in conmaquia tlaaltilli, ioan in tlaquechpaiotl iuhqui amatica, amatl in tlacuilolli, ioan ipoçulcac. In omocencauhtiquiz, nimã ic ceui in tletl: ça tlaiohoaian in quinqualtia tzoalli, necutitlan conaquitiuh: in quinqualtiaia nauhcamatl, ichtica in quixotlaia.

Auh in oquimonqualti: niman ic quintzõcuitiquiça, ce tlacatl tlapitztiquiça quipitztiquiça chichtli, quitotiquiça chich: çan quiuicaltitiquiça, inic tetzoncuitiquiça, intla ome intla ei, intla naui tlaaltilli, izquipa iuh quichioa: çan ic oalmoiaoalotiquiça, quauh-

1. Cf. this account in Anderson and Dibble, *op. cit.*, Book II, Chap 34.

2. In Sahagún (Garibay ed.), Vol. I, p. 180, *"A esta ofrenda llamaban* xalaquia, *porque el dia siguiente habia de morir."* Also cf. Anderson and Dibble, *op. cit.*, Book II, pp. 97, 133.

3. *Quintzõcuitiquiça*: also translatable as "he quickly took hair"; the same applies to other verbs in this passage ending in *-quiça*. See Andrés de Olmos: *Grammaire de la languae nahuatl ou mexicaine* (Paris: Imprimerie Nationale, 1875), p. 157, and Horacio Carochi: *Arte de la lengva mexicana* (Mexico: Imprenta del Museo Nacional, 1892), p. 481.

of one's head: if [there were] two, if three, if four bathed ones, as many times did he do so. At once [the whistler] came circling [the slaves], carrying the eagle vessel, in which he went casting the hair. And those who had taken the hair from the crowns of [the slaves'] heads then came shouting, crying out, striking their lips with the palms of their hands. Then swiftly he who had taken the hair [in the eagle vessel] quickly went away. [The host] came taking the incense ladle; he thereupon offered incense there in the middle of the courtyard. To the four directions he raised his incense ladle in dedication.

And the ceremonially bathed slaves, all during the night they lived, slept not.[4] And when the dawn broke, they thereupon gave them food. No more could they eat, although strongly did they urge them; it was as if they were anguished in spirit; they looked forward only to their death.

They were awaiting the time when Painalton would come; the time when he would come entering; when he would follow along the road; when he would describe a circle. He began at Tenochtitlan, then Tlatilulco; he proceeded to Nonoalco, Popotlan, Maçatzintamalco, Chapultepec, Tepetocan, Maçatlan; he joined the road which went straight to Xolloco, by which he entered Tenochtitlan.

And as he was already following the road, as Painalton already went, thereupon they conducted the bathed slaves to the outskirts of [the *calpulli* of] Coatlan, where they came upon the place of encirclement situated there at the temple courtyard.

When the ceremonially bathed slaves arrived, so were the encirclers arrayed, girt for battle. These same ones were chieftains, men of war who fought against the bathed slaves. It was not merely a skirmish; it was just like real fighting. The bathed slaves each had their shields [and] their obsidian-bladed swords. And if [the others] captured some bathed slaves, there at [the temple of] Uitzcalco, there their decision was rendered as to how great was the ransom of the slave. Once again the one who provided the banquet, the slave owner, paid as much ransom [as was required], so that his bathed slave was given to him. But if he had no large cotton capes with which to ransom him, [the captor] consumed his flesh there at Uitzcalco. In this manner did it come to pass, when there was encirclement.

caxitl quitquitinemi, oncan contentiuh in tzontli. Auh in iehoan oquimontzoncuique: niman ic tzatzitiquiça, hicaoaca, motenuitequi: niman hiciuhca iauh in ontetzoncuic, quicuitiquiça in tlemaitl, niman ie ic tlenamaca, in oncan itoalnepantla: nauhcampaisti coniiaoa in itlema.

Auh in tlaaltiltin aquenmã oncochi ceioal in nemi: Auh in otlauizcalleoac, niman ie ic quintlamaca: aocmo uel quiqua, in nellimach quincuitlauiltia, ça iuh quinnentlamati in iollo, ça iê quimatticate in inmiquiz:

quichisticate in quenman uitz, in quenman calaquiquiuh painalto, in otli quitocaz in tlaiaoaloz: oalpeoa tenochtitla, niman ie tlatilulco, quiçaia nonoalco, popotla, maçatzintamalco, chapultepec tepetoca: maçatlan quioalnepanoaia in otli inic oallamelaoa xolloco, ic oalcalaquia tenochtitlan.

Auh in ie otlatoca, in ie iauh painalton, niman ie ic quinuica in tlatlaaltiltin, oncan quioalnamiquia in tlaamahuiaia, in inacaztlan cohoatlan, oncan momanaia in teuitoalco.

In onaci tlatlaaltilti, ic omocencauhque, omoiauchichiuhque in tlaamahuique: uel iehoantin in tiacahoan, in oquichtin, in quiniauchioaia tlatlaaltilti, amo çan tlaiehecolli uel iui in iautihoa: in tlatlaaltilti inchichimal, inmamacquauh ietiuh. Auh intla ceme oquimacique in tlatlaaltilti: in oncan vitzcalco, oncan motzontequia in imîtoloca in quezqui ipatiuh tlacotli: oc ceppa no izqui ic quiquistia, in tecohoani in tlaaltile: ic oalmacoia in itlaaltil. Auh intlacaoctle iquach inic quiquistiz: ompa popoliuia in inacaio in uitzcalco. O iui in, in mochioaia inic tlaamahuiloia.

---

4. Corresponding Spanish text: *"en toda esta noche los esclauos que aujan de morir no dormjan."*

And when Painalton proceeded to emerge, thereupon [the bathed slaves] were placed in order, arranged in rows, before [the image of] Uitzilopochtli; there at the pyramid landing they four times took them in procession around the [pyramid] temple. And when they had been taken around it, once again they put them in file; they placed them one by one in order. Thereupon Painalton ascended to the top [of the temple of] Uitzilopochtli.

When he had ascended, thereupon the sacrificial papers came down. They laid them on the [so-called] banquet table of Uitzilopochtli. They raised them as an offering to the four directions. And when they had come to place them, then also descended [a priest within] a fire serpent. He came with his covering of paper [and] his tongue of flaming arara[5] feathers which came [as if] burning. When he had come down to the pyramid base, where the banquet table of Uitzilopochtli was,[6] he stood facing the sun. Thereupon he gestured toward it; to all four directions he did this.[7] And when he had gestured, then he placed [the fire serpent] on the sacrificial papers which were spread out. Then the fire serpent which he had come to leave, burned; then he ascended to the top of [the temple of] Uitzilopochtli. When he had ascended, thereupon the shell trumpets [and] long shell trumpets[8] were blown; the priests on top [of the temple of] Uitzilopochtli blew them.

And the common folk massed together; indeed all came to watch. They were spread about verily everywhere, seating themselves in the temple courtyard. None ate; indeed everyone fasted. When [the fast] ceased, the sun hung low. Later there was eating when the fast [had ceased]. When they had finished, the captives [and] the bathed slaves died.[9]

And Moctezuma remained seated by a wooden column on a seat with a back rest, which was on his ocelot skin carpet. And he was seated on a wolf skin covered seat upon which he was looking up to the top [of the temple of] Uitzilopochtli. Before him stood an artificial tree of reeds, sticks, and feathers,[10] with quetzal feathers outspread at the top. It seemed

Auh in oquiçato painalton: niman ie ic temanalo, tetecpanalo: in ispan Vitzilobuchtli, in oncan apetlac, nappa in quinteucallaiaoalochtiaia. Auh in ontlaiaoaloque: ie no ceppa quintecpana, ceceiaca quinmana: niman ie ic tleco in painalton, in iicpac vitzilobuchtli

in ontlecoc. Niman ie ic oaltemo in teteupooalli, oncan quimana in itlaquaia Vitzilobuchtli, nauhcampa in coniiaoa. Auh in ocõnmanaco, niman no ic oaltemo in xiuhcoatl, amatl itlaquen ietiuitz, in inenepil cueçalli tlatlatiuitz. In otemoco tlatzintla in oncan itlaquaia Vitzilobuchtli, quisnamictimoquetza in tonatiuh: niman ie ic coniiaoa in iscopa, nauhcampaisti iuh quichioa. Auh in oconiauh niman ipan quiteca in teteppoalli oncan mani: niman ic tlatla in oconcaoaco xiuhcoatl, niman ie tleco in icpac Vitzilobuchtli. In ontlecoc, niman ie ic tlapitzalo, tecuciztli, quiquiztli in quipitzaia tlamacazque in icpac Vitzilobuchtli.

Auh in maceoalli, uel tzitzica, uel isquich oallauh, in oallachiaia: uel nouian netecoia, netlaliloia in teuitoalco, aiac tlaquaia, uel mochi tlacatl moçaoaia: in necaoaloia ommopiloa tonatiuh, quin icoac tlaqualoia in onneçaoaloc, in ontlanque miqui mamalti tlatlaaltilti.

Auh in motecuçoma tlaquetzaltitlan motlaztica quecholicpalli in ipan ca oceloehoatl in ipepech ietica: auh in ipan in otlaztica cuitlachicpalli, in ipan tlachistica, in icpac vitzilobuchtli, ispan icac petlacotl, quetzalli in icpac mani: iuhquinma quitzontecontia teucuitlatl inic tlacuilolli, ioan in ie mochi tlaçoihuitl, ioan quetzalli in itzcue ieticac.

5. Cf. *supra*, Chap. 1, n. 2.

6. Corresponding Spanish text: *"En llegando al apetlac, que es donde se acaban las gradas del cu, que esta una mesa, de vn encalado grande: y de alli hasta el llano del patio: ay quatro o cinco gradas: a esta mesa llamã apetlatl, o itlaquaian in vitzilobuchtli."*

7. *Ibid.*: *"hazia vn acatamjento, hazia el nacimjento del sol."*

8. *Strombus gigas* and *Fasciolaria giganta* respectively. Ancona H. and Martín del Campo, *op. cit.*, p. 16.

9. Corresponding Spanish text: *"entonce comjan, despues de acabadas, todas las cerimonjas dichas, ante de matar los esclauos."* — The *Acad. Hist.* MS has *onnecaualoc* for *onneçaualoc*.

10. *Ibid.*: *"vn arbol hecho a mano de cañas y palillos, todo aforrado de plumas, y de lo alto del, salian muchos quetzales . . . parecia que brotaũa de un pomo de oro, que estaua en lo alto del arbol: en lo baxo tenja una flocadura de plumas ricas."* Jena, *op. cit.*, p. 239, translates *petlacotl* as *ein Gestell aus Mattenrohr.*

as if they provided the top with a tassel painted gold. And [the tree] had all manner of rare feathers, and quetzal feathers, as a skirt about its base.[11]

Thereupon Painalton descended; he took all those who were to die; he went escorting them up, so that they would die there on top [of the temple of] Uitzilopochtli. The slave owners accompanied their bathed slaves. And the ones who would perform the sacrifice were already awaiting them, each arrayed in his sleeveless jacket which he had put on, and they had put on their heads feathered head fans[12] [from which hung] pasted paper pendants; and their cheeks were reddened with red ochre — what they called the sacred red ochre. To slay one they cut open his breast with a broad, leather-hafted knife; this was a well-sharpened, flint knife.

When one who was to die came to their hands, thereupon they stretched him out on the sacrificial stone; four took him by the arms and legs to draw him taut. Thereupon they gashed his breast open, seized his heart, placed it in the eagle vessel. When they had seized his heart, they then rolled the captive over; they just rolled his body over, cast it hence, bounced it down. It fell to the base [of the pyramid] to the [landing] called *apetlac*. And the captor there took his captive. He himself took him. No one could take another's captive, nor could he take someone else's captive. Then he carried him off to his home. And thus was it done; thus did they take up those who were to die. For the time, those captives who went first formed a fundament for the bathed slaves.

And when the captives had come to their end, had died, then the bathed ones went at the very last to die. The owners of the bathed slaves went leading them. Whether they slew two, [or] three, [or] four, they took up feathered staves in fours. And if the wife of the bather of slaves were there, both ascended, carrying the feathered staves in couples, each holding them in their hands, each [staff] with its quetzal feathers arranged like corn tassels. But if the bather of slaves had no wife, if his beloved uncle were there, both of them ascended; in couples they carried the feathered staves. And if he had no uncle,

Niman ie ic oaltemo in painalton: quinoallana in isquichtin miquizque, quiniacantiuh inic tleco, inic ompa miquizque in icpac Vitzilobuchtli: quinhuica in tealtianime in intlaaltilhoan. Auh in iehoantin tlamictizque: ie quinchie, omocencauhcaque, inxixicol conmaquia; ioan apanecaiotl contlalia in imicpac, ioan amatlaxolocholli, ioan motenchichiloa tlauhtica, iehoatl in quitoaia teutlauitl inic temictia teeltetequi isquaehoatica iehoatl in tecpatl uellatentilli.

In oimac onacic in miquiz: niman ie ic ipan conteca in techcatl, quinauhcauia in quitilinia: niman ie ic coneltequi, conanilia in iiollo, quauhxicalco contlalitica in iollotli. In oconanilique iiollo: niman ie ic quioalmimiloa in mamalti, çaiio in inacaio quioalmimiloa, quioallaça, quioaltetecuichoa: tlatzintlan oaluetzi, itocaiocan apetlac. Auh in iehoatl tlamani: oncã conanilia in imal, uel iehoatl in conana, aiac uel temalcuilia, ano ac çan temal in conana: niman quiuica in ichan. Auh inic mochioa, in ie quintlecauia in miquizque: çan oc iehoantin in iacattiui, in mamalti: in inpepechhoan mochioa tlatlaaltilti.

Auh in ontlanque miqui in mamalti: niman iehoanti in tlaaltilti, ça ontlatzacutiui in miqui, quiniacantiui in tealtianime: Intla ome: intla ei, intla naui quimictia: nauisti quitlecauia in ihuitopillj. Auh intla onca icihoauh in tealtianj: omestin tleco, ohome quitqui in ihuitopilli, inmac tetentiuh, quetzalli in imimiiahoaio ietiuh. Auh intlacaiac icihoauh in tealti: intla ie onca itlatzin, omestin tlêco, ohome quitqui in ihuitopilli. Auh intlacaiac itatzin, intla onca ipiltzin: iehoatl quiuica omestin tleco: ohome quitqui in ihuitopilli. Auh intla noço onca iiauitzin: anoço icultzin, anoço icitzin, anoço itiachcauh, anoço iteiccauh: ie-

---

11. Read *itzincue*.

12. Cf. corresponding Spanish text. In the Garibay ed. Sahagún (IV, p. 321), *apanecayotl* is " '*Adorno en forma de travesaño.' Insignia de honor y ornato, consistente en una banda de plumas que atraviesa de hombro a costado.*" Seler has something similar for *anecuyotl* — "device worn on their backs" (citing Sahagún, 3, 1, § 1: *mamatlatquitl*), but another translation (citing Sahagún, 2, 24, and 2, 34) is "god's crown widening at the top . . . a basketlike plaited work" (*Collected Works*, Vol. II, Pt. 3, p. 40).

if his beloved son were there he took him; both went up; in couples they bore the feathered staves. And also, if perhaps there were his beloved aunt, or grandfather, or grandmother, or elder brother, or younger brother, he took up the two feathered staves to the top [of the temple of] Uitzilopochtli. They went putting breath to their heads.[13] So doing, they climbed up to the top [of the temple of] Uitzilopochtli. Only once they circled [the image]. All those spread out at the [pyramid] base watched them.

Thereupon [the slave owner] descended. When he had come to reach the bottom, when he had descended, they who helped the bather of slaves carried home for him the body of his bathed slave. Thereupon [the slave owner] went to his home.

And when he had gone [home], then they quickly prepared his bathed one. They cooked him in an *olla.* Separately, in an *olla,* they cooked the grains of maize. They served [his flesh] on it. They placed only a little on top of it. No chili did they add to it; they only sprinkled salt on it. Indeed all [the host's] kinsmen ate of it.

Thus it is that it was done in days of old when they bathed slaves in [the month of] Panquetzaliztli.

He who did so, who bathed slaves, for as long as he still lived on earth, always guarded his sacred reed box.[14] There he kept what had been the array of his bathed slave, all his adornment, all that has been mentioned: the cape, the breech clout, the sandals; the skirt, the shift, everything. Nothing was omitted; verily, all he guarded for himself. Indeed all the hair from the crowns of [the slaves'] heads he packed into the sacred reed box. And later, if the bather of slaves died, they burned [all this] for him.

hoatl quitlecauia in ome hihuitopilli, in icpac Vitzilobuchtli moquaiiauitiuh, inic tleco in icpac Vitzilobuchtli ça ceppa in quioaliaoaloa, mochi tlacatl quimonitta in tlatzintlan mani:

niman ie ic oaltemo, in oacico tlatzintlan, in ooaltemoc: in iehoantin quipaleuia tealtiani, oquiuiquilique in ichan in inacaio itlaaltil: niman ie ic iauh in ichan.

Auh in ooia: niman hiciuhca quichichiuilia in itlaaltil, quipaoaci: nonqua quipaoaci in tlaolli, in ipan quitemacaia, çan isco quitlatlaliaia achitoton: atle chilli quinamiquia, çan iio iztatl quipoeliaia: uel isquichtin quiquaia in ioaiolque.

O ca ihui, in, in mochioaia in ie uecauh inic tealtiaia in ipan panquetzaliztli.

In aquin iuh quichioaia, y, in tealtiaia: in quesquich cauitl tlalticpac oc nemia, isquich cauitl quipiaia in itepetlacal: in uncan quipiaia intlatqui in itlaaltilhoan catca: in inechichioaliz in isquich omito, in tilmatli, in mastlatl, in cactli, in cueitl, in uipilli, in ie mochi: atle mocaoa, mochi uel quimopieltia in ie isquich inpantzon quiteupetlacaltemaia. Auh quinicoac intla omic in tealtiani: ipan quitlatiaia.

---

13. Corresponding Spanish text: *"subiendo resollauan las manos, y ponjan el resoelo, en las cabeças."* Jena, *op. cit.,* p. 340, has *"Seinem Kopf bot er (das Gastgeber) Vitzilopochtli als Opfer dar"* (cf. *iyaua* in Molina, *op. cit.*).

14. Possibly *iteupetlacal* is meant.

Fifteenth Chapter. Here are mentioned all the makers of fine ornaments called master craftsmen: the goldworkers and lapidaries.[1]

And the first mentioned are the goldworkers [and] the gold casters. And these goldworkers were each divided, separately classed, as to their workmanship, their artisanship. Some were called smiths. These had no office but to beat gold, to thin it out; to flatten it with a stone. Wherever it was required, it was polished, it was thinned. And some were called finishers.[2] These were named the real master craftsmen. And hence were they separate; for their tasks were of two kinds, so that they deliberated separately.[3]

In times of old, the god of the goldworkers, whom they worshiped, was Totec. Each year they observed his feast day; they paid him honor there at his temple, a place called Yopico, in [the month of] Tlacaxipeualiztli.

And at that time a man arrayed himself to be the likeness of Totec; he put on the skin of a captive when they had flayed him. Hence was it called the Feast of the Flaying of Men. And in this manner was [the man] arrayed. They placed on his head his plumage of precious red spoonbill feathers; the precious red spoonbill feathers served as his headdress. And [he had] his gold nose crescent, and his golden ear plugs. And his rattle stick rattled as he grasped it in his right hand; when he thrust it in the ground it rattled. And he had with him his shield with a golden circle. And his sandals were red and adorned with quail feathers. Thus was the quail adornment:[4] quail feathers were strewn on the surface. And there were his three paper flags which

Inic castolli capitulo vncan motenehoa in isquichtin tlachichiuhque in moteneoa tulteca teucuitlahoaque tlatecque.

Auh in iehoantin achto motenehoa, in teucuitlaoaque, in teucuitlapitzque. Auh in iehoantin, in, teucuitlaoaque, nononqua quiztica, xexeliuhtica in intlachioal, in intultecaio. Cequintin motenehoa tlatzotzonque: iehoantin in çan ie no inchiuil, teucuitlatl quitzotzona, quicanaoa, tetica cana quipatlaoa: inic cana monequi mopetlaoa, motecanaoa. Auh in cequintin moteneoa tlatlaliani: in iehoantin uel tulteca moteneoa. Auh inic nõqua cate: ca vntlamantli in intequjuh inic nonqua monotza.

In iehoantin teucuitlaoaque: in ie uecauh iehoatl inteouh catca, iehoatl quimoteutiaia in totec: cexiuhtica in quilhuiquistiliaia, in quimauiztiliaia, in ompa iteupan, itocaiocan iopico: ipan in tlacaxipeoaliztli.

Auh in icoac ce tlacatl mochichioaia, quimixiptlatiaia totec: conmaquiaia in ieoaio malli, in icoac quixipeoaia inic moteneoa tlacaxipeoaliztli. Auh iui, in, in mochichioaia, iteuquecholtzon, itlauhquecholtzon contlaliaia in icpac: iuhquinma itzoncal pohuia in tlaçoihuitl teuquechol: ioan iteucuitlaiacametz, ioan iteucuitlanacoch, ioan ichicaoaz cacalacaia, imaiauhcampa quitzitzquiaia: in icoac tlalpan quitilquetza cacalaca, ioan ichimal ietinẽca teucuitlaanahoacaio: auh in icac tlatlauhqui, ioan moçolichiuh çolihuitl in isco quitzetzelo, ioan ei mani in iamapan quimamaia icampa cuecuetlacatiuh: ioan itzapocue, mochi tlaçoihuitl in tlachioalli: ieh in moteneoa chilchotic quetzaluitztli, tlauipantli, i cuecuentitoc inic tlacencaoalli, in izquican icac tlaçoihuitl, ioan iiehoacozqui,

---

1. In Chapters 15, 16, and 17, we are indebted to Mr. Dudley T. Easby, Jr., Secretary, Metropolitan Museum of Art, New York, for much help in technical points and terminology.

2. Corresponding Spanish text: *"que quiere decir, que asientan el oro, o alguna cosa en el oro o en la plata."* See Molina, op. cit., tlatlalia (*fabricar y componer algo*).

3. In the *Acad. Hist. MS*, this passage reads, *Auh ynic nonqua cate ynic nonqua monotza yn yehoantin teocuitlauaque yn ye uecauh. . . .*

4. In the *Acad. Hist. MS*, yoan is followed by *moçolichiuh: ynic.*

he carried on his back, which went rustling. And his sapote leaf skirt was made of all precious feathers, those known as pointed quetzal feathers,[5] the color of green chili, arranged — prepared — in rows; everywhere there were precious feathers. And his [human] skin collar was of gold beaten thin. And he had his sapote leaf seat.

And thus did they offer him gifts. They made a kind of *tortilla* by the name of *uilocpalli*.[6] They made — formed — *tortillas* not of lime-treated maize kernels, [but] only of ground dried maize kernels, of flour. And they gave all manner of maize ear clusters,[7] and all the first formed fruits and newly opened flowers. All this passed first before him to pay him honor.

And thus [the impersonator] exhibited [the devices]: he danced, he went brandishing his shield; and he went thrusting his rattle board into the ground. Later they skirmished with him; some harried him. They left him there at the place called Totecco. There, too, stood the image of Totec, standing carved of stone. There were spread out all who harried him. When the harrying of Totec ceased, then again he went from house to house.[8] Everyone[9] of the common folk called out to him; the women said to him: "Our lord, come here!" Then they came to place for him his sapote leaf seat. They awaited him everywhere. They gave him, they laid down before him the *uilocpalli* which had been made for him; perhaps they came to lay down before him clusters of maize ears, one or two bunches, and whatever food had arrived for him, [or] which he had come upon. They gave him all. But he did not eat it; it only came before him. They took it from him; they removed it elsewhere. They went taking it away; they carried it off in the folds of their capes. For thus were alms sought[10] when he went from house to house.

And when he had lived thus for twenty days, going about wearing the [human] skin, then it was removed, disposed of, destroyed. This was the time

teucuitlatl in tlatzotzontli, in tlacanaoallj ioan itzapoicpal.

Auh inic quitlamaniliaia: centlamantli tlascalli in quichichioaia, itoca uilocpalli, amo nestamalli in tlamantli, çan tlaoltestli, iotestli in quichioaia, in quitlascalohoaia, mochi ocholli quimacaia: ioan in isquich achtopa mochioaia suchiqualli, ioan in iancuican cueponi suchitl, mochi achtopa ispan quiçaia inic quimauiztiliaia.

Auh inic tetlattitiaia, mitotiaia, momamamantinemi in ichimal: ioan quitilquetztinemi in ichicaoaz. Çatepan quinecaliltiliaia, cauiltiaia cequintin, ompa concaoaia in itocaiocan Totecco: no ompa ihcaca ixiptla in totec tetl in tlaxixintli moquetzticaca: ompa moiaoaia in isquichtin cahuiltiaia: in onnecaoaloc cahuiltia totec: niman ie no cuel ie ic tepan cacalaqui, mochi tlatl quinotza in maceoalti: conilhuiaia in cihoa totectzin, ma oc ie nican timouicatz: niman ic quioallalilia in itzapoicpal, nouian quichieltiaia, ioan quioalmacaia, ispan quioalmana in uilocpalli, in ica ochioaloc, anoço ocholli, centlalpilli, ontlalpilli: ispan quioallalilia, ioan in çaço tlein tlaqualli ipan oacic, in oquipantili mochi quimacaia: auh amo quiquaia, çan tequitl ispan onquiça, concuiliaia, conjcoaniliaia in quiuicatinemi in quitlacuexanilhuiaia: inic tepan cacalaquia.

Auh in iuh nenca, y, cenpoalilhuitl, in onactinenca ehoatl: icoac moueuelohoaia, motlatlaliaia, moxixitiniaia, in icoac ehoatlatiloia, inic cempoliuj imehoaio,

5. Sahagún (Garibay ed.), IX, Adiciones xv, 7, h: "*y su faldellín de (hojas) de zapote, todo de hechura de plumas finas: eran las llamadas 'chiles' y 'espinas de quetzal.'*"

6. *Uilocpalli*: "*vna manera de tortas . . . de mahiz molido, sin cozer hechas*" (corresponding Spanish text); see also Anderson and Dibble, *op. cit.,* Book II, p. 53, n. 25.

7. *Ocholli*: "*manojuelos de maçorcas de mahiz, que apartan para semjlla*" (corresponding Spanish text).

8. Cf. Anderson and Dibble, *op. cit.,* Book I, p. 17; II, p. 49.

9. *Tlatl: tlacatl* in the *Acad. Hist. MS.*

10. In *ibid., ca yc motlatlayehuiaia* precedes *inic tepan cacalaquia.*

of the hiding of skins; when the skins of all the captives whom they had flayed vanished completely. They cast them into a cave. This was done in [the month of] Toçoztontli.

And there to the Temple of Totec, at the place called Yopico, there went any who suffered eye ailments. There they made vows to him so that he might cure them. Perhaps one would have dancers dance, provide a banquet in his home to feed the people, [or] have a cape made for him, called the cape with the colored fringe.

in isquichtin mamalti in oquixipeuhque, oztoc conmamaiahuia: ipan in mochioaia, y, toçoztontli.

Auh in ompa iteupan totec, in jtocaioca, iopico: ompa onhuiia, in aquin iscocoiaia, ompa iuic monetoltiaia inic quipatiz, anoço quitotiz in ichan tecoanotzaz, tetlaqualtiz quichiuiltiaia itilma, itoca tentlapalli.

Sixteenth Chapter. Here is told how the craftsmen who cast precious metals fashioned their wares.[1]

The craftsmen fashioned [and] designed objects by the use of charcoal [and clay molds] and beeswax [models] to cast gold and silver. With this [step] they made a beginning in their craft. To start with, he who presided distributed charcoal among them. First they ground it, they pulverized it, they powdered it. And when they had ground it, then they added it to, they mixed it with, a little potter's[2] clay; this was the clay which served for *ollas*. Thus they made the charcoal [and clay mixture] into a paste, kneaded it, worked it with the hands into a cohesive mass, so that it would dry and harden.

And also they prepared it: in just the same manner [as tortillas] they made it into flat cakes, which they arranged in the sun; and others were likewise formed of clay which they set in the sun. In two days [these cakes] dried; they became firm, they hardened. When they had dried well, when they had hardened, then the charcoal [and clay core][3] was carved, sculptured, with a small metal blade.

[If] a good likeness, an animal, was started, [the core] was carved to correspond to the likeness, the form in nature [that] it imitated, so that from it would issue [in metal] whatsoever it was desired to make — perhaps a Huaxtec, perhaps a stranger, one with a pierced, perforated nose, an arrow across the face, painted [tattooed] upon the body with obsidian serpents. Just so was the charcoal [and clay core] dealt with as it was carved, as it was carefully

Inic castolloce capitulo: oncã mitoa, in iuhquj ic tlachichioa, ĩ iehoantin teucuitlapitzque.

In iehoantin teucuitlapitzque: in tecultica, ioan xicocuitlatica tlatlalia, tlacuiloa: inic quipitza teucuitlatl, in coztic, ioan iztac: inic ompeuhtica intultecaio, achto iehoatl tlaiacana, quinpalehuia in teculli, achto uel quiteci, quicuechoa, quicuechtilia. Auh in oquitezque: niman connamictia quineloa achiton çoçoquitl, iehoatl in tlaltzacutli in comitl mochioa, ic quipoloa, ic quixaqualoa ic quimatzacutilia in teculli, ic tlaquaoa, in tepitzaui.

Auh no quicencauhque, çan oc iuhqui in quitlatlascaloa: tonaian quimamana, ioan cequi çan oqu iuhqui tlaçoquitlalilli, tonaian quitlatlaliaia: omihuitl in oaqui, tepioaqui, tepitzoaqui, tepitzaui. In icoac ouel hoac, in otlaquaoac: çatepan moxixima, mocuicui in teculli, ica tepozhuictontli:

çan misnenpehoaltia, moiolcapeoaltia in mocuicui, ça mishuia, moiolhuia, inic ipan quiçaz, in çaço tlein mochioaz, in aço cuestecatl, aço toueio, iacahuicole, iacacoionqui, istlan mihoa, motlaquicuilo itzcohoatica: niman iuh motlaliaia in teculli inic moxiximaia, inic motlatlamachia: itech mana in catlehoatl motlaehecalhuia in quenami iieliz itlachieliz motlaliz, in aço aiotl: niman iuh motlalia in teculli in icacallo, inic molinitiez, iticpa oalitztica in itzontecon: moli-

---

1. An earlier tentative version of our translation of this chapter was analyzed by Herbert Maryon, O. B. E., the British Museum's expert on ancient metalwork, with whom Anderson consulted in 1955 during research in Europe made possible by a Fellowship of the John Simon Guggenheim Memorial Foundation. Also we have exchanged ideas with Dudley T. Easby, Jr., who has written extensively on pre-Columbian goldwork and goldworkers, defending Sahagún as an accurate technical reporter. See "Sahagún Reviviscit in the Gold Collections of the University Museum," *University Museum Bulletin*, Vol. 20, No. 3 (Philadelphia, 1956), pp. 3ff.; "Ancient American Goldsmiths," *Natural History*, Vol. LXV, No. 8 (New York, 1956), pp. 401ff.; "Orfebrería y orfebres precolombinos," *Anales del Instituto de Arte Americano*, Vol. 9 (Buenos Aires, 1956), pp. 21ff.; and "Sahagún y los orfebres precolombinos de México," *Anales del I. N. A. H.*, Vol. IX, 1955 (México, 1957), pp. 85ff. Cf. also Sahagún (Garibay ed.), Vol. III, pp. 67-72; Seler: "L'orfèvrerie des anciens mexicains," pp. 402ff.; and M. H. Saville: "The Goldsmith's Art in Ancient Mexico," *Indian Notes and Monographs* (New York: Heye Foundation, 1920), pp. 125-142.

2. *Çoçoquitl*: cozçoquitl is intended. In the *Acad. Hist. MS* the term is conçoquitl, equivalent to cozçoquitl; cf. Ignacio de Paredes: *Compendio del arte de la lengua mexicana* (Mexico: Bibliotheca Mexicana, 1759), p. 2.

3. Easby has suggested that Sahagún uses the word "charcoal" frequently as a short-hand name for objects in the process which contain charcoal, and that its meaning must be determined from the context. In this part, Sahagún is obviously referring to the core of the mold, made of the mixture of charcoal and potter's clay. See "Sahagún y los orfebres precolombinos de México," p. 88.

worked. It was taken from whatsoever thing was intended to be reproduced; howsoever its essence or appearance, so would it become [in metal]. If it were, perchance, a turtle, just so was the charcoal [and clay core] modeled: its shell, in which it can move; its head, which is peering forth from it; its neck, which is moving; and its feet, which are as though extending. Or if a bird were to be fashioned of gold, just so was the charcoal [and clay core] carved, so was it shaped, to give it feathers, wings, tail, feet. Or [if] a fish were to be made, just so was carved the charcoal [and clay core] to give it its scales; and its side fins were formed and its tail stood divided. Or [if] a lizard[4] were to be made, its feet were formed. So was the charcoal [and clay core] carved for whatsoever creature was imitated. Or else a radiating, golden necklace would be completed, with bells about its edge, each designed, decorated, with flowers.

When the charcoal [core of the mold] had been prepared, designed, carved, then the beeswax was melted. It was mixed with white *copal,* so that it would [become firm and] harden well. Then it was purified, it was strained, so that its foreign matter, its dirt, the impure beeswax, could fall.[5] And when the beeswax had been prepared, it was then flattened, rolled out, upon a flat stone with a round piece of wood. It was a very smooth, flat stone on which [the wax] was flattened [and] rolled.

When it was well flattened, just like a cobweb, nowhere of uneven thickness, then it was placed over the [carved] charcoal [and clay core]; the surface was covered with it. And carefully it was placed on [the core]; cautiously little pieces [of wax] were cut off or pared away. By this means a little [wax] entered hollows, covered eminences, filled depressions in places where the charcoal [and clay core] had been carved away. By means of a stick [or sliver of wood] they went making it adhere [to the core].[6]

And when it was prepared, when everywhere the beeswax was placed, then a paste of powdered charcoal[7] was spread on the surface of the beeswax. Well was the charcoal ground, pulverized; and a rather

nitica in iquech, ioan in ima, in iuhqui ic mamaçouhtica: in anoço tototl ipan quiçaz teucuitlatl, niman iuh mocuicui, iuh moxima in teculli inic mihuiiotica matlapaltia, mocuitlapiltia, mocxitia: anoço michin in mochioaz, niman iuh moxima in teculli inic moxincaiotia, ioan motlatlalilia in ipatlania iiomotlan, ioan in iuh hicac icuitlapil, maxaltic: anoço cuetzpalin: mochioa, motlalia in ima, inic moxima teculli: in çaço catlehoatl motlaiehecalhuia ioioli: anoce teucuitlacozcatl iecauiz, chaiaoacaio tencoiollo, tlatlatlâmachilli tlasuchiicuilolli.

In icoac omocencauh teculli, in omicuilo, in omocuicuic: niman mopaoaci in sicocuitlatl, moneloa iztac copalli, ic uellaquaoa, çatepan moiectia motzetzeloa: inic uel uetzi in itlaiello, itlallo, in çoquixicocuitlatl. Auh in icoac omocencauh xicocuitlatl: çatepan itztapaltepan mocanahoa, momimiloa ica quanmaitl mimiltic: ie in uel xipetztic tetl, in texixipetztic, ipan mocanaoa momimiloa.

In icoac uel omocacanauh: in ça iuhqui tocapeiotl, in aoccan chicotilaoac, niman itech motlalia in teculli, ic onmisquimiloa: auh amo çan iliuiz in itech motlalia, çan ihuian achitoton mocotontiuh, motectiuh: inic çan ipan oncacalaqui iueuetzian onmotlaça, icacalaquian, iaaquian: onmaquia: in oncan omocuicuic teculli, tepiton quauhtontli inic onmoçalotiuh.

Auh in icoac omocencauh, in ie nouiian itech omotlali in sicocuitlatl: çatepan teculatl isco moteca in sicocuitlatl, uel moteci mocuechtilia in teculatl: auh istilaoac in isco ommoteca xicocuitlatl.

4. *Anoço chacalin* [shrimp], *anoço cuetzpalin,* in the *Acad. Hist. MS.*

5. That is, be eliminated.

6. At this point, in the case of hollow castings it was frequently necessary to transfix the wax by pegs, perhaps of wood or thorn, to anchor the core in place within the mold when the wax was later melted out. This was an essential step where the core was not in direct contact with the outer shell of the mold. It may or may not be implied from the context. — *D. T. Easby.* Cf. Easby, "Sahagún Reviviscit," p. 6, and "Sahagún y los orfebres," pp. 90ff., 97, 116-117; see also Pl. 47.

7. Cf. "Sahagún Reviviscit," p. 8. Seler, *op. cit.,* p. 405, refers to *charbon pulvérisé,* and, on pp. 415f., to *eau de charbon.* — The latter is technically correct and is accepted foundry practice today, except that an aqueous emulsion of graphite, instead of charcoal, is used. — *D. T. Easby.* Cf. also discussion in Easby, "Sahagún y los orfebres," p. 94.

thick[8] coating [of paste] was spread[9] on the surface of the beeswax.

And when it was so prepared, again a covering was placed over it, to wrap, to envelop completely the [thus far] completed work, in order for the gold to be cast. This covering was also of charcoal, also mixed with clay — not pulverized but relatively coarse. When the mold was thus covered, thus completely enveloped, it dried for another two days, and then to it was affixed what was called the *anillotl*,[10] likewise of beeswax. This would become the channel for the gold, for it to enter there [into the mold] when it was molten. And once more [the mold] was laid out; it was placed [in] what was called the crucible [a charcoal brazier],[11] also made of charcoal [and clay] hollowed out. Then thus was the melting. The charcoal fire was laid. There the gold was placed in a crucible; it was melted, so that then it entered into the channel [in the mold], there to be led along, flow, spread out into the interior.

And when it was cast, whatsoever kind of necklace it was which had been made — the various things here mentioned — then it was burnished with a pebble. And when it had been burnished, it was in addition treated with alum; the alum with which the gold was washed [and] rubbed was ground. A second time [the piece] entered the fire; it was heated over it. And when it came forth, once more, for the second time, it was at once washed, rubbed, with what was called "gold medicine."[12] It was just like yellow earth mixed with a little salt; with this the gold was perfected; with this it became very yellow. And later it was polished; it was made like flint, to finish it off, so that at last it glistened, it shone, it sent forth rays.

It is said that in times past only gold [was known to] exist. It was taken advantage of. The gold-workers cast it; they made it into necklaces, and the

Auh in ie iuhqui in omocencauh: oc ceppa itech motlalia tlapepecholoni, ic moquimiloa mocentlapachoa. In oiecauh tlachioalli: inic mocopinaz teucuitlatl, inin tlapepechaloni çan no teculli, no tlanelolli tlaltzacutli, amo cuechtic, çan papaiastic. In icoac ic omopepecho, inic omocenquimilo tlacopinaloni: oc no omilhuitl in hoaqui: auh çatepan itech motlalia itoca amilotl, çan no sicocuitlatl: iehoatl in ipiazio mochioa in teucuitlatl, inic oncan calaqui, in icoac oatis: auh oc ceppa ipan momana, motlalia, itoca tlacasxotl, çan no teculli in tlachioalli, tlacomololli: niman iuh mati motlalia in teculli, oncan mocasxotia matilia in teucuitlatl, ic çatepan calaqui itech amilotl: inic oncan mopiaziotia, inic ontotoca tlaticpa onnoquihui.

Auh in icoac omopitz in çaço tlein cozcatl oiecauh: in izquitlamantli nican omoteneuh, niman ic mopetlaoa ica texalli. Auh in omopetlauh: ie no cuele motlalxocohuia moteci in tlalxocotl, ic maaltia ic momamatiloa in teucuitlatl in omopitz: oppa in tleco calaqui, ipan mototonia: Auh in ohoalquiz, oc ceppa ie no cuele ic maaltia, ic momamatiloa itoca teucuitlapatli: çan no iuhquin tlalcoztli moneloa achiton iztatl ic mocencahoa ic cenca coztic mochioa in teucuitlatl: auh çatepan ic mopetlaoa motecpauia, ic uel mocencaoa, inic iequene uellanestia, pepetlaca, motonameiotia.

Mitoa, in ie uecauh çan oc ie in coztic teucuitlatl nenca, in mauiltiaia: in quipitzaia teucuitlahoaque, in quichioaia cozcatl: ioan in quitzotzonaia in qui-

8. *Achi yxtilauac* in the *Acad. Hist. MS*; this is in keeping with what would be required.

9. Probably with a brush, in order to work the paste into all the minute interstices in the wax. — *D. T. Easby.*

10. In Sahagún, *op. cit.*, p. 69, *anillotl* is translated as *tubo para el oro*; Seler, *op. cit.*, p. 406, uses the term *échenal* (sand basin for fused metal). The term may be related to the Spanish *anillo* (ring), since the native artisans had, by the time the *Florentine Codex* was compiled, adopted some Spanish terms (cf. *esmeril, infra*). This must be the "pour" and entrance channels mentioned by Easby in "Sahagún Reviviscit," p. 7. Some sort of venting to allow air and gases to escape was frequently necessary, and may be implied by the term *anillotl*, but is not specifically mentioned. Cf. also Easby, "Ancient American Goldsmiths," p. 406, fig., and "Sahagún y los orfebres," pp. 92f.

11. The mold was pre-heated in a brazier (a) to melt out the wax, (b) to dry the mold out thoroughly before pouring in the molten gold, and (c) to assure that the molten gold would flow more freely to all parts of the mold. *Tlacasxotl* seems to be an error in transcribing *tlecaxitl* (small brazier); or it may be used here with the secondary meaning given by Molina, "something like a crucible" (a brazier). "Crucible," as we use the word today, makes little sense in this context. — *D. T. Easby.*

12. Cf. Easby, "Sahagún Reviviscit," p. 9. The context of the MS might indicate that a mineral was used, unless the phrase *çan no iuhquin tlalcoztli* refers only to the color.

goldbeaters hammered it, flattened it, into the devices which they required.[13] Silver was not yet in use, though it existed; it appeared here and there. It was highly valued. But today, on the other hand, all is silver; they want gold; it is much treasured.

The goldcasters and beaters[14] who work now also require copper, though only a little, a measured amount. They add it to silver [solder][15] to give it binding power, to make it adhere.[16] For if only silver were melted [to use as solder], the article joined would only shatter; it would only break [at the seams]. There where the article was soldered, [the seams] would not everywhere bind [and] come together.

And the goldbeaters, in times of old, hammered only gold. They smoothed it, they burnished it, with a stone, and they worked out a design along a black line with a stone. First the feather workers made them a design, and then they chased the design with a flint knife [as a tracer]. They followed the black line to form the design with a flint knife. They embossed it, they went making relief work, copying just as was the [black line] pattern. In the same way they manufacture objects today, wherever their work is needed. Perhaps feather mosaic [or other] feather work is required. [The goldworkers] join with [and] are instructed by the feather workers who cut all manner of feather work[17] which may come their way.

Today the goldworkers work thus. They require sand — fine sand. Then they grind it, they pulverize it well; they also mix it with potter's clay. Then they set it out [in the sun], in the very same manner as they form the clay so as to bring forth, to cast, whatsoever they would make. And in two days it is dry.

When it is well dried, then with a potsherd the surface is rubbed, smoothed,[18] polished, burnished, shined, so that the surface is smoothed. Then it is carved — sculptured — with a metal knife, as is told elsewhere. In either two or three days [the work] is finished, made good, perfected.[19]

canaoaia teucuitlatzotzonque, in itech monequia tlauiztli: aiatle catca in iztac teucuitlatl, tel onnenca, çan oc canin necia: uel motlaçotlaia. Auh in ascan ie no cuele ça moche in iztac teucuitlatl quinequi, in coztic ie uel motlaçotla.

In iehoantin teucuitlapitzque, ioan tlatzotzonque, in ascan ic tlachichioa: no quinequi in chichiltic tepuztli, tel çan tlaisiehecolli, tlatamachioalli: in ipan quitlaça iztac teucuitlatl ic caltia, ic tzictia. Auh intla çan miscahui, mopitza iztac teucuitlatl: çan tlatlapaca, tzatzaiani in tlachioalli, amo uel nouiampa monanamique, mocacamapiqui in oncan çaçaliuhtiuh, ic tlatlamachilli.

Auh in iehoantin teucuitlatzotzonque: in ie uecauh çã quiscahuiaia in teucuitlatl quitzotzonaia, quitealaoa, petlaoa, ioan quiteicuiloa tlilanpa: achtopa quimicuilhuiaia in amanteca: auh çatepan iehoantin quiteicuilohoaia, ica tecpatl, quitocatiui in tlilantli, inic tlatecpaicuiloa quitotomoloa, quitotomolotihui: itech cantiui in quenami machiotl. Çã ie no iuh tlachichioa in ascan: inic cana monequi intlachioal, aço ihuitlacuilolli, ihuitlachioalli itech monequi: quinepanhuia quimottitia in amanteca, inic quitequi, in quexisquich quinamictiuh, ihuitlacuilolli.

In ascan ie ic tlachichioa teucuitlahoaque, quinequi in xalli, in xalpitzaoac: çatepan quiteci, uel quicuechoa, no quineloa in tlaltzacutli: niman ic quimana, çan oc iuhquin quiçoquitlalia, inic ipan quiçaz inic mocopinaz, in çaço tlein quichioazque: auh omilhuitl in oaqui.

In icoac ouelhoac: çatepan tapalcatica mischichiqui, mixiqui, motapalcauiia, motapalcachichiqui, motapalcaichiqui, inic misxipetzoa: niman ic moxima mocuicui tepuzhuictica: in iuh omoteneuh cecni, aço omilhuitl, anoço eilhuitl in mocencahoa in moiectilia in moiectllio.

---

13. See the plaques illustrated in S. K. Lothrop: "Metals from the Cenote of Sacrifice," *Memoirs of the Peabody Museum*, Vol. X, No. 2 (Cambridge, 1952). See also Pls. 53-56.

14. *In yehoantin teocuitlauaque yn tlepitzque yoan yn tlatzotzonque*, in the *Acad. Hist. MS.*

15. Herbert Maryon, personal communication, July 20, 1955: "a seam made with silver only as the solder would not make a good joint. . . . . a solder composed of silver and copper would make a stronger and more continuous joint."

16. *Yc çalia yc tzictia*, in the *Acad. Hist. MS.* Cf. *çaçaliuhtiuh*, near the end of the same paragraph, *Florentine Codex*.

17. *Yhuitlachiualli*, in the *Acad. Hist. MS.*

18. *Mixichiqui*, in *ibid.*

19. *Moiectlalia* is intended; cf. *ibid.*

When [the core] is prepared, then powdered charcoal paste is spread on its surface, and the surface is made smooth with a clay paste. Then the beeswax[20] is melted; it is mixed with white *copal,* as was mentioned. When cooled, when purified, then it is flattened, rolled out on a flat stone with a piece of wood. Forthwith it is placed upon — joined to — the clay object to form the shape of the gold, whatsoever is to be made, perhaps a jar or an incense burner, which they call *perfumador.* It is painted; it is designed with a beautiful design.

They especially esteem beeswax; they use it especially to form patterns, to produce works of art. But first, somewhere, a model of beeswax is made. When it has been well prepared, the mold is pressed upon it [to make the wax model].[21] For there is a model [in wax] of all they make, whether birds' wings,[22] or flowers, or leaves of plants, or whatsoever beautiful design.

By means of a small wooden stick, called a thorn stick, [the wax] is pressed on; it is made to adhere [to the core of the mold].[23] In perhaps two days it is perfected; it is made good.

When it has been prepared, when in all places the [modeled] beeswax has been made to adhere [to the core], then on its surface is spread [a thin paste of powdered charcoal].[24] When it is dried, then in addition a covering is placed upon it, of only coarse charcoal [and clay], in order to envelop the model [of wax with its coating of powdered charcoal paste]. In perhaps two days it dries. Then to it is placed the beeswax channel, called the round *anillotl.* First it is rounded. This becomes the channel for the gold, for it to enter there.

And when the channel has been set in, once more [the mold] is arranged [in] something like a crucible[25] where the gold is [to be] cast. When they are this far, when all is prepared, then [the mold] is placed on the fire; it is thoroughly heated. Then flows out burning the beeswax [model] which has been placed within it. When the beeswax has come

In icoac omocencauh: niman teculatl isco moteca, ioan tzacutli ic onisxipetziui: ic niman mopaoaci in xicotlatl, moneloa in iztac copalli, in iuhqui omoteneuh: in oceuh, in omoiecti, niman mocanaoa itztapaltepan, quanmatica momimiloa: ic niman itech motlalia, itech moçalohoa in tlatlalilli, çoquitl inic mocopinaz teucuitlatl: in çaço tlein mochioaz, in aço Jarro, anoço tlapopochhuiloni, in quitocaiotia perfomador, ic micuiloa, ic motlatlamachia in qualli tlacuilolli:

oc cenca ie quimati in xicocuitlatl, oc cenca ie tlahuica inic tlacuilolo, inic tultecatioa: ca tel achto cecni mocopina in xicocuitlatl. In icoac ouel mocencauh: ipan onmopachoa in tlacopinaloni: ca oncân câ icopinaloca in isquich tlamachtli, in aço totoatlapalli, anoço suchitl, anoço quilatlapalli, in çaço tlein qualnezqui tlacuilolli

ic onmopachotiuh ic onmoçalotiuh quauhtontli quitocaiotia quauhuitztli, aço omilhuitl in iectia in moiectlalia.

In icoac omocencauh, in onouiiampa moçalo xicocuitlatl: niman ic isco moteca in teucuitlatl: in ohoac, ie no cuele itech motlalia in tlapêpecholoni, in ça papaiastic teculli, inic mocenquimiloa in tlacopinaloni, aço omilhuitl in oaqui, niman ic itech onmotlalia in xicocuitlatl, in itoca anillotl mimiltic, achtopa momimiloa: iehoatl ipiazio mochioa in teucuitlatl, inic oncan calaqui.

Auh in omotlalli anillotl, ie no cuele ipan momamana in tlacasxotl in oncan atiiec teucuitlatl. In icoac ie iuhqui in omochi mocencauh: niman ic tleco motlalia mocentotonia: oncan quiça oncan tlatla in xicocuitlatl in tlâtic omotlalica. In icoac oquiz, in otlatlac xicocuitlatl, niman moceuia, ic ie no cuele pani onmoteca in xalli, çan papaiastic: icoac iequene mopitza,

20. *Xicocuitlatl* is intended; cf. *ibid.*

21. That is, parts of the wax model were pressed in molds and then applied to the core, instead of the wax being modeled free-hand on the core (as is generally done). — *D. T. Easby.*

22. *Totocuitlapilli* follows *totoatlapalli* in the *Acad. Hist. MS.*

23. Here possibly the wax was transfixed by pegs as noted *supra,* n. 6.

24. *Teculatl,* in the *Acad. Hist. MS.*

25. The word appears to be corrected in the MS to read *tlacasxotl,* for which Molina gives "crucible for melting metal, or a similar object" (possibly a brazier). It may be an error in transcribing *tlecaxitl,* "a small brazier." In any event, a brazier and not a crucible would have been used to pre-heat the mold. See Pl. 62, and n. 11, *supra.*

forth, when it has burned, then [the mold] is cooled, for which purpose it is once more set out over sand, quite coarse sand. Then immediately the casting takes place; there [the mold] enters the "fire pot" [a charcoal brazier][26] on a charcoal [fire]; and the gold, which is to enter there [into the mold], is melted separately in a ladle [and poured].

Here this ends; thus the work is finished. And when the piece has been formed, when it has been cast, when it comes forth, then it is treated with alum; in a copper vessel it is boiled. And if somewhere the piece has cracked, has split, that is the time to mend it. That which is to be joined [soldered] is mended. And then it is rubbed so that like copper it shines.[27] Once more it goes into [and] is treated with alum. So thereafter it is cleaned; it is made like flint, so that it glistens brightly.

oncan oncalaqui in tlecomic, ipan onmotlalia in teculli: auh in teucuitlatl in oncan calaquiz, nonqua tlemaco matilia:

oncan tlami, y, inic iecaui tlachioalli. Auh in otlacat, in omopitz, in oquiz tlachioalli: niman motlasxocohuiia tepuzcaxic, ipan moquaqualatza: auh intla cana otzâtzâia oihitlacauh tlachioalli, çanioca oncan mopâpâtia ic moçaloa in tlaçaloloni: auh çatepan ic michiqui, iuhquinma tepuztli, ic mopetlaoa: oc ceppa tlalxocotitlan calaqui motlasxocohuia, ic çatepan mocencahoa, motecpahuia inic uel mopetlahoa.

---

26. Sahagún uses the word *tlecomic*. Although Molina gives "crucible for melting gold" for *tlecomitl*, the word appears to be a compound of *tletl* (fire) and *comitl* (pot), or "a brazier." See n. 11 and n. 25, *supra*. This implies that the mold was heated twice, once to burn out the wax and a second time to assure that the molten gold would fill the mold before freezing or solidifying. — *D. T. Easby*.

27. *Yuh i matepuztli*, in the *Acad. Hist. MS* (as [with] a little metal adze).

Seventeenth Chapter. Here are discussed the lapidaries who worked precious stones.

There were four grandfathers [and] fathers of the lapidaries in times of old: devils whom they regarded as gods. The name of the first was Chiconaui itzcuintli; and her names were [also] Papaloxaual and Tlappapalo. So three names were hers. And the name of the second of their gods was Naualpilli. The name of the third was Macuilcalli. The name of the fourth was Cinteotl. The feast days of all these occurred only once; they celebrated the feast day for all four. And the feast day was celebrated, [and] they acknowledged [these gods] at the time that the day count called Nine Dog set in.

Of these, the first mentioned, their god[dess] named Chiconaui itzcuintli, Papaloxaual, Tlappapalo, was a woman. Thus was she arrayed. Her face was painted with her butterfly face painting, whence came her name. At her right she bore her hand-staff, and at her left rested her shield. Thus was the painting of her shield: a foot stood on it. And [she had] her golden ear plugs and golden butterfly nose pendant,[1] and her shift of variegated red [and white]; just the same was her skirt. [She had] her obsidian sandals, also bright red, so called obsidian sandals [because] obsidian serpents were their design.[2]

All and each of the persons who represented [the deities] died when the feast day was celebrated.

And the one [called] Naualpilli was adorned just like a Huaxtec. He was of disordered, unkempt hair, uncombed, disheveled; in elflocks. And gold was his forehead disc,[3] which rested on his brow; and his ear pendants were of gold. And [he had] his feathered staff, and his shield with feather patches on the four sections.[4] And his sleeveless jacket was all variegated red [and white],[5] fringed. And bright red were his sandals.

Inic castolli omome capitulo: vncan mitoa in tlatecque in quichichioa tlaçotetl.

In iehoantin tlatecque, in ie uecauh in inculhoan, in intahoan catca: nahuintin in quinmoteutiaia diablome. Inic ce, itoca, chicunaui itzcuintli, ioan itoca papaloxaoal, ioan tlappapalo ic eteisti itoca. Auh inic ome inteouh catca: itoca naoalpilli. Inic ei itoca macuilcalli. Inic nahui itoca cinteutl. In izquintin in, çan cenquiçaia in imilhuiuh: nahuistin ilhuiquistililoia: auh in iehoatl ipan ilhuiquistililoia, ipan quimattihuia, in icoac moquetza cemilhuitlapoalli in itoca chicunaui itzcuintli.

In iehoanti achto moteneoa inteouh in itoca chicunaui itzcuintli papaloxaoal tlappapalo cihoatl: inic mochichioaia, inic michiuh ipapaloxaoal ic necia in itoca in immaiauhcampa quitquiticaca imacpaltopil: auh in iopuchcopa ichimal ieticac inic tlacuilolli ichimal itech icac ce icxitl, ioan iteucuitlanacoch, ioan iteucuitlaiacapilpalouh, ioan iuipil tlappoiaoac: çan no iuhqui in icue, itzcac, çan no chichiltic (inic mitoa itzcac) tlaitzcoaicuilolli.

In izquintin cecenme tlaca quinmixiptlatiaia: izquintin miqui, in icoac ilhuiquistililoia.

Auh in iehoatl naoalpilli: çan iuhquin cuestecatl ic mochichioaia, moquatzitzintiaia, quatatapatic, quatzomatic, quapaçoltic, moquaxelolti: ioan teucuitlatl in isquatechimal isquac manca, ioan inacazpipilol teucuitlatl, ioan ihuitopil, ioan ichimal ihuichachapanqui nauhcanpa ioan ixicol: çan tlappoiaoac tenchaiaoac, ioan chichiltic in icac.

_____

1. *Iteucuitlaiacapilpapalouh* is intended.
2. Corresponding Spanish text: *"vnas cotaras, tambiẽ coloradas, con vnas pinturas que las hazian almenadas."*
3. *Ibid.: "vna lamina de oro, delgada como papel."*
4. *Ibid.: "vna rodela, como de red hecha, y en quatro partes tenja plumas ricas, malpuestas."*
5. *Ibid.: "vna xaqueta tejida de blanco, y colorado, con rapacejos, en el remate de abaxo."*

And Macuilcalli they also represented as a man. Thus was he adorned. His head was provided with a crest; quetzal feathers stretched in a row at the crown of his head, [to form] his crest.[6] He had golden plates placed on his temples.[7] And [he had] his necklace of wooden discs with shells,[8] as well as his feathered staff [and] his shield provided with red discs.[9] And, likewise, he was anointed with red ochre. He also had his bright red sandals.

And also Cinteotl was represented as a man, with his turquoise [mosaic] mask and his turquoise rays, and his mist jacket of [light] blue, as if netted, and his wind jewel necklace. And they formed for him his resting place, whence he looked forth, called his maize house; indeed all of maize stalks they formed his hut.[10] And [he had] his white foam sandals; with down feather [laces] were they tied.[11]

To these four [gods], so they said, they attributed the art [of the lapidary]. Their creations were lip pendants, lip plugs, and ear plugs, ear plugs of obsidian, rock crystal, and amber; white ear plugs; and all manner of necklaces; bracelets; the manner of designing, of inlaying, with green stones; and the drilling, the polishing. It was, so they said, their creation, their invention.

And at that time, when their feast day arrived, [their] old men, all the master lapidaries, provided song [and] held vigil during the night for those who were to die at dawn — all the likenesses [of these gods]. All rejoiced; they enjoyed the feasting.[12]

And this took place there at Xochimilco, because the grandfathers [and] fathers of all the lapidaries came from there. There was the beginning; there they took their origin. It was their native land.

* * *

The master lapidaries[13] cut rock crystal, and amethysts, and green stones, and emerald-green

Auh in macuilcalli no toquichtin in quimixiptlatiaia: inic mochichioaia, moquachichiquilti, quetzalli in iquanepantla uipantoca, in iquachichiquil, teucuitlatl in icanahoacan quimomamanili: auh in icozqui quappaiaoalolli, tecuciztli, no ihuitopil, ioan ichimal tlauhtemalacaio: auh çan no motlaoçac, no chichiltic in icac.

Auh in cinteutl, no toquichtin in ipan mixehoaia ixiuhxaiac, ioan ixiuhtlanes, ioan iaiauhxicol texotli, iuhquin tlalpilli, ioan iecacozqui: ioan itlapech quitlaliliaia, oncan oalitzticatca, motenehoa içincal: çan moche in toctli quixacallaliliaia, ioan ipoçulcac, çan iztac, potonqui inic tlatlapilli.

In nahuintin y, iuh quitoa, ca iehoatl intech quitlamiaia in tultecaiotl; iehoatl intlachioal, in tezçacatl, in tentetl, ioan in nacochtli, in itznacochtli, in teuilonacochtli, apoçonalnacochtli, iztac nacochtli: ioan in ie mochi cozcatl, in macuestli, inic micuiloa, inic moteicuiloa chalchiuitl: ioan inic momamali, inic mopetlaoa, iuh quitoa ca iehoatl intlachioal intlanestil.

Auh in icoac, y, in imilhuiuh quiçaia: in iueueiohoan, in isquichtin tulteca tlatecque, ioaltica quincuicatiaia quitozçahuiaia in ie oallathui miquizã, in izquintin teixiptlahoan mochintin papaquia, ilhuitlamatia.

Auh inin mochioaia, ompa xochmilco iehica in isquichtin tlatecque, ompa oallaque in inculhoan, in intahoan: ompa nelhoaioticate ompa antica in innelhoaio: ca inquizcan iniolcan.

* * *

In tlatecque, tulteca: inic quitequi in iztac teuilotl, ioan tlapalteuilotl, ioan chalchiuitl, ioan quetzalitztli,

6. Ibid: "los cabellos cortados, por medio de la cabeça, como lomo, que llamã quachichiquile: y este lomo no era de cabellos sino de pluma ricas."

7. Ibid.: "en las sienes, vnas planchas de oro delgado."

8. Ibid.: "vn juel colgado al cuello de marisco redondo, y ancho, que se llamava quappaiaoalolli."

9. Ibid.: "vna rodela, con vnos circulos de colorado unos dentro de otros que se llamava tlauhtemalacaio."

10.. Ibid.: "ponjanle, en vn tablado alto, de donde estaua mjrando, el qual llamava cincalli, compuesto con cañas de mahiz, verdes, a manera de xacal."

11. Ibid.: "las ataduras dellas, erã de algodon floxo"; tlatlapilli should be read tlatlalpilli (cf. Acad. Hist. MS). In the Acad. Hist. MS, yoan ycintopil follows quixacallaliliaia.

12. Corresponding Spanish text: "de noche dezian sus cantares, y hazian velar por su honrra a los captivos, que aujan de morir: y se holgauã en su fiesta."

13. Cf. Elizabeth Kennedy Easby and Dudley T. Easby, Jr.: "Apuntes sobre la técnica de tallar jade en Mesoamérica," Anales del Instituto de Arte Americano, No. 6 (Buenos Aires, 1956); Foshag: "Mineralogical Studies on Guatemalan Jade," Smithsonian Pub. No. 4307 (1957); Sahagún (Garibay ed.), III, pp. 72ff; Seler: "L'orfèvrerie des anciens mexicains," pp. 418ff.; and M. H. Saville: "Turquoise Mosaic Art in Ancient Mexico," Indian Notes and Monographs (New York: Heye Foundation, 1922), pp. 31-33.

jade,[14] with[15] abrasive sand, and hard metal.[16] And they scraped them with a worked flint tool. And they drilled them; they bored them with a metal tubular drill.[17] Then they slowly smoothed the surfaces; they polished them; they gave them a metallic luster. And then they finished them off with a piece of wood [and very fine abrasive]. They polished them so that they gleamed, they sent forth rays of light, they glistened. Or with a piece of fine cane [containing silica] the lapidaries polished, finished,[18] perfected their artifacts.

And in just the same way was amethyst worked [and] finished. First the master lapidaries broke it;[19] they shattered it with a piece of metal, so that they could put aside the good [pieces], of good color, of pleasing aspect.[20] Thereupon they placed them where they were needed, when they had removed the rough parts with a piece of metal. And then they abraded it, smoothed the surface, and gave it a metallic luster; and they polished it with a piece of wood, a polisher, with which they embellished it. So they finished it.

And what is called blood[-speckled] flint [bloodstone][21] is very hard and resistant. It could not be cut with abrasive sand, but could only be broken up, beaten with a stone; and its rough pieces,[22] which were no good, which could not be polished, were cast away. Only that was taken, was sought, which was good, which could be polished: the blood-colored, which was well speckled. It was abraded with water and with a very hard stone which came from Matlatzinco, because they were suitable to each other. The rock was just as hard as the flint so that together they cut each other. Afterwards the surface was smoothed with abrasive and given a metallic luster with a [finer] abrasive.[23] And then it was

ioan teuxalli: ioan tlaquaoac tepuztli. Auh inic quichiqui, tecpatl tlatetzotzontli. Auh inic quicoionia, inic quimamali tepuztlacopintli: niman ihuiian quisteca quipetlahoa, quitemetzhuia: auh in ie ic quicencaoa: itech quauitl in quipetlaoa, inic pepetlaca, inic motonameiotia, inic tlanestia: anoço quetzalotlatl in itech quipetlaoa, inic quicenca, inic quiiecchioa in intultecaio tlatecque.

Auh çan no iuhqui in tlapaltehuilotl inic mochioa, inic mocencaoa: achtopa quimoleoa, quihuipeoa tepuztica, in tlatecque, in tulteca: inic iioca quitlatlalia in qualli, in motquitica tlapaltic, in ilacqui: çã niman iuh quitlalia in campa monequiz, in icoac quimoleoa tepuztica: auh niman quichiqui, quisteca, ioan quitemetzhuia, ioan quipetlaoa itech quauitl in tlapetlaoaloni: inic quiiectilia, inic quicencaoa.

Auh in iehoatl in motenehoa eztecpatl: cenca tlaquaoac, chicahoac, camo ma uel motequi in ica teuxalli: ca çan motlatlapana moteuiia, ioan motepehuilia in itepetlaio, in amo qualli, in amono uel mopetlaoa: çan iehoatl mocui motemolia in qualli, in uel mopetlaoa in eztic, in uel cuicuiltic, michiqui atica: ioan itech tetl, cenca tlaquaoac, ompa hoallauh in matlatzinco: ipampa ca uel monoma namiqui, in iuh chicaoac tecpatl, no iuh chicaoac in tetl, inic monepan mictia: çatepan misteca ica teuxalli, ioan motemetzhuia, ica esmelir. Auh çatepan ic mocencaoa, ic mopetlaoa in quetzalotlatl: inic quicuecueiotza, quitonameiotia.

---

14. Cf. *supra*, chap. 4, n. 10.

15. *Ioan*: possibly *yca in* in the *Acad. Hist. MS.*

16. Seler, *op. cit.*, p. 418: bronze; Sahagún (Garibay ed.), III, p. 74: *un metal duro.*—A hard metal, however, would not have held the abrasive sand so well as a soft metal; hammer-hardened copper would have been satisfactory. Wood and bone were also used with abrasives. On the nature of the abrasive sand, cf. Durán, *op. cit.*, lvi (p. 442), on Moctezuma's embassy to the south to secure special sand requested by the lapidaries.— D. T. Easby.

17. Cf. Siméon, *op. cit.*; also Easby and Easby, *op. cit.*, p. 11. Seler, *op. cit.*, p. 419: *pointe de cuivre nue*; Sahagún, *loc. cit.*: *punzŏn de metal.*

18. *Quicencaua* in *Acad. Hist. MS.*

19. *Quihuipeoa* reads *quihuipena* in the *Acad. Hist. MS.*

20. *Ilacqui*: *itaqui* in *ibid.*

21. Cf. Foshag, "Mineralogical Studies," p. 47, n. 11. Also see Emmart, *op. cit.*, p. 61, and Reccho, *op. cit.*, pp. 337, 339. — Flint (*tecpatl*) and bloodstone (*eztecpatl* or *eztetl*) are both cryptocrystalline varieties of quartz, and both are equally hard stones (7 on the Mohs scale, on which diamond is 10). Jasper falls in the same group as flint and bloodstone, but the term "jasper" should not be used here, since it is clear that Sahagún is talking about bloodstone and nothing else. — D. T. Easby. See also Sahagún (Garibay ed.), III, p. 337.

22. Cf. *tepetlaio* in Molina, *op. cit.*

23. Emery probably was not used in Mexico before the Conquest; Sahagún uses it as a generic term to include a number of abrasives; cf. Sahagún, *op. cit.*, III, p. 341. — D. T. Easby.

finished, polished, with a piece of fine cane [containing silica], with which they made it gleam; they made it send forth rays of light.

And what was called humming-bird flint [Mexican opal][24] is by nature of many kinds; it is multicolored: white, and green, and like fire or like a star, and like a rainbow. It is quite small, it is abraded, it is polished, with only a little sand.

And the so-called round turquoise is not hard.[25] No hard abrasive is needed to grind it down, to smooth its surface, to give it a metallic luster. And to polish it, it is rubbed with a piece of fine cane, so that it may give forth rays of light, may glisten.

And fine turquoise is not very hard. With just a little sand it is polished; with it, it is embellished. And also, it may be given brilliance, radiance, [with] another tool called a turquoise-burnisher.

Auh in iehoatl motocaiotia uitzitziltecpatl: niman iuh ioli tlacati, miec tlamantli inic mocuicuilohoa: iztac, ioan xoxoctic, ioan iuhquin tletl, anoço iuhquin citlalin, ioan iuhquin aiauhcoçamalotl, çan tepiton: xalli inic michiqui, inic mopetlaoa.

Auh in iehoatl motocaiotia xiuhtomolli ca no tlaquaoac, camo esmellir itech monequi, inic michiqui, inic misteca, ioan inic motemetzhuia: ioan inic mopetlaoa, inic moquetzalotlahuia, inic motonameiotia, motlanesiotia.

Auh in iehoatl teuxihuitl, ca amo cenca tlaquaoac: çan no tepiton xalli, inic mopetlaoa inic moiectilia. Auh in uel no ic motlanestilmaca motonameiomaca, oc centlamantli, itoca xiuhpetlaoaloni.

---

24. Cf. Foshag, *op. cit.*, p. 48, n. 15.

25. *Ca no*: read *camo*; mineralogically, turquoise is not regarded as a hard stone, being about 6 on the Mohs scale. The "round turquoise" is probably a reference to that found as nodules rather than in veins or seams. — *D. T. Easby*.

Eighteenth Chapter. Here are mentioned the inhabitants of Amantlan, ornamenters who worked precious feathers and many other kinds of feathers.

Accounts have been heard as to the manner of the narratives, the traditions, of the old men of Amantlan, as they counseled one with another. They told how they took [and] worshiped as their god one named Coyotl inaual. It is said, then, that [as] they carried him here, he came advising the old men, those who first came here, the newcomers, the progenitors, the Mexicans.[1] When they had established themselves, settled, multiplied themselves, begotten their sons, their grandsons, then they made — they set up — a statue; they made it of hewn wood. And they raised his temple for him; they named his *calpulli* Amantlan. There they paid him honor; they made him offerings.[2]

And thus did they array and adorn the one they named Coyotl inaual when it was the time of his feast day.[3] That which was put on was a prepared coyote skin, a product of the inhabitants of Amantlan. It was provided with a [coyote] head from which was peering the face of one resembling a man. Gold were its teeth and fangs. All were thus. And his sword-shaped staff was set with obsidian blades, and his shield of bamboo sticks had a [light] blue border, and he bore an *olla* with quetzal feathers upon his back. His shells, his rattles, they placed on his feet, and his yucca fiber sandals showed that he was one lately arrived, a newcomer. As they said, he was a Chichimec.[4]

And not this one alone did they worship as a god. For seven were arranged in their *calpulli* when the inhabitants of Amantlan arranged their images. Five were the representations of men, and two were made

Inic castolli omei capitulo: vncan motenehoa in amāteca, in tlachichiuhque, in quichioa tlaçoihuitl: ioan oc cequi miec tlamantli ihuitl.

In mocaqui tlatlatolli, in iuhca innenonotzal, in inpiel catca, ueuetque, amanteca, inic mononotzaia: quitoaia, inic canque, inic quimoteutique inteouh, in itoca Coiotl inaoal: quilmach niman quioalhuicaque quinoalnotztia in ueuetque, in achto oallaque in econi in tlacapixoani mexiti, in icoac omotecaque inic onoque, in omotlapiuique in otlapiuisque inpilhoan imishuihoan: niman ic quixeuhque quitlacaquetzque, quauitl tlaxixintli in quichiuhque: auh quiquechilique iteucal, icalpul, quitocaiotique amantlan vncan quimahuistiliaia, quitlamaniliaia.

Auh inic quichichioaia, inic quicencahoaia, icoac ilhuipan inic quitocaiotia coiotl inaoal: iê in onmaquiaia coioehoatl tlachichioalli, intlaiectlalil catca in amanteca, tzontecometicaca, ompa oalitztica in ixaiac tlacatlachie, teucuitlatl in itlancoch, ioan itlancoiolomiuh mochiuhtoc, ioan imacquauhtopil itztzo, ioan iiotlachimaltentexoio, ioan quetzalcomitl in quimamaticac, icoiol itzitzil contlaliticac in icxic, ioan icçocac ic quinestiaia in çan oallani, in econi iuh quitoa ca chichimecatl.

Auh amo çan ie iio y, in quimoteutiaia, ca chicomen manca in incalpulco, inic quinmanaia inixiptlahoan amāteca: macuiltin in oquichtin impan mixehoaia: auh omenti cihoa mochiuhtimanca: iehoatl

1. Corresponding Spanish text: *"a estos llamaron econj, y tlacapixoanj, mexiti, que quiere dezir los que primero poblaron que se llamaron Mexiti, de donde vino este vocablo mexico."* Sahagún (Garibay ed.), III, p. 75: *"los antiguos que primeramente vinieron, la migración, la formadora de linaje de hombres, los mexicanos."*

2. Corresponding Spanish text: *"edificaronla vn cu, y el barrio donde se edifico llamaronle amantla. En este barrio honrrauan, y offrecian a este dios, que llamauan coiotl inaoal: y por razon del nombre del barrio, que es amantlan, tomaron los vezinos de alli este nombre amanteca."*

3. Coyote disguise; in Sahagún, *loc. cit.,* he who has a coyote as his double.

4. [I]icçocac (icçotl, cactli); icçotl, Yucca albifolia Y. sp. (Sahagún, *op. cit.,* IV, p. 337). Corresponding Spanish text: *"ponjāle vnas cotaras texidas o hechas de hojas de vn arbol que llamā icçotl, porque quando llegarō a esta tierra vsauan aquellas cotaras: componjanle siempre con ellas para dar a entender, que ellos erā los primeros pub* ladores chichimecas, que avian publado en esta tierra de Mexico."*

like women. Coyotl inaual was the one who took the very lead, who headed them all. One named Tiçaua followed him; he took second place. And one named Macuil ocelotl took third place; he stood in third place. One called Macuil tochtli took fourth place; he stood in fourth place. Then the two women followed; they came closing the line. The name of one was Xiuhtlati; the name of the second was Xilo. And still another, who was in seventh place, stood facing the others; his name was Tepoztecatl.

All these were thus arrayed. The five [men] all bore *ollas* with quetzal feathers on their backs; just as Coyotl inaual stood, just so were the rest.[5] Only Tiçaua wore nothing as his disguise; he bore upon his back only the *olla* with quetzal feathers, and his chalk [colored] ear pendants [were] made of thin, elongated shells. Then he had placed on his radiating ornament of turquoise, his feathered staff, and his shield, his rattles, and his foam sandals.

And Macuil ocelotl was wearing as his disguise the head of a wild beast, from which was peering his face. Also he bore upon his back the *olla* with quetzal feathers; [he had] his radiating ornament of turquoise, his feathered staff, his shield, his rattles, his foam sandals.[6]

And in just the same way Macuil tochtli also wore his disguise, like the head of a rabbit. Also he bore upon his back the *olla* with quetzal feathers in which the feathers scattered out, and [he had] his feathered staff, his shield, his rattles, his foam sandals.

And Xiuhtlati wore her light blue shift, and the shift of Xilo, the younger, was made bright red, scarlet, very red. Both had their shifts sprinkled, scattered with divers kinds of feathers. Thus they were sprinkled, thus were they scattered with all manner of precious feathers: the blue cotinga, the tail feathers of the blue cotinga, [feathers of] the red spoonbill, those the color of the corn silk flower;[7] and eagle feathers—fine eagle feathers; also trogonorus feathers; green, pointed quetzal feathers; and the yellow

uellaiacatiaia teceniacanaia in coiotl inaoal, contoquiliaia, cononcaiotiaia itoca tiçahoa: auh tlaiecaiotiaia, tlaiecaiopan icaca: itoca macuil ocelotl: tlanauhcaiotiaia tlanauhcaiopā icaca: itoca macuil tochtli: ic niman iehoantin quimontoquiliaia quintzacutimanca in omentin cihoa: ce itoca xiuhtlati, inic ome itoca xilo: auh in oc ce intechiconca, çan teisnamicticaca itoca tepuztecatl.

In izquintin, y, ihuin in mochichioaia, macuiltin in moch quetzalcomitl quimamatimanca in iuhqui iqu jcac coiotl inaoal: çan no iuh mama in oc cequinti çan ie iio in tiçaoa atle onmaquiaia inaoal, çaniio quimamaia in quetzalcomitl, ioan ititiçanacoch tecuciztli in tlachioalli in tlacanaoalli, çan papatlachtic, niman ie ixiuhtlanes contlaliticac ihuitopil: ioan ichimal, itzitzil ioan ipoçolcac.

Auh in macuilocelotl onacticaca in inaoal in tequani itzontecon: ompa oalitztica in ixaiac, no quetzalcomitl in quimama ixiuhtlanes, ihuitopil, ichimal, itzitzil, ipoçolcac:

çan ie no iuhqui in macuiltochtli, no onacticac in inaoal, in iuhqui tochin itzōtecon, no quimamaticac in quetzalcomitl, xoquiuhtimani in quetzalli, ioan ihuitopil, ichimal, itzitzil, ipoçolcac:

Auh in xiuhtlati, itexouipil in onacticaca: auh in xilo in xocoiotl mochiuhticac chichiltic in iuipil, tlanochezpalli, tlatlapalpalli: onteisti nepapan ihuiio in inuipil, nepapan ihuitzetzeliuhqui nepapan ihuimoiaoac ic tzetzeliuhtoc, ic moiahoatoc in ie mochi tlaçoihuitl, in xiuhtototl in xiuhtototcuitlapilli, in tlauhquechol xilosuchitic ioan in quauiuitl in quauhteuitztli: niman iehe in tzinitzcan in chilchotic quetzaluitztli ioan in toztli, in toztapacatl, in tozcuicuil in piliuitl. Auh in aiopal in ielihuiio, xiuhtototl, uel no-

5. For *mama*, the *Acad. Hist. MS* has *mania*.

6. Corresponding Spanish text: "*solamēte el dios que se llamaua tiçaoa no le componian de pellejo de coiotl: solamēte lleuaua a cuestas el jarro con los quetzales: y vnas orejeras de concha de marisco: lleuaua tambien su baculo, y su rodela, y sus caracolitos, en las piernas, y vnas cotaras blancas.*"

7. *Xiloxochitl*: milky corn silk flower, according to Emmart, *op. cit.*, p. 300: *Calliandra anomala* (Kunth) McBride. *Pachira insignis, Calliandra grandiflora*, or *Bombax ellipticum* H. B. K., according to Santamaría, *op. cit.*, II, p. 149 (*jilosúchil*: "*los pistilos son largos hilos sedosos, finos, delicados, de color rosado o lila, solferino, morado, etc., y estilo más grueso y de color más encendido, formando todos en conjunto un haz suelto, al que protegen largas bracteas, del color del conjunto por dentro y verde amarillento de musgo por fuera.*"). *Ceiba pentandra* (L.) Gaertn., *Bombax pentandrum* L., *C. casearia* Medic., *Eriodendron anfractuosum* DC, *E. occidentale* Don (silk cotton tree), *B. ellipticum* H. B. K., *Carolinea fastuosa* DC, or *B. mexicanum* Hemsl. (corn silk flower), according to Standley, *op. cit.*, Vol. 23, Pt. 3, pp. 791, 793-794. Cf. also Sahagún, *op. cit.*, IV, p. 368.

parrot, neck feathers of the yellow parrot, varicolored parrot feathers; feathers of young birds; and the yellow breast feathers of the blue cotinga. Indeed their shifts were everywhere covered with feathers, whereby they were made marvelous, wonderfully finished, perfected. And on their borders, a feather fringe was made of soft eagle feathers; thus were they pasted with feathers. Also her sandals were everywhere sprinkled with divers precious feathers.

In the hands of both of them lay their maize stalk staves. Some say quetzal bird fans were in their hands. Golden were their breast pendants, like cut discs of gold. And their golden ear pendants were constantly trembling, gleaming. No *ollas* with quetzal feathers did they bear upon their backs. Only their paper headdresses with billowing quetzal feathers did they arrange, and they set their radiating turquoise ornaments in place. And both their arms were feathered with divers feathers; their feathering reached to their wrists. Likewise their legs were feathered with divers feathers; their feathering ended at their ankles. And with their yucca fiber sandals they showed that they were Chichimec women who had just arrived.

uiian ic ihuitzetzeliuhqui in inuipil, inic tlamauizçotilli, tlamauizchichioalli, tlacencaoalli. Auh in itenco inic tenihuiio mochioa ie in quauhtlachcaiotl ic tlapotonilli, no ic tzetzeliuhtoc in izquican icac tlaçoihuitl nepapan ihuitl

omestin inmac oonoc, incicintopil in cequintin quitoa quetzaltotoecacehoaztli in inmac mamanca teucuitlatl in imelpancozqui iuhquin comalli ic tlatectli teucuitlatl ioan inteteucuitlanacoch, uiuiiontimani cuecuecueiocatimani: aoc tle quimama tequetzalcomitl, çaniio imaamatzõ inpopoquetzal conmamantimani ioan inxiuhtlanes contlalitimani: ioan innenecoc inmac, nepapan ihuitica in mopotonique, in maquechtlan oallacicitica in innepotonil: çan no iui in imicxic, no nepapan ihuitica in mopotonique, in xoquechtlan tlatlami in innepotonil: auh no imicçocac, ic quinestiaia ca chichimecacihoa ca çan oallaque.

Nineteenth Chapter. Here is told how the inhabitants of Amantlan, ornamenters who made feather articles, celebrated a feast day to their gods.

And thus did they celebrate a feast day [to their gods]. They paid honor to them twice: when it was [the month] called Panquetzaliztli; secondly, when it was [the month] called Tlaxochimaco — when the women gave one another flowers. It was in Panquetzaliztli that they slew the likeness of Coyotl inaual.

If no one had succeeded in securing a victim to be bathed [and slain], the inhabitants of Amantlan invited guests; they brought [them] together; they strengthened their numbers with guests in order to buy a slave whom they would slay. Everyone gathered [and] presented the large cotton capes which were the price of the slave.[1]

But if some inhabitant of Amantlan succeeded in securing a victim to be ceremonially bathed, this same one took [and] bathed the likeness of Coyotl inaual. He arrayed him; he adorned him. He placed on him all the array, the personal insignia [of the god]. If he made a great thing of the ceremonial bathing, perhaps he took [and] slew a number of likenesses of all their gods; perhaps he killed two; perhaps three. But if he did not make a great thing of it, if it was not highly regarded, he took [and] slew only the likeness of Coyotl inaual.

And when this happened, all the old men of Amantlan, every one, gathered there in their *calpulli* temple; there they provided song, they held vigil for all who were to die as likenesses [of the gods]. They said that in order that they would not fear, that they would not dread death, they first made them drink what they called the obsidian medicine. It is said that apparently by means of it they deprived them of their senses, of their consciousness, so that no longer would they be afraid at the time that they cut open

Inic castollonnaui capitulo: vncan mitoa, inic quimilhuiquistiliaia in inteuhoan, in iehoantin tlachichiuhque in amanteca in ihuitl quichioa.

Auh inic quimilhuiquistiliaia: oppa in quinmauiztiliaia: icoac in motenehoa panquetzaliztli: inic oppa icoac in mitoa tlasuchimaco, cihoa mosuchimaca in ipan panquetzaliztli, icoac quimictiaia in ixiptla coiotl inaoal:

intlacaiac ipanti in icoac tealtiz, çan quicohoachioaia, quicohoauicaia, quicohoaotlatoctiaia in amanteca: inic quicoaia ce tlacotli in quimictizque, quinechicoaia mochi tlacatl quinestiaia in quachtli in ipatiuh tlacotli.

Auh intla aca amantecatl, oipantic tealtiz: çan niman iehoatl conana, caltia, in ixiptla coiotl inaoal, quichichioa, quicencaoa: isquich itech quitlalia: in inechichioal in inetlamamac. Intla quiiueichioa itealtiliz, aço quezqui quimonana, quinmictia in imixiptlahoan, izquintin inteuhoan aço ome, aço ei quimictia. Auh intlacamo quiiueichioa, intlacamo cenca omouelitta: çan iehoatl conana, quimictia in ixiptla coiotl inaoal.

Auh in icoac, y, in isquichtin in ueueiohoan, amanteca: mochintin oncan cenquiça in incalpulco, oncan quincuicatia quintozçauiia in quezquinti miquizque, teixiptlaoan, iuh quitoa: inic amo miquizmauhque iezque, inic amo quimacacizque miquiztli, achtopa quimitiaia in quitocaiotiaia itzpactli: quilmach iuhquin ic quiniolpoloaia: ic quiniolmictiaia, inic aocmo momauhtizque: in icoac quimeltetequizque, iuhquinma ic ihuinti: tlapoloa in iniollo. Conitoa, in aca tlaaltilli: iuhquin iollotlaueliloc muchioa, ça mono-

1. Sahagún (Garibay ed.), III, p. 77: *"se cotizaban, hacían una cooperación, formaban un grupo de gasto común...."*

their breasts. It was as if they were besotted; they lost their senses. They say that some of the bathed ones became deranged; quite of their own wills they climbed — ran — up to the top [of the temple] of the devil, longing for — seeking — [death], even though they were to suffer, to perish.

And when for the second time their feast day arrived, when it was [the month] called Tlaxochimaco, none died. They concerned themselves only with paying honor to the two women, Xiuhtlati and Xilo, although in doing so they did honor to all their gods. Wherefore all the women, the women of Amantlan, every one, assembled there in the temple of their *calpulli;* there they danced with interlocked arms. This was what was called the interlocked arms dance: the women were pasted with feathers; their faces were painted. The colored feathers with which they were pasted reached to their ankles. Similar were their arms. But only the legs of the men were pasted with colored feathers; their pasted feathering reached to their thighs.

On this occasion the inhabitants of Amantlan pledged all their children as offerings. If it were a boy, one asked that he might serve as a priest, to grow up there in the priests' house, and that when matured he would acquire understanding, artisanship.[2] But if it were a girl, one asked that she might embroider well; might dye articles well; might tint rabbit fur; might tint well the varicolored rabbit furs wherever they were placed; or might dye feathers in varied colors: azure, yellow, rose red, light blue, black; [that] she might judge colors, so that she could work her feathers.

The *calpulli* temple [and] the priests' house of these inhabitants of Amantlan extended by, were paired together with, the *calpulli* temple of the merchants. Likewise their gods were placed together; they put together, placed in twofold division, those named Yacatecutli and Coyotl inaual; because the glory, the renown of the merchants, the vanguard merchants, was equal; they were always placed near together, in proximity. Thus were they arranged in line: the merchants' row of houses was arranged in line at one side; likewise the feather artisans' row of houses [was] on [the other] side;[3] because they

matlecauia, motlalotitleco in icpac Diablo: coneleuia, conmonectia in macuele ontlacoti ompopoliui.

Auh in icoac ic oppa imilhuiuh quiçaia: icoac in motenehoaia tlasuchimaco, aocac miquia, ça miscauiaia in quinmauiztiliaia vmētin cihoa in xiuhtlati ioan xilo: tel ic quincenmauiztiliaia in inteuhoan: iehica in isquichtin cihoa, in amanteca cihoa, mochintin oncan cenquiçaia in incalpulco in inteupā oncan tlanaoaia: inic mitoa tlanaoaia: mopotoniaia, moxaoaia in cihoa in xoquechtlan tlatlamia in tlapalihuitl ic mopotoniaia: no iui in īmac. Auh in oquichtin çaniio imicxi in mopotoniaia, tlapalihuitica, inmetzpan tlatlamia in innepotonil:

ic oncan quinnetoltiaia in isquichtin impilhoan amanteca: intla oquichtli quitlaitlaniaia inic oncan tlamacazcatiz mohoapaoaz calmecac, auh in quauhtic uel quicuiz in istli in iollotli in tultecaiotl: auh intla cihoatl quitlaniaia inic uel tlamachioaz, ioan uellapaz tochomipaz, uel quipaz in izquican icac tlapapaltochomitl, anoço ihuitl quipaz tlatlapalpaz, tlamatlalpaz, tlacozticapaz, tlaxochipalpaz, tlatexopaz, tlaiiappalpaz, tlapaltica tlatlatlapalpoaz inic quitlatlamachiz ihuiuh.

In iehoantin, y, amanteca in incalpul, in incalmecauh: çan monetechanaia onteistin manca in incalpul puchteca: no iui in inteuhoan nehoan manca quinnehoanmanaia, quimomemanaia in itoca iiacatecutli ioan coiotl inaoal. Ipampa in puchteca in oztomeca çan centetl catca in inmauizço in innemauiztiliz mochipa netloc nenaoac motlaliaia: inic motecaia centlapal incalma in puchteca, no centlapal incalma in amanteca, iehica achi moneneuilitiuia, inic mocuiltonoaia, inic tealtiaia. Ca in puchteca in oztomeca: iehoan quioalcalaquiaia, quioallaxitiaia, in isquich tlaçoyhuitl, in nepapan ihuitl.

2. Corresponding Spanish text: *"si era varon el que se prometian de meterle, en el calmecac, para que alli se criasse: y despues quando venjan años de discrecion, enseñauanle, para que deprendiesse el officio de tultecaiotl, con la ayuda de aquellos dioses."*

3. Cf. Sahagún, *op. cit.,* p. 79.

were almost equal in their wealth, in their bathing [of sacrificial victims]. For the merchants, the vanguard merchants, were the ones who introduced, who secured, all the different precious feathers.

And in the hands of the inhabitants of Amantlan were used, were taken apart, the feathers of the quetzal, the troupial, the red spoonbill. In their hands were taken apart indeed all the precious feathers. They displayed well, they made attractive, the precious feathers, thereby preparing artistically all the splendid shields which were the gifts of the rulers;[4] nothing common; all covered, pasted over, with precious feathers; [pasted with yellow parrot feathers, with trogonorus feathers];[5] painted, decorated, designed with those of the blue cotinga, the hummingbird, the red spoonbill; with gold; tufted with parrot feathers on the border; rimmed with hanging ornaments; with pendants radiating from the [lower] rim; with eagle down,[6] with quetzal feathers, with those of the troupial, with those of the red spoonbill; with grasshopper figures on the ends of the pendants.[7] And verily all the devices, indeed all, were made of nothing but precious feathers, in which they looked beautiful: perhaps the quetzal feather crest-like device, or the Xolotl head, or the yellow parrot feather shirt; the blue parrot feather one[8] with wavy lines in grackle feathers;[9] the scarlet parrot feather shirt,[10] the green feather one,[11] the heron feather one, etc.: whatsoever they made. For many were the forms of devices.

And it is said that before there were precious feathers with which the inhabitants of Amantlan could practice their craft, could decorate the objects, all that they required[12] were the common feathers, like those of the heron, and black bird feathers, and white bird feathers, and duck feathers. Only heron feathers corresponded to those of the quetzal; [with them] they made the forked heron feather device in which the winding dance was performed. They

Auh in amanteca inmac poliuia, inmac puztequia in quetzalli, in çaquã in tlauhquechol inmac teinia in ie isquich tlaçoihuitl, iehoan uel quiuelnestiaia, quiiectlaliaia in tlaçoihuitl, inic tlatultecatia, in isquich in mauizçochimalli in tlatoque intenemac catca: atle nemiuhqui mochi tlaçoihuitica tlapepecholli, tlatzaqualli [toztica, tzinitzcantica tlatzacualli,] xiuhtototica vitzitziltica, tlauhquecholtica teucuitlatica icuiliuic, icuiliuhqui, tlatlacujlolli, toztenoloio, tentlapilollo, tlapiloltica tenchaiaoac, quanmoloctica, quetzalpuztectica, çaquantica tlauhquecholtica iacachapollo in tlapilolli: ioan in ie mochi tlauiztli, çan ie moche in tlaçoihuitl, ic uel necia in aço quetzalpatzactli, anoço quaxolotl, anoço tocehoatl, cuitlatexoehoatl tzanatica motlotlouitec, chamolehoatl, coçoehoatl, aztaehoatl, etc. in çaço tlein quichioaia: ca miec tlamãtli in tlauiztli catca.

Auh mitoa, in aiatle tlaçoihuitl, inic tultecatizque, inic tlauelnestizque amanteca: çan oc moch ehoatl in quinequia, macehoalihuitl, in iuhqui aztatl, ioan tliltic totolihuitl, ioan iztac totolihuitl, ioan canahuihuitl: in aztatl, çan oc iehoatl quetzalpouiia, aztaxelli quichioaia in ipan cuicoianaloia totolquechtapalcatl in tlateloloiotl in quichioaia: auh in tlapilolli iê in canauhihuitl quipiloaia.

4. Sahagún (Garibay ed.), III, p. 79: "Todo lo hermoso de los escudos era atributo exclusivo de los reyes."

5. The addition in brackets is found in the *Acad. Hist. MS.*

6. If *quauhmoloctli*, soft eagle feathers (cf. Anderson and Dibble, *op. cit.*, Book II, p. 87). According to Seler, *op. cit.*, p. 437 and n. 86, "*les plumes brunes et blanches de la Piaya cayana*," "*du coucou à queue longue.*"

7. Compare Seler, *Gesammelte Abhandlungen*, II, pp. 665-666, with Sahagún, *loc. cit.* The versions vary slightly.

8. *Cuitlatexoehoatl*: see *supra*, Chap. i, n. 2.

9. *Tzanatl*: boat-tailed grackle — *Cassidix mexicanus* (Gmelin). Friedmann *et al.*, *op. cit.*, Pt. II, p. 279.

10. Cf. *supra*, Chap. i, p. 1.

11. *Coçoehoatl*: read *cochoehoatl*. Although the white-fronted parrot, *Amazona albifrons* (Sparrmann) is white, red, turquoise and green in color, its plumage is predominately green. Cf. Friedmann *et al.*, Pt. 1, p. 129.

12. *Yevatl* in *Acad. Hist. MS.*

made feather balls of turkey breast feathers; for pendants they suspended duck feathers.

And to cut them [they used] obsidian blades, which they applied against a bald cypress[13] [board] on which they cut the feathers.

But when the precious feathers came to appear, so it is told, it was later, in the time of the ruler Auitzotl. Those who discovered them, who came upon them, were his noble travelers, his vanguard merchants, who had become trading merchants when first they penetrated the land of Anauac. Then, later, gradually, they discovered, they invented, they put to use[14] —

Auh inic tlatequia çan oc iê in itztli aueuetl quinamictiaia in ipan quitequia ihuitl.

Auh in necico tlaçoihuitl, iuh mitoa: quin ipan in auitzotl tecutli, iehoan quinestico, caxitico in itecunenencahoan, in ioztomecahoan mochiuhque puchteca, inic iancuican quipetlaque anaoacatlalli, icoac quin no iuian quinestique quiiocusque quinenemilique.

---

13. Aueuetl: *"Sabino, árbol prócer de la Mesa Central. . . .* Taxodium mucronatum" (Sahagún, *op. cit.*, IV, p. 320); cf. also Santamaría, *op. cit.*, I, p. 65. According to Standley, *op. cit.*, Vol. 23, Pt. 1, p. 60, bald cypress.

14. The break seems arbitrary here; there is none in the *Acad. Hist. MS.*

Twentieth Chapter, which telleth the manner in which these inhabitants of Amantlan, the ornamenters, worked feathers for adornment.

—all their tools for ornamenting: the copper scalpel, the knife to cut the feathers, and the bone blade[1] for gluing, and the painting tools, the paint dish with which to paint, to outline, their patterns, and the wooden block[2] on which the feathers were cut; to the copper they opposed hard red wood.

And when finally the craft [of] feather design became important, it came to pass in the time of Moctezuma. For when he ruled, precisely when he was reigning, then quetzal feathers arrived, and all kinds of precious feathers. In just his time [this commerce] flourished. So he settled, he housed separately, those who were his feather workers, who pertained to him. He gave them a house of their own. The feather artisans of Tenochtitlan and Tlatelolco mingled with one another.

And these specialized only in making the array of Uitzilopochtli, which they called the divine cape: the quetzal feather, the hummingbird, the blue cotinga capes, designed, intricately worked, so that indeed all different parts were of precious feathers.

And they made the array which was Moctezuma's own, which he gave, with which he showed favor, to his guests, the rulers over cities, wherefore [the craftsmen] were called, were named, feather workers of the palace, artisans of the ruler. And some were known as feather workers of the treasury store house; their domain was everything which was in Moctezuma's treasury store house. They made that which was the dance array of Moctezuma, in which a dance was danced. When a feast day came, they displayed for him, they made attractive to him, whatsoever one he might want, in which to dance. For each separate article completed, made, remained in a certain place. His majordomos guarded them.

And some were known as private feather workers. These specialized exclusively in devices which they

Inic cempoalli capitulo: itechpa tlatoa inic tlachichioa in iehoantin amanteca in tlachichiuhque in quichioa ihuitl inic tlachichihoa.

In isquich intlachichioaia: in tepuzuictli, tepuztlateconi, inic motequi ihuitl, ioan in omihuictli inic moçaloa, ioan in tlacuiloloni, in tlapalcaxitl inic quicuiloa, quitlilania in inmachiouh, ioan in quauhtlateconi in ipan motequi ihuitl quinamictique in tepuztli tlaquaoac quauitl in tlatlauhqui.

Auh in iequine uel ueis tultecaiotl: in ihuitlacuilolli ic mochioa, quin ipã in motecuçoma: ipampa in icoac tlatocatia, ie uel ipan totocac, inic oallacia quetzalli: ioan in ie mochi tlaçoihuitl uel ipan tlapiuis ic nonqua quintecac, quincalten centetl calli quinmacac iniscoian iiamãtecahoan catca in itech pouia: nepan istoca in tenochtitlan amanteca ioan in tlatilulco amanteca.

Auh in iehoantin, y, çan quiscahuiaia in quichioaia itlatqui vitzilobuchtli in quitocaiotiaia teuquemitl, quetzalquemitl uitzitzilquemitl, xiuhtotoquemitl, ic tlatlacuilolli, ic tlatlatlamachilli in ie mochi in izquican icac tlaçoihuitl.

Yoan quichioaia in iscoian itlatqui motecuçoma: in quinmacaia, in quintlauhtiaia icoahoan in altepetl ipan tlatoque, ic monotzaia motenehoaia tecpan amanteca itultecahoan in tlacatl. Auh in cequintin, motenehoaia calpiscan amanteca, itech pouia in izquitetl icaca icalpiscacal motecuçoma: iehoatl quichioaia, in tlein imâcehoallatqui motecuçoma in ipan macehoaia, mitotiaia: in icoac ilhuitl quiçaia, quitlatlattitia, quitlanenectiaia, in çaço catlehoatl queleuiz in ipan mîtotiz, ca cecentlamantli iecauia, cecentlamantli quichioaia in izquicacan catca icalpiscahoan in quitlapieliaia.

Auh in cequintin motenehoaia calla amanteca: in iehoantin, y, çan quiscauiaia in tlauiztli quichioaia

---

1. *Plegadera* in Sahagún, *op. cit.,* III, p. 80.
2. Literally, axe for cutting wood. In *loc. cit., cortador de palo;* according to Seler, "L'orfèvrerie," p. 426, *coupoir de bois.*

made [and] sold: perhaps shields, or shirts of yellow parrot feathers — whatsoever they made.

But today, although devices are no longer much required, in the same way the making, the ornamenting, of articles proceed; they advance. As the ancient feather workers left [and] established their traditions, so [those of today] go on learning their craft; for the same expert work is demanded for ornamenting today. Shields covered, overlaid, with feathers are made when required; and insignia borne on the back are made, with which there may be dancing; and all the dance array, gear, and ornaments: the quetzal feathers, head ornaments, bracelets for the upper arm with precious feathers, gold bands for the upper arm; fans — fans of heron, of red spoonbill,[3] of troupial, of crested guan, of quetzal feathers; and hand banners, quetzal feather hand banners with troupial feathers in alternating bands, heron feather banners, gold banners tufted with quetzal feathers at the tips.

And particularly here, the craftsmanship, the art of feather design, is apparent; for any sort of image is made [of feathers].[4]

And in the ornamentation, in the working with feathers, two methods [were used]. In the first, the feathers were fastened with glue to complete the work. And in the second, with only cord, with maguey thread, were the works completed, perfected. In these ways was [feather] craftsmanship undertaken; thus the feather workers started their work.

quimotiamictiaia, aço chimalli, anoço tozehoatl: in çaço quenami quichioaia.

Auh in ascan, maciui in aocmo cenca monequi tlauiztli: ca çan ie iuh otlatoca, çan ie iuh motocatiuh in tlachioalli, in tlachichioaliztli: in iuh otlacauhtiaque, otlanelhoaiotitiaque in amanteca ueuetque inic quitziui intultecaio: ca çan iee in imis, in iniollo motitlani, inic tlachichioalo ascan, ca mochioa in chimalli: ihuitica motzacoa mopepechoa in icoac monequi: auh mochioa in tlamamalli in ipan mâcehoalo, ioan in isquich mâcehoallatquitl, in netotiloni, in nechichioaloni in quetzalli, in icpacxochitl, in machõcotl, in matemacatl in êcacehoaztli, aztaecacehoaztli, quauhquecholecacehoaztli, çaquanecacehoaztli, coxolêcacehoaztli quetzalecacehoaztli, ioan macpanitl, quetzalmacpanitl çaquantica tlatlapanqui, uiuiltecqui, aztapanitl, teucuitlapanitl, quetzaltzontecomaio:

ioan in uel oncan neci tultecaiotl, in ihuitlacuilolli, ca mochioa in itla tlaixiptlaiotl.

Auh inic tlachichioalo, inic amantecatioa, ontlamantli: inic centlamantli, iê in tzacutica moçaloa ihuitl, inic iecaui tlachioalli. Auh inic ontlamantli çan mecatica ichtica in iecaui in mouellalia tlachioalli. Iui, y, in nelhoaiohoa in ompehoa tultecaiotl inic quipehoaltia intlachichioal amanteca.

---

3. *Quauhquechol*: read *tlauhquechol*.

4. Seler, *op. cit.*, p. 429: "*Et c'est particulièrement dans les mosaïques en plumes que l'habileté de ces artisans se révèle. Car on fait des vraies images en plumes.*"

Twenty-first Chapter. Here is told how those of Amantlan, the ornamenters, performed their task.

The feather workers, who painted with feathers, who rejoiced in feather [work], thus began their creations. First of all, they saw, by the pattern, how they would make it. They who first drew it were the scribes.

When they had seen how it was designed, that it was well done, that the painting was sufficiently detailed,[1] then on a maguey leaf they reinforced cotton: they strengthened it with glue. They called this the reinforcement of cotton.

They sought a good [maguey leaf],[2] of smooth, shiny surface, with no knobs; and even,[3] not raised [or] depressed. On it they reinforced the cotton.

First they put glue on the surface; with their hands they covered the surface with glue. Then on this they laid, they stretched out, they pressed down the carded cotton. First they carded it well; they stretched it repeatedly; they thinned it out. When this was just like a cobweb, like the mist, they pressed it down upon the maguey leaf, and set it out in the sun. Only a little did the surface dry. When the surface had dried, once again they spread glue on the surface, thereby making the surface of the cotton glossy, shiny. So no more was to be carded, since the glue was well hardened in it.

And when it had dried, when it crackled with its dryness, then [the cotton] was peeled off. Then [the cotton] was spread, placed on the painted pattern. On [the cotton] was painted, delineated, on it one went tracing, the painting which appeared from underneath.

And when finished, when the cotton was painted all over, when nothing of all the completed pattern had been forgotten, then [the cotton] was glued on a piece of paper, coarse paper,[4] so that [this] reinforced

Inic cempoalli oce capitulo: vncan motenehoa in quenī quichioa intequiuh in iehoãtin in tlachichiuhque in amãteca.

In iehoan amanteca, in ihuitica tlacuiloani, in ihuitl quimauiltia: inic peoa intlachioal, oc achto q̃tta in machiotl in quenami quitlalizque: iehoantin achto quicuiloa in tlacuiloque.

In icoac oquittaq̃ inic tlamachca, inic tlatlamachilli, in aço uel testitoc tlacuilolli: niman ic mepan quioapaoa, quitzacuoapahoa in ichcatl, quitocaiotia, ichcatlaoapaoalli:

quitemoa in qualli in isxipetztic, in istetzcaltic, in amo isçahoaio, ioan in pechtic, in amo copiltic, copichtic: ipan quioapaoa in ichcatl,

achto conistzacuuia, conistzacumato: nimã ic ipan conteca conçoa, compapachoa in ichcatlapuchintli: achto uel quipochina, cahana, quicanahoa, icoac in ça iuhqui tocapeiotl, in ça iuhqui aiauitl mepan compachoa: auh tonaian conmana, çan achi onishoaqui: in icoac oonishoac, oc ceppa conistzacuuia, ic onispeti, ic onistetzcaui, ic onispetziui in ichcatl, inic aocmo çan pochintoz, ic uel ipan onhoaqui in tzacutli.

Auh in icoac ohoac, in ocacalachoac, niman ic mocoleoa: icoac ipan ommoçoa, onmomana in tlacuilolmachiotl, ic ipan micuiloa, motlilania, iehoatl ipan onmotztiuh in tlanipa oalneci tlacuilolli:

auh in icoac omocencauh, in onouiian micuilo ichcatl, in atle omolcauh, in isquich ic tlatlalilli machiotl: niman ic ipan onmoçaloa ce amatl, quaoamatl, ic mocenoapaoa ic chicaoa in ichcatlaoapaoalli. Auh niman

---

1. *In aço uel testitoc*: *aço* appears as *oço* in the MS.

2. In the *Acad. Hist. MS*, *metl* follows *qualli*.

3. In *ibid.*, *yxpechtic* follows *pechtic*.

4. *Quaoamatl*: cf. von Hagen, *op. cit.*, p. 60: *cuah-amatl*, "coarse, thickly-fibered paper, more difficult to fashion than the fig tree variety"; product of *Acacia cornigera* ("bull's horn acacia"). The bark is used. Seler, in *Collected Works*, II, Pt. 3-4, p. 59, refers to it as *papel de la tierra* (citing Tezozomoc); in Fr. Bernardino de Sahagún: *Historia general de las cosas de Nueva España* (México: Editorial Pedro Robredo, 1938), V (Appendix), p. 213 (*quauhamatl* or *texamatl*), he attributes it to paper made from the bark of some *ficus* tree; and in "L'orfèvrerie," p. 431, he calls it bark paper. In Sahagún (Garibay ed.), III, p. 83, it is *papel de amate*.

cotton was completely strengthened, so that it was given support. And then was started the trimming, the gouging, with a metal blade where [the outline of] the painting was projecting [or] was drawing in.[5] It was cut, trimmed, on a small piece of wood called a cutting board. All was cut on this; feathers were broken, evened off,[6] rounded off at the top.

And when the paper pattern had in all parts been trimmed to be like the [original] painting, then it was spread out upon a maguey leaf; on this was traced the pattern which had been cut.[7]

When the maguey had been painted,[8] then it was covered with glue; cotton was applied to it; thereby the [second] reinforcement of cotton was strengthened with glue. The outline of the painting was put on it. Again it dried in the sun.[9] Later, upon it were placed, one by one, the feathers called "the glue-hardened ones," those which had been glued, dried.[10]

But first, quite apart, on a maguey leaf, the feathers had been cut,[11] one by one; glue-hardened, one by one. They were known as the glue-hardened feathers. The feathers were suspended, dipped, in glue; later they were stuck to the maguey leaf; their surfaces were smoothed with the bone blade.

This so-called glue-hardening was all of common feathers; for they came first of all, at the start, in order to accomplish the feather work. This, to begin with, became the basis, the bed, on which all the precious feathers were bedded. Perhaps yellow dyed ones were glue-hardened, or heron, or scarlet ones, or blue parrot,[12] or green parrot feathers,[13] or some feathers dyed in one color, dyed in many. They took note, they tried out, they matched whatsoever kind would harmonize, would serve as the basis for the precious feathers. Blue cotinga were provided blue parrot feathers as a basis; they [also] matched scarlet macaw feathers.[14] And for trogonorus, they used green parrot feathers as a basis. And for the red spoonbill,

ic mopeoaltia in tepuzuictica mocui: motacalotiuh in umpa cacalactica, xoxomolactica tlacuilolli, ipan motequi, mocuicui tepiton quauhtontli in itoca quauhtlateconi: isquich ipan motequi, moteinia, moquapaiania, moquaiaoaloa in ihuitl.

Auh in icoac ie onouiian mocuicuic amamachiotl: in iuhqui ic ca tlacuilolli: niman ic mepan onmomana, vncan ipan ic micuiloa in metl, motocatiuh in uncan omocuicuic machi machiotl:

In icoac omocuicuilo metl: niman ic onmitzacuuia, ipan onmochcauia, ic motzacuoapaoa, in ichcatlaoapaoalli, in ichcatl itech oalmoteca in tlilantli, in tlapalli, oc no hoaqui tonaia: çatepan ipan moteteca in ihuitl, moteneoa tzacoatzalli, tlatzacuoatzalli,

tel achtopa oc nonqua mepã çan oc cecentetl motequi, motzacuoatza in ihuitl, motenehoa tlatzacoatzalli: tzacutica mopiloa, motzacupiloa in ihuitl, çatepan mepan moçaloa, omiuictica ommisxipetzoa.

Inin motenehoa tlaoatzalli: çan oc moche in maceoalihuitl, ca iehoatl uel quiiacana, quiiacatia inic iecaui ihuitlachioalli: iehoatl achto tlapepechiotl, ipepech mochioa quimopepechtia, in isquich tlaçoihuitl, aço coztlapalli in motzacoatza, anoço aztatl, anoço chamolin, anoço cuitlatexotli, anoço cochoihuitl, anoço itla ihuitl çan tlapalli, tlatlapalpalli: ipan mouelitta, moiehecoa, monanamictia, in catlehoatl quimonamictiz, quimopepechtiz tlaçoihuitl, in xiuhtototl, iehoatl mopepechiotia, in cuitlatexotli ihuiio: iehoatl quisoaltia in alo: auh in tzinitzcan, iehoatl quimopepechtia in cochoihuitl: auh in tlauhquechol: iehoatl ipepech mochioa in çan ie no ie iialapachio tlauhquechol, anoço tlatlapalpalli ihuitl auh in toztli ipepech mo-

---

5. This procedure is the cutting out of the painted design or picture to provide a stencil or a templet. The illustrations (Pls. 91 and 92) seem to indicate that it was a templet.

6. *Acad. Hist. MS*: *moquapania*.

7. *Machi machiotl*: so it appears in the MS.

8. *Acad. Hist. MS*: *omicuilo*.

9. See Fig. 92.

10. *Tzacoatzalli, tlatzacuoatzalli*: the first word is *tlavatzalli* (dried out) in the *Acad. Hist. MS*. In Seler, *op. cit.*, p. 432, it is translated: *"plumes maigres ou collage maigre."*

11. *Acad. Hist. MS*: *moteteca*.

12. Cf. *supra*, Chap. I, n. 2.

13. *Anoço chochoihuitl*: *aço cochoyvitl* in *Acad. Hist. MS*.

14. *Alo*: Scarlet macaw, *Ara macao* (*Linnaeus*), in Friedmann *et al.*, *op. cit.*, Pt. I, p. 125.

the moulted feathers[15] of the same spoonbill, or red dyed feathers, became the basis. And for yellow parrot feathers, yellow dyed feathers became the basis; in the same way, they used moulted yellow parrot feathers to form the basis.

These feathers, which were called yellow dyed, were only dyed; dyed, tinted yellow. The yellow color cooked on the fire; it boiled; alum[16] was added; and then it was provided with saltpeter.

When [the color] had been provided with saltpeter;[17] when [the feather base was] finished; when on all parts stood the glue-hardened feathers for the basis; when everywhere each one had been laid out on the painted cotton on the maguey leaf, had been glue-hardened, then it was lifted off.[18]

And then a thin board was set out; a paper was glued on it; on this once again was painted the trimmed pattern, which had become the work design. On this was the feather work completed; on it all the feather base was glued, perhaps to be pictures of flowers, or of plants, or of some image which was to be made, of whatever design which was pleasing.

When the pattern on the board had been painted, when it had been outlined, then began the gluing, the arranging.

First the glue was dissolved, mixed. There was dissolving, making of glue. The preparation of the glue was the task of the children who were being trained. They dissolved the glue for [the workers]; they dissolved the glue.

Then the black outline was cut away in order to mark, to delineate, the feather painting. This came at the very beginning. First the [outline] feathers were glued, pressed on with the bone blade. The black outline was made of grackle feathers, or scarlet ones, the glue-hardened scarlet feathers. Then followed the cutting of its bed of glue-hardened feathers, which became the bed of the feathers according to the kind of feathers with which they first began, according to the pattern: perhaps the blue cotinga, or trogonorus, or red spoonbill, or the yellow ones,[19]

chioa in coztlapalli ihuitl, çan no ie quimopepechtia in tozcuicuil,

in ihuitl in motenehoa coztlapalli, çan mopa, mocozticapa, mocozpa tleco icucic ipan quaqualaca in tlapalli, çacatlascalli, tlasxocotl monamictia: auh çatepan motequisquiuia,

in icoac in omotequisquiui, in ie omocencauh, in izquicac icac tlapepechiotl, in ihuitlaoatzalli: in ie nouian omotetecac, omotzacoaz, in ipan ichcatl mepan tlacuilolli, çatepan mocoleoa.

Auh in icoac centetl momana: oapaltontli ipan moçaloa ce amatl, oc ceppa ipan micuiloa in omocuicuic machiotl, in tlacuicuitl omochiuh: iehoatl ipan iecaui in ihuitlachioalli, ipan mocençaloa in ihuitl oapalli, aço suchitlacuilolli, aço quillacuilolli, anoço itla tlaixiptlaiotl in mochioaz, in çaço quenami tlamachtli, intla uel ittalli.

In icoac omicuilo, in omotlitlilani oapalpan machiotl, niman ic peoa in tlaçaloliztli, in tlachichioaliztli:

achto mopatla, moneloa in tzacutli, tzacupatlalo, netzacupatililo: iehoan intequiuh in tzacupatlaliztli in tepilhoan, in izcaltiloni, tetzaucpatilia, tzacupatla:

niman ic motequi in tlilli in tlilantli, inic motlillotia, motlilancaiotia, in ihuitlacuilolli: ca iehoatl uellaiacana, achto onmoçaloa, onmopachoa omiuictica: iehoatl in tlilantli muchioa, ihuiio tzanatl, anoço chamolin, chamoloatzalli: niman ic contoquilia, motequi in itlaoatzallo, in ipepech mochioa in quenami ihuitl, in catlehoatl achto ompehoa in iuhqui ic ca machiotl, aço xiuhtototl ompeoa, anoço tzinitzcan, anoço tlauhquechol, aço aiopal, anoço xiuhuitzili, uitzitzili, quetzaluitzitzili, tleuitzilin: in ie izquican icac ihuiio itlachieliz in iuhqui ic xotla, ic pepetzca

---

15. *Acad. Hist. MS*: *yalapachyo*.

16. Cf. Book XI, Chap. xi, of the *Florentine Codex*; also Arthur J. O. Anderson: "Pre-Hispanic Aztec Colorists," *El Palacio*, Vol. 55 (1948), pp. 22-23. *Tlasxocotl*: probably *tlalxocotl* is intended.

17. The *Acad. Hist. MS* does not repeat *omotequisquiui*.

18. See Pl. 97.

19. Cf. *ayopal teuilotl* (*amatista*), in Molina, *op. cit.* In Sahagún, *op. cit.*, III, p. 84, *ayopal* is *pluma amarilla fina;* in Seler, *op. cit.*, p. 434, *l'oiseau couleur de topaze,* and in n. 68, Seler writes: *"De la couleur de la fleur de courge, c'est-à-dire un jaune foncé, ayopal-teuilotl est traduit dans la partie espagnole du dictionnaire de Molina par 'Cristal amarillo,' dans la partie aztèque — erronèment? — par 'Amatista piedra preciosa.' Il paraît que ce terme signifiait la 'topaze fumée.'"*

or the turquoise hummingbird, the [ordinary] one, the quetzal-green one, the flame-colored one. One by one they went matching the [precious] feathers, each being placed in position according to its appearance, as it glowed, shimmered. The mentioned glue-hardened feathers formed the bed in all places. They continued consulting the pattern, how it was painted, noting the different colors appearing on it.

When the glue-hardened feathers had been fastened down with the bone blade, then on its surface were set the precious feathers, going placed, glued in order, set in position by means of the bone blade; just so proceeding, the covering continuing, the feathers proceeding to cover the glue-hardened ones. And on it the trimmed paper pattern went being laid, being tested. Lest somewhere the work might be warped, lest it be distorted, the pattern went on being compared as the gluing of the feathers proceeded.

Just so was made, completed, the feather painting which was made with glue.

But there was still another manner of work which was finished only with cord, with maguey thread. These were such as fans, quetzal feather fans, feathered bracelets for the upper arm, devices borne upon the back, yellow parrot feather shirts, etc.; then pendants, tufts of feathers, balls of feathers, tassels — all things with which the fans were beautified [and] laden.

And to complete these, first a frame was bound together. Then it was covered over to strengthen it. On this were laid out the quetzal feathers. And in this way did they set out the quetzal feathers. First their bases were provided with pieces of stout cane; a piece of cane was bound to it to strengthen it. Then they were provided with maguey thread; they were bound with maguey thread. The base ends were provided with maguey thread to make fastening places by which they could be arranged, could be tied, with cords.

And when they were arranged in order, then nooses were applied; they were provided at the midpoints; they were bound at the middle with fine maguey fiber,[20] so that the quetzal feathers could be set in order, assembled, gathered together; so that they would not spread [or] scatter; so that they could be gathered, be pressed, together.

And as the quetzal feathers were placed, and indeed all the feathers arranged in order, they were

monanamictiuh, inic ommotectiuh tlapepechotl, in izquican icac tlaoatzalli omoteneuh, ipan onmotztiuh in machiotl, in iuhqui ic iuiliuhqui, in quezquitlamantli tlapalli ipan motta.

In icoac omoçalo omiuictica tlaoatzalli: niman isco onmoquetza in tlaçoihuitl, motecpantiuh, moçalotiuh, omiuictica onmoquetztiuh, çan iuh otlatocatiuh, mopepechotiuh in ihuitl commopechtitiuh in tlaoatzalli: auh ipan onmomantiuh in amamachiotl tlacuicuitl, ipan onmoiehecotiuh, inic amo cana necuiliuiz tlachioalli, inic amo quipatiliz, çan uel onmonamictitiuh in machiotl: inic onmoçalotiuh ihuitl.

Oca çan ihui in, in mochioa in iecaui in ihuitlacuilolli in tzacutica mochioa.

Auh in oc centlamantli tlachioalli, in çan mecatica, ichtica iecaui: iehoatl in iuhqui ecacehoaztli, quetzallecacehoaztli, machoncotl, tlamamalli tlauiztli, tozehoatl Etc.[a] Niman ic tlapilolli, tlatecomaiotl, tlateloloiotl, tlaiacac pilcacaiotl, moch ic mouelnestia, ic motlamamaca in ecaceoaztli.

Auh inic ecaui achto molpia in colotli: çatepan misquachuia ic chicaoa, iehoatl ipan momana in quetzalli: auh inic momana in q̄tzalli, achto môtlaiotia in itzintlan, otlatl itech micuia, inic chichicaoa, çatepan mochiotia, ichtica moolpia, motzinichiotia, ic motlaanaltia: inic mouipanaz, mecatitech molpitiaz:

In icoac omouipan, niman ic mouicoloa meluicoloa, melilpia quetzalichtica, inic uel mocenmana, mocentema mocenquistia quetzalli, inic amo xexeliuiz, momoiaoaz, ic uel onmocentecpichoa monenetechmana.

Auh inic momana quetzalli, ioan in ie muchi ihuitl tlauipãtli nenecoc momauictia, q. n. in umpa moma-

20. Cf. Siméon, op. cit., quetzalichtli.

shaken back and forth in the hand. That is to say, if, there, the feathers were properly set — if, there, they were gathered — they were what he looked for. But if they were there matted, tangled, they dropped down into place.[21]

When they were in order, provided with nooses, then they were sewn to the frame. So was done to all the feathers; a covering was given them in the making of their bases. If eagle down or troupial came next after the quetzal feathers, they were at first provided maguey thread, placed in order, provided a noose; then they went to be sewn on to the frame, pressed, reinforced at their bases with cord, so that they followed the interrupted sequence of quetzal feathers. And then red spoonbill formed the border covered at the bottom with white, soft feathers. All were first set in order; then they went sewn on the frame. All were so completed; the rest of the devices were thus made.

And if some animal, a small animal, were to be made, first was carved *colorín* wood[22] to make its skeleton. But if it were only a small creature like a small lizard, or a dragon-fly,[23] or a butterfly, this was given a skeleton of dried maize stalk, or strips of paper; then the outside was covered with pulverized maize stalk made into a dough with glue. The powdered maize stalk thus formed a covering over the strips of paper. Then it was scraped, it was rubbed, with a piece of porous, volcanic stone,[24] by which it was made handsome, smooth. And then, on the surface, it was covered with a lining of cotton on which was the design, the design to be worked, so that it served as a basis for the feathers. On this was placed whatsoever insect was to be tried, whatsoever was to be designed.

Never[25] were the copper knife and bone blade omitted. With them alone the feathers were cut, whatever sort were needed. And with the bone blade they were fastened down, they were set in place.

In just this way did the feather workers adorn articles.

End of the Ninth Book

ihmati, in umpa motecpichotiuh ihuitl itlachisca muchioa. Auh in umpa ma paçoltic, ma çolonqui tlanipa motlaça:

in icoac omouipan, omouicolo, niman ic itech onmitzommana in colotli, çan moch iuh mochioa in ihuitl in itlatlatocio muchioa in itzintlachioallo: intla quanmoloctli, anoço çaquan contoquilia quetzalli, muchi achto muchiotia mouipana, mouicoloa çatepan ipan onmitzontiuh in colotli, onmotzinmecapachotiuh, onmomecatoctitiuh: ic ie no cuele contoquilia in quetzalpuztec tlauipantli: auh niman ic tlauhquechol, isquamul muchioa, iztac ihuitl molonqui ic onmotzinpachoa much achto mouipana, çatepan colotitech ommiitzontiuh, ça much iuh iecaui, in oc cequi tlauiztli ic muchioa.

Auh intla itla ioioli, ioioliton motlali: achto moxima in equimitl, in tzonpanquauitl, ic momiiotia. Auh intla çan ioioli, in iuhqui cuetzpalton, anoço cincocopi, anoço papalotl, iehoatl momiiotia in ooaquauitl, anoço amatlapilintli, çatepan pani mooaquauhtesxotia, tzacutica tlapololli in ooaquauhtestli ic mopepechoa in amatlapilintli, çatepan michiqui, moteçouiia, ic moiectlalia, ic xipetziui: auh çatepan pani mochcauia ipan ommicuiloa, in uncan motlatlamachitiuh, inic mopepechotiuh ihuitl: itech mana in quenami motlaiehecalhuia ioioli, in quenami ic mocuicuilo

aquēman ommocaoa in tepuztlateconi, ioan in omiuictli, çan ic ommotectiuh in ihuitl in quenami monequi, ioan ic ommoçalotiuh ic ommoquetztiuh in omiuictli.

Ca çan iui, in, in tlachichioa amanteca.

fin del libro nono

21. The *Acad. Hist. MS* has *Nenecoc momavictia, q. n. (quitoz nequi) yn vmpa momaymati, yn vmpa matecpichtic yvitl ytlachixca muchiua, auh yn vmpa mapaçoltic, maçolonqui tlanipa motlaça.*

22. Santamaría, *op. cit.*, I, 615 (*equimite*); III, 321 (*zompancle*); they are the same tree (*Erythrina coralloides, E. americana*), known also as *colorín*. See also Anderson and Dibble, *op. cit.*, Book XII, p. 100, n. 7. The light, white wood is now used to make corks, etc. Cf. also Seler, *Collected Works*, II, Pt. 3, p. 174. Maxímino Martínez, in *Las plantas medicinales de México* (México: Ediciones Botas, 1933), pp. 74-75, discusses the toxic qualities of the seeds. Seler, "L'orfèvrerie," p. 438, has *Budleia salicifolia.*

23. However, cf. *Florentine Codex*, XI, cap. 13, fol. 248v, gloss: "*Mayz falso que parece mayz y no lo es.*" Seler, *loc. cit.*: *l'image de la plante de maïs*; Sahagún, *op. cit.*, III, p. 86: *libélula.*

24. Cf. Molina, *op. cit.*, *teçontli.*

25. *Auh quenman* in the *Acad. Hist. MS.*